Textbook on Horticulture

Textbook on Horticulture

Textbook on Horticulture

Rajaneesh Singh
Head
Department of Horticulture
Tilak Dhari Post Graduate College
Jaunpur- 222 002
Uttar Pradesh

Bijendra Kumar Singh
Assistant Professor
Department of Horticulture
Tilak Dhari Post Graduate College
Jaunpur- 222 002
Uttar Pradesh

New Delhi – 110 034

A Paperback Division of

NEW INDIA PUBLISHING AGENCY

101, Vikas Surya Plaza, CU Block, LSC Market
Pitam Pura, New Delhi 110 034, India
Phone: + 91 (11)27 34 17 17 Fax: + 91(11) 27 34 16 16
Email: info@nipabooks.com
Web: www.nipabooks.com
Feedback at feedbacks@nipabooks.com

ISBN : 978-93-89571-77-6

Composed and Designed by NIPA

World Noni Research Foundation

64, Third Cross Street, Second Main Road, Gandhi Nagar, Adyar, Chennai-600 020 Telefax: 044-2442 3601 E-mail: mail@worldnoni.org Website: www.worldnoni.org

Dr. Kirti Singh
FNASc, FNAAS, FNABS
CHAIRPERSON

Foreword

Realizing the significance of services it renders to mankind, horticulture has played its major role in ensuring food and nutritional security of the country. It has become an entirely separate division in almost all agricultural universities of the country. As for basic knowledge of the subject is concerned it includes all the facets of horticulture, may it be fruits, vegetables, ornamental, medicinal and aromatic plants, plantation crops, post harvest etc. Such branches of the subject makes the study difficult and readers have to consult different type of text book for locating of a particular interest. The present book entitled "**Textbook on Horticulture**" deals with basic elementary information which is essential at undergraduate and postgraduate levels for the students of horticulture. This book fulfills the gap and provides all aspects of the basic horticulture. It covers fundamental aspects of science of horticulture which are lacking in many books available on the subject in the market.

In my opinion, this text book shall be extremely helpful to the students of horticulture in various colleges and universities as well as to the teachers engaged in teaching the subject. I have great pleasure to complement and congratulate the authors for their enthusiasm and hard work in bringing out useful and informative publication.

Date: 08-01-2020
Place: Jaunpur

(Kirti Singh)
Former Vice-Chancellor

Preface

Being at the forefront among the national agricultural discipline, horticulture has played its major role in ensuring food and nutritional security of the country. They are not only delicious and refreshing but are also the chief source of vitamins, minerals and proteins.

The book is primarily meant for the student of graduate and postgraduate in the field of horticulture of all agricultural universities in India and neighbouring countries. The information included in this book is considered to be of utmost value to student of horticulture fruit & vegetable growers, nursery man, gardeners, subject matter specialist and other person's engaged in the field of horticulture. In this edition I have shared my personal experience on horticultural crops acquired during last nineteen year.

The book will proved boon for student contesting Indian Council of Agricultural Research Junior and Senior Fellowship, Agriculture Research Services examination and NET in the field of horticulture. I am highly thankful to management of the college and principal for providing me always moral support in writing of this book. We have great pleasure in acknowledging moral support, encouragement valuable suggestion and connective criticism received from Dr. Hari Baksh, Mr. Raj Pandey and all agriculture faculty members, Tilak Dhari P.G. College, Jaunpur.

I am highly grateful to Prof. Anil K. Singh (BHU), Prof. Ranveer Singh, Prof. J.P. Tiwari and Prof. Hari Har Ram who always encouraging me for preparing this manuscript. We appreciate the efforts of Mr. Sumit Pal Jain, M/s. New India Publishing Agency, New Delhi for printing the book in the nice form.

We fill immense pleasure to express our heartfelt gratitude to my elder brother Prof. I.S. Singh, Mr. Avaneesh Singh and all family members who always inspiring, guidance, encouragement and blessing.

At the last but not the least I can never forget the co-operation rendered by Dr. Bijendra Kumar Singh (Dept. of Horticulture), my wife Smt. Priya Singh and my children Pranjal Singh and Kishlay Singh without his co-operation this task cannot be completed.

Jaunpur **(Bijendra Kumar Singh)** **(Rajaneesh Singh)**

Contents

Contents

Chapter 1

Introduction to Horticulture

The term 'Horticulture' is derived from two Latin words, *Hortus* meaning Garden and *Cultura* meaning Cultivation. In ancient days the gardens had protected enclosures with high walls or similar structures surrounding the houses. The enclosed places were used to grow fruits, vegetables, flowers and ornamental plants. Horticulture differs from agriculture and forestry in specializing the cultivation of garden crops. The garden crops include fruits, vegetables, flowers, ornamental trees, spices, plantations, medicinal and aromatic plants. Horticultural crops do not give food grains. The products of horticultural crops such as fruits and vegetables are highly perishable so that they are utilized in the fresh state. In general horticultural crops need more intensive cultivation (i.e. need more work) than the agricultural crops.

Special Features of Horticulture

1. As horticultural crops generally need intensive cultivation, they require a large input, capital, labour and technology per unit area of land.
2. Many cultural operations are specific to horticultural crops. The cultural operations such as propagation, fertilization, training, pruning, harvesting and marketing are skilled operations and these are specific to horticultural crops.
3. Mostly the horticultural products are utilized in the fresh state and are highly perishable.
4. Most of the horticultural crops are the rich sources of vitamins and minerals.
5. Gratification or aesthetic sense is an exclusive phenomenon for horticultural science.

Division of Horticulture

The cultural operations are unique to each and every group of horticultural plants. Based upon the method of cultivation, horticulture has been grouped into the following divisions.

i. **Pomology-** Pomology is the cultivation of fruit crops. It deals with propagation, improvement, cultivation, training, pruning and protection of fruit crops and harvesting, storage and marketing of the fruits. Pomology is concerned with the cultivation of major fruits and many under exploited fruits.

   The major fruits are widely grown as important crops in many parts of the world. Some fruit crops are cultivated only in small areas of the country. Hence they are known as underutilized (minor) fruits.

ii. **Olericulture-** Olericulture refers to the cultivation of vegetable crops. It deals with the propagation, improvement, cultivation, training, aftercare and protection of vegetable crops. Importance is given to storage, processing and marketing of the harvested vegetables. Vegetables are used in culinary preparations and salad.

iii. **Floriculture-** It refers to the cultivation of plants which give economic flowers. Growing jasmines, roses, chrysanthemum etc. on commercial scale for cut flowers or for extraction of essential oils in the important aspect of floriculture. Flower arrangement and dry decorations constitute the display of cut flowers, this is yet other aspect of floriculture.

iv. **Gardening-** Growing ornamental plants to decorate indoor and outdoor areas is called gardening. Foliage plants, flowering annuals, biennials, perennials, climbers, succulents, cacti, palm, ferns, etc. are grown in garden to have a good scenery in these places. Laying out of garden in the interior of house and other building is called indoor gardening. Laying out of gardens in parks, outside the building and open places to imitate the natural scenery is called outdoor gardening or landscape gardening.

v. **Arboriculture-** Growing of tree species alone in specific locations is called arboriculture. Places where such trees are grown are called arboreta. These arboreta are extensively used for aesthetic, educational and scientific purpose.

vi. **Plantation crops-** Plants that are usually grown in large stretches of lands are called plantation crops. Coconut, arecanut, coffee, tea and rubber are important plantation crops grown in India.

vii. **Spices crops-** Spices are plants products used in cookery to season or flavour food. Plants yielding spices are called spice crops e.g. ginger, turmeric, clove, cinnamon, pepper etc.

   Some spices add flavour as well as taste to the foods and are called condiments e.g. coriander, cumin, mustard etc.

viii. **Medicinal and aromatic plants-** Plants which give active principles used in drugs are called medicinal plants. The active principles may be alkaloids or steroids, which are responsible for preventive and curative action of drugs e.g. foxglove, opium, rauvolfia, senna, ashwagandha, etc.

ix. **Nurseries-** A nursery is a place where young plants are raised for planting or sale. The young plant may be raised from seed, grafts, cutting, layering etc. They may be grown in seed pans, earthen pots, plastic or polythene bags containing a suitable pot mixture. After attaining a suitable height, the plants are transplanted in the field or send for sale.

x. **Post harvest technology-** Fruits and vegetables are collected during the cropping season and processed to preserve them for making them available while there no cropping. Such processing industries show rapid development in recent years. They process fruit into jam, jelly, marmalades, squashes, syrup etc.

Recent Trends in Horticulture

With rising pressure on the land and haunting environmental crisis, maintaining sustainability in agri-horti system has been much sought after aspect. To ensure livelihood security to the native population vis-a-vis nutritional security to the mass at large, horticulture sector has been recognized as the best viable alternative. Though, horticultural crops cover 15 per cent of the total area under agriculture, they contribute to about 20.4 per cent of the GDP from agriculture. These crops account for 37 % of the total exports of agricultural commodities. Due to planned emphasis laid on horticulture, India is accredited as the second largest producer of fruits and vegetables, largest producer and consumer of cashewnut, tea and spices, third largest producer of coconut, fourth largest producer and consumer of rubber and sixth largest producer of coffee in the world. Horticulture has emerged as sustainable and viable ventures especially for small and marginal farmers. However, attempts are underway to make horticulture more and more remunerative at the cost of per unit input used and resources utilized in course of harvesting the produce.

Hastened use efficiency of inputs synergizing more harvest while restoring overall health of soil and environment and maximizing return has been focused attention in horticultural research and development nowadays. Accordingly, initiatives are being undertaken to popularize hi-tech horticulture.

Hi-tech Horticulture

As the name indicates, hi-tech horticulture is technology intensive production system. It is time and space dimensions compatible system of production in which inputs and resources are combined judiciously so as to maximize return many times more than the conventional system of production. Use of micro-irrigation system, use of plastics, protected cultivation, precision farming, high density planting, integrated nutrient management (INM), integrated pest management, (IPM), mechanization, organic farming, contract farming, etc. are important facts of hi-tech horticulture.

Micro-irrigation

The term micro-irrigation implies to application of water to the plants by drippers/ emitters. At present, many modifications of micro-irrigations are available and micro-sprinklers, micro-jets, micro-tubes, misters, foggers, micro-jets, fanjets etc. are some of them. This technology has been found of worth increasing productivity by 30-100 per cent while saving water to the extent of 70%. To enhance water use efficiency and to fulfill rising demand of irrigation water, micro-irrigation is getting popularity. Drip irrigation has got maximum coverage under fruit crops (35%) followed by plantation crops (18.5%). In fruits maximum area is under grape, followed by mango, pomegranate and banana. About 275.8 lakh ha area has been brought under micro-irrigation.

Use of Plastics

Use of plastics in agriculture is widely referred to as plasticulture. Plastic is used invariably in production and post-harvest handling of horticultural produce. Green house, net house, nurseries, roof top gardening, off-season cultivation, mulching, micro-irrigation, propagation, packaging etc. depend heavily on plastics. Different grades of plastic material are in use. Low Density Polythene (LDPE), Linear Low Density Polythene (LLDPE), High Density Polythene (HDPE) pipes for drip irrigation, plastic sheets of varying thickness for mulch, ultraviolet (UV) radiation stabilized, UV radiation blocked, sulphur diffused, anti-drip film for cladding in greenhouses etc. are some common grades of plastics. Plasticulture offers many benefits: minimized maintenance of the system, efficient management of water and energy, minimized temperature and moisture fluctuations, better nutrient application, minimized wastage, controlled soil erosion etc. are increasing day by day.

Protected Cultivation

It is also called as green house cultivation. Actually, constrained by rhythmic change in climate to grow the crop whenever needed, the concept of protected cultivation gets sensitized and with rising trade in horticulture, it is getting popular progressively. In protected cultivation, attempt is made to avert incompatibility of climate using artificial means and its benefit is harnessed in terms of harvesting produce out of their normal growing season. Demand of a particular produce all the year round has provided due back-up to the protected cultivation.

Green house cultivation was adopted in USA and Europe during 19th century. At present, China and Japan are leading countries in protected cultivation. Besides these, Netherland, Israel, Egypt, Spain, etc. Canada are another important countries where protected cultivation is widely practised.

Green house is a framed or inflated structure constructed using glass or plastic material in which growing environment is controlled suitably to grow the crops. With boom in retail sector, protected cultivation is catching fast momentum in India. High value, low volume crops are preferential for green house. A variety of vegetables, short duration-short growing fruits and flowers have been found suitable for green house cultivation. Strawberry, capsicum, baby-corn, tomato, cucumber, rose, gerbera, chrysanthemum, cactus, anthurium, orchids etc. are under cultivation in green house. The crop grown under remains protected from wind and rains also. Such condition favours harvest of good quality. Green house hastens maturity of the crops, increases yield, improves quality and in many instances reduces the load of insects and pests. However, high investment incurred in erecting is major bottleneck in popular adoption of green house technology. The technology being worth increasing yield by as high as 300 per cent, it needs due adoption.

Precision Farming

As the name suggests, precision farming is a technique of cultivation which lays emphasis on maximum precision in production minimizing wastage of inputs and resources in harnessing production potential and utilizing the crop for vested economic attributes. It involves use of technologies to manage spatial and temporal variability associated with all aspects of horticultural production while improving environment quality. The system takes into account efficient management of resources through location specific interventions. It promotes deploying variable management practices within a field according to site conditions. Global positioning system (GPS), geographic information system (G1S), remote sensing, yield monitoring devices, soil, plant and pest sensors, variable rate technologies for application of inputs are enabling technologies in precision production system. Micro-propagation, micro-irrigation, fertigation, mulching, protected cultivation, organic farming, integrated nutrients, water, pests and diseases management, use of modified crop varieties, hi-tech post harvest handling etc. form the part of precision farming.

High Density Planting (HDP)

Accommodating more number of plants per unit area in comparison to normal planting is referred to as HDP. It was attempted successfully in Europe during early sixties in under-taking apple plantation following the use of dwarfing rootstocks. Besides Europe, HDP is in commercial practice to grow temperate fruit crops in Australia, America, Japan, New Zealand and Israel. In present day scenario when land: man ratio is declining sharply, HDP needs due popularity. HDP offers high productivity per unit area both in short duration as well as perennial horticultural crops. It is achieved by resorting (i) use of dwarf rootstock/ inter-stock (ii) adoption of dwarf scion varieties (ii) use of growth regulators (iv) proper training and pruning and (v) suitable crop management practices. In India, HDP has been successfully attempted in apple, peach, pear, banana, pineapple, papaya, guava, mango and citrus etc.

Meadow Orcharding (MO)

Meadow orcharding are defined as the planting of high stemmed fruit trees that stand scattered on meadow, pastures or waysides. As the trees stand well spaced out, the area can be used for cattle herding, for example. The apple and guava trees planted in such orchards are old species with an intensive taste and aroma. The meadow orchard ecological value as features of our cultural landscape worthy of preservation is well known.

Planting intensities

In HDP, planting intensity is maintained many times higher than normal planting. Accordingly, it is named differently, as:

Semi-intensive- 500-1,000 trees/ha

Intensive- 1,000-10,000 trees/ha

Super-intensive/Meadow orcharding- 20,000-1,00,000 trees/ha

Advantage

- Efficient utilization of inputs-seeds, plants, manures, fertilizers, chemicals, pesticides, machineries, tools, labours etc. and resources-soil, water, solar radiation etc.
- Higher yield
- Higher economic return
- Easy canopy management
- Convenient farm mechanization
- Easy harvest
- Improved quality of harvest

Suitable dwarfing rootstocks

HDP is possible only using dwarfing rootstocks. In this regard suitable rootstocks for different fruit trees are as under:

Apple: Dwarfing/semi-dwarfing-M4, M7, M9, M26 and MM106,
Ultra-dwarfing - M27

Mango: Vellaikolumban

Guava: Pusa Srijan, *Psidium friedrichsthalianum*

Suitable dwarfing scion cultivars

Apple: Red Spur, Star Crimson Spur, Gold Spur, Well Spur, Oregon Spur, Silver Spur, Red Chief and Hardi Spur.

Papaya: Pusa Nanha

Banana: Dwarf Cavendish

Peach: Red Heaven

Mango: Amrapali

Sapota: PKM 1 and PKM 2

Training System

Training is a new practice in which tree growth is directed into a desired shape and form.

Suitable training systems

Central leader system- Walnut, Pecan nut

Open center or vase shaped system- Peach, Japanese plum, Nectarine

Modified leader system- European plum, Sweet cherry, Pear

Bower system- Grape

Espalier system- Apple

Cordon system- Peach

Single stem system- Citrus, Fig, Annona

Multiple stem system- Pomegranate

Two arm kniffin system- Passion fruit.

Pruning System

Pruning is the removal of a portion of a tree to correct or maintain tree structure. Prunings are found in two ways are:

1. **Thinning out-** Removal of undesirable shoots or branches without leaving any stub e.g. mango, loquat, olive etc.
2. **Heading back-** Removal of terminal portion of the shoots, branches or limb leaving its basal portion.

Special pruning techniques in fruit crops

i. **Root pruning-** Removal of roots 40cm away from the plant e.g. mandarin.

ii. **Ringing-** Removal of complete ring of bark from a branch or a trunk e.g. mango, grape.

iii. **Dehorning-** To removal of overcrowding and intermingling of branches e.g. mango.

iv. **Notching-** Partial ringing of a branches above a dormant lateral bud e.g. poona fig.

v. **Nicking-** Partial ringing of a branches below a dormant bud e.g. apple, poona fig.

vi. **Smudging-** Practice of smoking the tree e.g. mango.

vii. **Bending-** Bending of branches of shoot e.g. guava.

viii. **Thinning-** Removal of part of flower bud or small fruits from a heavy crop e.g. grape, peach, plum, quince.

ix. **Girdling-** Removal of 2-3mm white strip of barks around the them e.g. grapes.

x. **Leaf pruning-** Removal of old and senescence leaves e.g. datepalm.

xi. **Top working or top grafting or top budding-** Changing the established plants, trees, shrubs or vine with a desirable cultivars e.g. mango, apple.

Integrated Nutrient Management (INM)

It is a system of maintaining fertility of the soil ensuring judicious use of different sources of nutrients enabling better availability of nutrients to the plants so as to harvest desired productivity of the crop on sustainable basis. Under INM strategy, attempt is made to conjugate use of organic and inorganic sources of nutrients so that without jeopardizing innate fertility level of soil, optimum yield level can be achieved. Recently, among organic inputs, bio-fertilizer is receiving commercial acceptability. It improves uptake and availability of essential macro and micronutrients. The demand of bio-fertilizer is on the rise and necessary initiations have to be taken for adequate supply of bio-fertilizers.

Integrated Pest Management (IPM)

IPM strategy envisages using cultural, mechanical, chemical and biological methods simultaneously in combating pest's problem. At present much emphasis is being given on integrated approach primarily due to aggressiveness of pest population and rising demand of health safe produce.

Mechanization

Cheap and ample availability of labour is a constraint nowadays especially in agriculture. This necessitates mechanization. Automation of various farm activities are required to accomplish the work within time. Machines are available for digging of pits for planting, application of fertilizers, spray of chemicals, weeding, training and pruning, micro-irrigation, harvesting, sorting, grading, waxing, packing and for value addition.

Organic Farming

An approach of farming without use of chemical input is termed as organic farming. Increasing demand for green safe food has attracted the attention of people towards organic farming. It emphasizes upon management practices- agronomical, biological and mechanical for sustainable production, with no reliance on synthetic inputs. For manuring FYM, compost, vermi-compost, oil cakes, green manuring etc. are utilized in the field. Incorporation of leguminous crop in farming help assists in maintaining nitrogen level in the soil. Botanicals are used as protectant in combating pests/diseases problem. To claim any product organic, certification is required. The product labelled as organic fetch premium price in the market.

Contract Farming

It is getting popularity day by day with economic liberalization process. Under this system a farmer grows selected crops under buy back arrangement with an agency. The agency further trade or process the products. It has been successful attempted in potato, chilli and tomato in Punjab, in hybrid seed production in Punjab and Karnataka, in oil palm in Andhra Pradesh etc. With such type of tie-up farming system, the farmers get better and ensured return out of their produce.

Export-Import Trade in Horticulture

India is leading producer of horticultural crops. Even-though, its share in global trade is merely 0.5 %. The country exports fruits, vegetables, processed products, flowers, seeds and planting materials, spices, cashewnut, tea and coffee etc. The export of cashewnut occupies dominantly higher position followed by spices, tea and coffee. Fresh fruits and vegetables comprise about 35 % of the world trade in horticulture. Among fresh fruits grapes, mango, citrus, banana, apple, etc. are exported in maximum magnitude. Among vegetables, which constitute 22 % in the world trade in horticulture, onion, tomato, pea, bean, potato, mushroom, asparagus and capsicum are prominent ones. Export growth of fresh fruits and vegetables in term of value is 14% and of processed fruits and vegetables is 16 %.

Chapter 2

Importance and Scope of Horticulture

Horticulture means the cultivation of garden plants. The garden plants are comprised of fruits, vegetables, ornamentals etc. The culture covers the operation from raising and planting of saplings to the ultimate use of the produce and as such, it is the most intensive of all the agricultural [illegible]

[illegible]

Chapter 2

Importance and Scope of Horticulture

Horticulture means the cultivation of garden plants. The garden plants are comprised of fruits, vegetables, ornamentals etc. The culture covers the operation from raising and planting of saplings to the ultimate use of the products and, as such, it is the most intensive of all the agricultural sciences. However, the concept of growing plants in garden or in an enclosure does not fit well in the changed perspective where large scale cultivation of fruits, vegetables and flowers extending over several square kilometers, in many a place nowadays, delimits the boundary of garden.

Importance of Horticulture

The importances of horticulture are established not only as a source of nutritious foods but also in many other ways which are narrated in the following points:

1. **Social-** Due to the long association, the fruits are seen to have a permanent seat in the social life of man. As a consequence, various fruits have acquired their place in art, music, literature, customs and habits of various nations of the world. The description of fruit as symbolic insertion in the poems and literatures, the use of whole fruit plant or part thereof in various social festive and public gathering, and conferring titles to individuals in the name of fruits or naming a region or whole district after the name of a fruit are nothing but an indication of their popularities and social position in various countries.

2. **Art and culture-** The sculpture of mango tree on the walls of tope at Sanchi in India, the paintings of fruit trees in various caves and galleries throughout the world, and the moulding of earthen pitchers in the shape of cherimoya by Inkas in central America are the indications of acceptance of fruits in the art and cultural themes of man living in various parts of the world. Nevertheless, the fruit plants and the flowers are considered in many countries as symbols of expression of human themes. Some of them are symbols of majestic pomp, rivalry, magnanimity, modesty or simplicity. The importance of fruits for expression of human theme and attitude clearly exemplifies their position in the cultural life of various nations.

3. **Religious-** Some of the fruits are also considered as symbols of religious cultures in many countries. It is also interesting that some fruits or the whole plants are attributed as symbols of certain god or goddess in different parts of the world and worshipped accordingly. Apart from these, some nations observe religious festivals in the name of fruits. The Mandruin Festival of China, Cherry Blossom Festival of Japan and others indicate the importance of fruits in the religious life of various nations.

4. **General utility-** The fruit trees, from the time immemorial, are providing not only foods to the man and domestic animals but also shelter to the animal kingdom, timbers for manufacture of furniture, leaves for thatching the roofs, medicines against ailments, structures for transports, protection against soil erosion and natural hazard, maintaining the bearing capacity of the earth by improving the ecological balance, and saving the atmosphere from various pollutions. The fruits also provide taste to the tongues, pleasure to the vision and aroma to the nasal organs. It is a question, if Adam was first attracted by any of the qualities or by all of them. That is why, while considering the importance of fruits or fruit trees, the overall importance of them cannot be ignored.

5. **Nutritive value-** Still then, the importance of fruits is primarily considered in the context of their nutritive values. Fruits are suitable diets for people of all age groups. It is a common proverb. "Take an apple a day and keep the doctors away". It points out the nutritive as well as medicinal properties of fruits to provide balanced food to the different working classes of the society. Fruits are attributed as protective foods and these provide kinetic energy to the body. The essential characters of good food like good taste, nutrition, storability, blend ability, palatability and preservability are seen in most of the fruits. In addition, they are easily consumed as fresh when they are ripe, and thus, the cumbersome process of cooking is avoided to satisfy the appetite. Most of the fruits have their characteristic aroma developed from various organic constituents. The aroma may develop from phenolic, alcoholic, turpentine or other compounds inside the fruits, depending on their composition, with the advancement of ripening. The aroma has a pleasant smell which enriches the taste of the fruit, as taste is not merely a combination of sugar and acid but something else, which increases the interest of eating and gives pleasure to the oral organs. Most of the fruits are good source of carbohydrate in the form of soluble sugars like glucose and fructose. However, sucrose and others are also seen in some ripe fruits although in smaller quantity. The sugars available from the fruits are easily digestible, and many a times, are recommended for the healthy person as well as for a patient, for a child as well as for an old man to meet the calorie requirements

of the body. Some of the fruits are also, good source of protein and fat. However, majority of the fruits are good source of the vitamins and minerals. Amongst the vitamins, the vitamin B complex which is required in abundance for various metabolic process of the body, is available from the fruits adequately. Vitamin A, vitamin C and vitamin K are also available in appreciable quantity from many of the fruits. Minerals like calcium, phosphorus, iron etc. are required in appreciable quantity for the growing young's and the sedentary people as well. These minerals are adequately available in many of the fruits. In short, it may be said that daily consumption of fruit is a must to have a balanced diet.

Most of the fruits are easily stored for reasonable period. However, there is difference in duration of storability of fruits growing in various temperature regimes. Storability is nothing but deferred usability which helps in consuming the materials in future. Mature fruits once harvested take some time to ripe and further longer period to break down or spoil. In general, the acidic fruits are stored for a longer period than the sweet fruits. It is thought to be due to gradual bio-conversion of acids to sugars with the advancement of ripening. Some of the fruits are still consumable when the sugars are further oxidized to alcohols. This state of transformation is known as fermentation and comes under fruit processing which will be dealt later.

Many of the fruits are easily blended with the other fruits. So also, it may be blended with other food, fresh or processed. However, some sour fruits like lime, lemon etc. cannot be blended with all the foods. On the other hand, the preparation of fruit salad or apple pie is good example of the blend ability of fruits with other food. In the process of blending, it is a specialized technique to make a preparation of varied taste, aroma and texture to increase the palatability and to bring a variety in taste.

The techniques for fruit processing in terms of preparation of alcohol, resins etc. are very old. Further, research and development through centuries have generated the methods of preparations of powder, pickles, cider, jam, jelly, marmalade, sauce, dehydrated fruits etc. in the long past. Although, the duration of preservation varies with different methods, yet the concept of delayed use of fruits, even after their ripening, to the ancient man, through fruit preservation, was a long way forward to plan a civilized life by adoption of newer technology in the field of horticulture.

6. **Economical-** The economic profitability of an enterprise depends on its meaningful utilization. Fruit orcharding is a very expensive and skillful job. During the earlier part of establishment of an orchard, the major expenditure is incurred for saplings, planting as well as the cost of protection, in addition to those there are some recurring expenditures. However, these costs, many

a times, are compensated by growing other crops in the same field throughout the year during the early part of orcharding. The initial high cost generally tends to decrease as the fruit plants develop and start production. Depending on the nature of the fruit trees, the longevity of the orchards in terms of economic production varies to a great extent. The annual and seasonal fruits, on the other hand, do not develop the concept of orcharding. The quick growing fruits having shorter life span in comparison to most of the tree fruits develop orchards but for a shorter duration. On the contrary, the trees having longer life give a good standing for the orchards, sustaining for a century or more. The orchard operators, even after the expiry of the productivity of fruit trees, get a good return from the timbers. The economic productivity of the fruit plants per unit area is no less than any of the agricultural crops. Moreover, some of the fruit plants have a very high and encouraging production. In this regards, the production of 50 tones of grapes, 45 tones of pineapple or 80 tones of papaya from a hectare of land per annum is no wonder and these may compete with any other agricultural crop enterprises. It has been reported that the horticultural crops with their meager share of 2-3% of land area, in most of the countries, contribute 5-7% of gross food production and 10-35% of the national income from the crop enterprise.

The high productivity of fruit trees gives higher economic return per unit area. This also provides higher calorie return from the same area of land. It is logical that higher production also increases the production of higher quantity of essential minerals and vitamins for human consumption from the unit area. It is unthinkable, in this context, that how the man can solve the problem of scarcity of aerable land and food in this earth without fruit culture, which is gradually becoming over taxed with population pressure. The higher production with choicest quality of food and higher economic return per unit area purport the logic of sustenance of living standard on a smaller portion of aerable land in comparison to the field crops. In other words, as the pressure of population will increase, the nations will have to develop agricultural policies based on fruit crops or other horticultural crops which will provide food for the empty stomach with delicacy of taste, shelter against the natural hazards, good environment for living and improved quality of life.

It is a common observation that the tree fruits take longer period to come to production after transplanting. But, this is not true for the annual fruit crops. On the other hand, the quick growing as well as the long term tree fruits, generally, gives rise once over annual production which, often, compels the orchard operator to wait for the entire year for the produce and as in case of most of the agricultural crops, the growers are to depend on the whims of the nature. The problem of dependence on nature or the annual once over harvest are, generally, avoided by the growers by adoption of inter cropping or multistoried cropping system provided other factors for raising these crops are favourable. The initial poor and slow return from the orchards are compensated by the former cropping system. But, a much higher productivity of the land or orchard and more riskless practice is followed, if multistoried cropping system is adopted in the orchards. The practice of growing 2-3 crops of various altitude in an orchard which will sustain for a longer duration and share the natural resources like sunlight, water, nutrition etc. which otherwise would have been lost in the nature, is a unique technique derived by man from the tropical rain forest of the world. As such, this cannot be practiced in the orchards of quick growing or annual fruits. The total production in a multistoried orchard is additive where the atmosphere is not at all affected rather enriched with the sharing of the resources. The multiple cropping system in the orchards also generates more avenues for employment either in the operation or otherwise. The intensive horticultural practices may accommodate skilled and trained personals in the developing countries where unemployment is a serious problem.

The management of orchards as well as harvesting and the subsequent operations need a large number of manpower of various age and sex group throughout the year. This provides a unique opportunity to the young people to learn the various techniques starting from planting and propagation of plants to ultimate use of the produce, even from their boyhood and engage their spare time in creative works. The old and working people may engage themselves to this work of creativity of various natures to break the monotony of life. Thus, the growing of fruits may employ people of various age and sex groups. It may also provide relaxation and induce diversion from the daily monotonous routine work. In this juncture, the immense scope for employment of family labour may be emphasized where workers of various age and sex groups are available under the same roof. If the family labours are employed, the young generations in a family learn discipline and harmony of work from the elder people and the old people undergoes light exercises for health. The importance and essentiality of these are admitted by almost all the sensible people in the various societies of the world.

7. **Trade and industrial-** As stated earlier, the oldest industrial use of fruits was the preparation of alcohol, resins etc. with the advancement of technology, a large number of products have been developed. The increased production of fruits has widened the scope of their industrial use which helps in preserving the fruits, through processing for future use. The fruits,

in these types of industry, are directly utilized as raw materials. In certain countries these are developed as cottage industry, while in others as small or medium scale industries which make a satisfactory contribution in the national economy with an annual turnover of several billion of dollars. These industries provide job opportunity and extend the export potentiality of those countries.

Apart from these, a large number of ancillary industries and trade sectors are also developed. The fresh fruits are generally stored either in an air conditioned warehouse, or regulated atmosphere (RA) or controlled atmosphere storage (CA) such as, these infrastructure help in prolonging the shelf-life of the commodities. The processed fruit products are also stored in cold storage or RA or CA storage which also provides some employment opportunity. Finally, the trade of the fruits which requires market processing likes sorting, grading, packaging, labeling, transportation or auctioning also increases job opportunity to a great extent, if properly organized. In conclusion, it may be said that the fruit production has a great possibility in trade and industrial development of any country of the world.

8. **Ecological balance and pollution control-** Environmental pollution is endangering the habitation of the entire animal kingdom nowadays in this earth. The sources of pollution are industrial refuses, automobile fumes, unscientific use of fertilizers and agro-chemical etc. which are not only poisoning the atmosphere but also disturbing the ionosphere of this universe by piercing the ozone layers. As a consequence, various ailments are cropping up in human life. Due to disturbance in ionosphere, some cosmic rays which are detrimental to the skin, are penetrating this globe. The animals have natural immunity against these odds. So, scientists are trying to overcome these problems by introducing social forestry, agro-forestry etc. or in other word, by increasing the proportion of forest in comparison to agricultural land which should ideally be around 21 per cent of geographical area. By introduction of fruit plants of suitable types in appropriate regions, the purpose of increasing forest area may also be attained which will serve the dual purpose by providing guard against pollution as well as food and medicine for the millions for a reasonably longer period.

   In this way, by inclusion of perennial fruit plants having faster growth rate, the ecological balance may be maintained and the bearing capacity of this earth may be improved for a longer period for the man, and domestic and beneficial animals. In addition, the fruit crops may fit well in crop diversification programmes in various scales, ranging from organized large orchards to a few trees in the waste land or backyard of homestead or elsewhere. Naturally, these plants may be successfully utilized for reclamation of waste lands.

Horticulture is important due to the following considerations

1. As a source of variability in produce.
2. As a source of nutrients, vitamins, minerals, flavour, aroma, alkaloids, oleoresins, fibre, etc.
3. As a source of medicine.
4. As an economic proposition as they give higher returns per unit area in terms of energy, money, job, etc.
5. Effective utilization of waste land through cultivation of hardy fruits and medicinal plants.
6. As a substitute for family income being the component of home garden/ kitchen garden.
7. As a foreign exchange earner, has higher share compare to agriculture crops.
8. As an input for industry being amenable to processing, especially fruit and vegetable preservation industry.
9. Aesthetic consideration and protection of the environment.
10. Religious significance in the country.

In short and sweet horticulture supplies quality food for health and mind, more calories per unit area, develops better resources and yields higher returns per unit area. It also enhances land value and creates better purchasing power for those who are engaged in this industry. Therefore, *horticulture is important for health, wealth, hygiene and happiness.*

Other importance

1. Similar to forest trees these horticultural trees will maintain the ecosphere.
2. They help in transforming the micro climate.
3. Provides shelter to birds, reptiles and other micro organisms and add to the geo-ecological diversity on the land.
4. Provides thrust to the writers, poets, thinkers and analysts there by keeps their cultural impulse alive.
5. Adds to the survival of life-spheres of living entity.

Scope of Horticulture

Like any other things, scope of horticulture depends on incentive it has for the farmers, adaptability of the crops, necessity and facilities for future growth through inputs availability and infrastructure for the distribution of produce/ marketing etc.

1. Incentive for the farmer

- The biggest incentive for the farmer is money.
- Horticultural crops provide more returns in terms of per unit area of production, export value, value addition compared to agricultural crops.

2. Adaptability

- India is bestowed with a great variety of climatic and edaphic conditions as we have climates varying from tropical, subtropical, temperate and within these humid, semi-arid, arid, frost free temperate etc.
- Likewise we have soils from loam, alluvial, laterite, medium black, rocky shallow, heavy black, sandy etc., and thus a large number of crops can be accommodated with very high level of adaptability. Thus, there is lot of scope for horticultural crops.

3. Necessity

- After having achieved the self sufficiency in food, nutritional security for the people of the country has become the point of consideration/priority.
- To meet the nutritional requirement in terms of vitamins and minerals horticulture crops are to be grown in sufficient quantities to provide a bare minimum of 120 g of fruits and 300 g of vegetables per head per day with a population of above 120 crores.
- Good land is under pressure for stable food, industry, housing, roads and infrastructure due to population explosion and only wasteland had to be efficiently utilized where cultivation of annuals is a gamble due to restricted root zone and their susceptibility of abiotic stress. These lands can be best utilized to cultivate hardy horticultural crops like fruits and medicinal plants.
- At present our share in international trade of horticultural commodities is less than one per cent of total trade. Moreover, these commodities (spices, coffee, tea etc.,) fetch 10-20 times more foreign exchange per unit weight than cereals and therefore, taking advantage of globalization of trade, nearness of big market and the size of production, our country should greatly involve in international trade which would provide scope for growth.

4. Export value

- Among fresh fruits-mangoes and grapes; in vegetables- onion and potato; among flowers, roses; among plantation cashewnut, tea , coffee, coconut, arecanut, and spice crops like black pepper, cardamom, ginger, turmeric, chilies, etc., constitute the bulk of the export basket.
- *European* and *gulf* countries are major importer of horticultural produce.

Table 2 : Major countries for export of horticultural produce from India

S.No.	Commodity	Major importer	Share value (%)
1	Fruits and vegetables	United Arab Emirates	28.00
2	Flower crops	U.S.A	37.70
3	Processed products	Soviet Union Countries	14.60
4	Spices	U.S.A	43.50
5	Cashew	U.S.A	40.00

- **In the recent past communication and transport system have improved, investment in food industry has increased which will support growth of horticulture through quick deliverance and avoidance of waste.**

Reasons for scope of horticulture in India are:

1. To exploit the great variability of agro climatic conditions in the country.
2. To meet the need for fruits, vegetables, flowers, spices, beverages in relation to population growth based on minimum nutritional security and for other needs.
3. To meet the requirement of processing industry.
4. To substitute import and increase export.
5. To improve the economic conditions of the farmers and to engage more labourers to avoid the problem of unemployment.
6. To protect environment.

Chapter 3

Horticulture Crops for Human Nutrition

Fruits and vegetables play an important role in balanced diet. These provide not only energy rich food but also provide vital protective nutrients/elements and vitamins. Comparatively fruits and vegetables are the cheapest source of natural nutritive foods. Since most of Indians are vegetarians, the incorporation of horticulture produce in daily diet is essential for good health. Realizing the worth of fruits and vegetables in human health, Indian Council of Medical Research (ICMR) recommended the use of 120g fruits and 300g vegetables per capita per day. With the growing awareness and inclination towards vegetarianism worldwide the horticulture crops are gaining tremendous importance.

Functions of fruits and vegetables in human body

1. Fruits and vegetables provide palatability/taste.
2. Improves appetite and provides fiber to overcome constipation.
3. They neutralize the acids produced during digestion of proteins and fatty acids.
4. They improve the general immunity of human body against diseases, deficiencies etc.
5. They are the important source of vitamins and minerals for used in several bio-chemical reactions occur in body.
6. Fruits and vegetables provide higher energy value per unit area compared to cereals.
    - Fruits are also a good source of energy eg. Avocado, Olive etc.,
    - Fruits are also a good source of enzymes which are helpful in metabolic activities leading to proper digestion of food eg. Jamun and Papaya.
    - All fruits have one or the other medicinal value.
    - They should be eaten in adequate quantity.

- Regular consumption of fruits reduces obesity, maintain health and increase the longevity of life.
- Fruits are attractive in appearance, delicious in taste and easily digestible. Therefore, they are liked by young and old alike.

Importance of fruits and vegetables in human diet

- For balance diet fruits and vegetables play an emperor role in health, happiness and prosperity.
- Fruits and vegetables are the rich source of mineral and vitamins without which human cannot maintain their proper health and resistance to diseases.
- Deficiency of mineral and vitamins causes disturbances of metabolism and resulting ill health beside these protein and cellulose are found in the fruit with stimulate the intestinal activity and protect the human body against various type of disorder.
- Man cannot survive bread alone therefore at least 120 g fruit capita per day and 300 g vegetables capita per day is required in addition to pulse, cereals, milk etc.
- For keeping the body system fit, use of fruits and vegetables have become must in daily diet, especially in present era of environment pollution.

Some of the essential nutrients provided by different fruits and vegetables are:

Vitamins/ Minerals	Role in human body	Sources
Vitamin-A	1. Essential for growth and reproduction. 2. Helps in resistance to infections, increases longevity and decreases senility. 3. Deficiency causes, night blindness, xeropthalmia, retardation in growth, roughness in skin, formation of stones in kidney.	Mango, Papaya, Persimon, Dates, Jack fruit, Walnut, Oranges, Passion fruit, Loquât etc. Beet leaf, Spinach and Fenugreek leaves, Carrot, Coriander leaves, Colocasia leaves etc.
Vitamin-B_1	1. For maintaining good appetite and normal digestion. 2. Necessary for growth, fertility, lactation and for normal functioning of nervous system. 3. Deficiency causes beri-beri, paralysis, loss the sensitivity of skin, enlargement of heart, loss of appetite and fall in body temperature.	Walnut, Apricot, Apple, Banana, Grapefruit, Plum and Almond etc. Chilli, Colocasia leaves, Tomato (red) etc.

Vitamin-B_2	1. Important for growth, health of skin and for respiration in poorly vascularised tissue such as the cornea. 2. Deficiency causes pellagra and alopecia, loss of appetite, loss of weight, sore throat, and development of cataract, swollen nose and baldness.	Bael, Papaya, Litchi, Pomegranate, Wood apple and Pineapple etc. Fenugreek leaves and Amaranthus etc.
Vitamin-C	1. Deficiency causes scurvy, pain in joints, swelling of limbs, unhealthy gums, tooth decay, delay in wound healing and rheumatism.	Barbados cherry, Aonla, Guava, Lime, Lemon, Sweet oranges, Ber, Pineapple and Pear etc. Drumstick leaves, Coriander leaves, Chilli and Tomato etc.
Fat		Walnut, Almond, Avocado etc.
Fibre		Guava, Pomegranate, Aonla, Grape, etc. Amaranth, Mustard, Beet leaf, Spinach etc.

Some minerals are essential for the growth and development for the human body:

Minerals	Deficiency causes	Sources
Calcium	Causes Rickets, Osteomalacia.	Sitaphal, Ramphal, Fig, Phalsa, Citrus, Sapota, Grapes, West Indian Cherry etc. Curry leaf, Amaranthus, Fenugreek, Radish leaves, Coriander leaves, Agathi etc.
Phosphorous	Essential for cell multiplication of bones and soft tissues. Helps in liberation of energy on oxidation of carbohydrates.	Wood apple, Avocado, Dates, Pomegranate and Grape raisins etc. Agathi, Amaranthus and Coriander leaves etc.
Proteins	Important for body growth, formation and maintenance of body tissues	West Indian cherry, Avocado, Custrad Apple, Banana, Apricot, Guava, Grapes etc. Pea, Cowpea and Indian bean etc.
Iron	Act as oxygen carrier in the body.	Karonda, Date palm, Grape raisins, West Indian Cherry, Guava, Sitaphal, Avocado, Sapota, plum etc. Agathi, Amaranthus and Coriander leaves etc.

Importance and Scope of Horticultural Crops

Fruits and vegetables growing is one of the important and age old practices, practiced in India since ancient times. Cultivation of fruits and vegetables crops plays an important role in overall status of the mankind and the nation. The standard of living of the people of a country is depending upon the production and per capita consumption of fruits and vegetables. Fruit growing have more economic advantages.

1. Economic importance

- **High productivity:** High yield per unit area: From a unit area of land more yield is realized from fruit crops than any of the agronomic crops. The average yields of Papaya, Banana and Grapes are 10 to 15 times more than that of agronomic crops.
- **High net profit:** Through, the initial cost of establishment of an orchard is high it is compensated by higher net profit due to higher productivity or high value of produce eg- Grapes/Mango/Banana yield 20-40 tones/ha. Which cost about 1.5-2.5 lakh/ha.
- **Source of raw material for agro based industries:** Fruit farming provides raw materials for various agro based industries- canning and preservation (fresh fruits), coir industries (coconut husk), pharmaceutical industry (Aonla, Papaya, Jamun) transporting and packaging industries etc.
- **Efficient utilization of resources:** Growing of fruits being perennial in nature, enables grower to remain engaged throughout the year in farm operations and to utilize fully the resources & assets like machinery, labour, land water for production purpose throughout the year compared to agronomic crops.
- **Utilization of waste and barren lands for production:** Although, most of the fruits crops require perennial irrigation and good soil for production, there are many fruit crops of hardy in nature, Mango, Ber, Cashew, Custard apple, Aonla, Phalsa, Jamun etc. which are grown on poor shallow, undulated soils considered unsuitable for growing grain/ agronomical crops.
- **Foreign exchange:** Many fresh fruits, processed products and spices are exported to several countries earning good amount of foreign exchange.

2. Nutritional importance

Importance of fruits in human diet is well recognized. Man cannot live on cereals alone. Fruits and vegetables are essential for balanced diet and good health. Nutritionist advocates 120g of fruits and 300g vegetables per capita per day in addition to cereals, pulses, egg etc. fruits and vegetables are good sources of vitamins and minerals without which human body cannot maintain proper health and develop resistance to disease they also contain pectin, cellulose, fats, proteins etc.

3. Fruits have medicinal value

The fruits like Aonla, Pomegranate, Kokum, Jamun, Bael, Ber etc., have great medicinal value.

1. Papaya reduces night blindness.
2. Citrus juice reduces acute dihorrhea.
3. Aonla triphala (chawan prash) for digestion.
4. Jack fruit (Jackoline) for prevents AIDS.

4. Other importance

Fruit and vegetable growing in kitchen gardens helps to reduce family budget on purchase of fruits and vegetables.

- Planting of fruits trees, maintains ecological balance and to increase precipitation of the locality.
- Fruit tree farming also reduces soil erosion, silting and air pollution.
- Generate employment being highly intensive and skillful enterprise generates employment even for trained persons.

Chapter 4

Classification of Horticultural Plants

Classification is system of placing an individual or a member in various groups or to categories them according to particular plan or sequence which is in conformity with the nomenclature. From time-to-time for purposes of convenience plants or fruits have been classified in various ways that makes possible to refer them to a large number of kinds under a group name without enumerating or specifying individually. The basis of these groupings varies according to the features of fruits or growth of the fruit plants that have been under classification at the time.

Knowledge of classification of horticultural plants is very useful to the horticulturists because it serves: (1) to identity and name them, (2) to afford at least some idea of the closeness of their relationship i.e. line of descent to other kinds, (3) to suggest with what other kind they possibly may or may not be interbred or crossed, (4) to suggest the kinds with which they possibly may or may not be inter-grafted, and (5) often to suggest certain soil and the cultural requirements, climatic adaptations etc. However, the classification of fruit trees or fruits and vegetables on the basis of consumer's rating also gained attention in recent years. The consumers' rating is mainly based on the size, shape, nutritive value and marketability of them. Each of these classifications is quite different from the other classification or groupings.

Basically, the fruit trees, as suggested by many authors, have been classified on the basis of their botany comprising of taxonomic ancestry, morphologic features, physiological functions, adaptability etc. or on the basis of agricultural and horticultural requirements. But the consumers' rating has not been properly covered in the earlier classification. Generally based on botanical relationship the plants are classified as under.

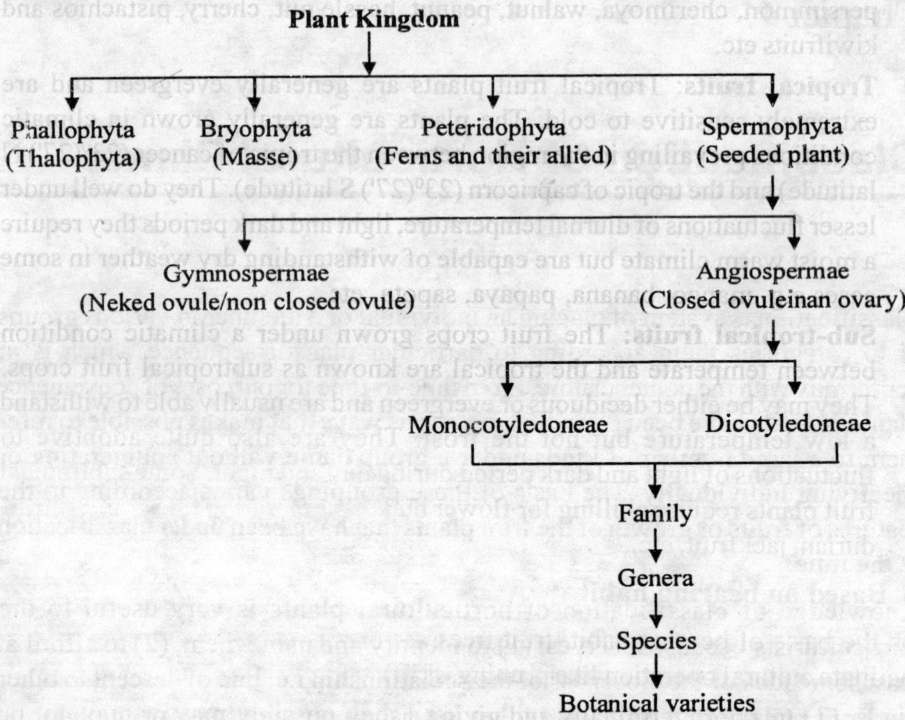

The detailed classification of various kinds of horticultural plants is as under:

A. CLASSIFICATION OF FRUITS

Classification is the system of grouping or placing of an individual according to nomenclature. It is very useful to the pomologist, it helps to:

- To identify and naming the crop.
- To study the close relationship.
- To know their hybrids and crossing behavior.
- To know their compatibility & inter grafting ability.
- To know their adoptability to soil & climate.

A. Based on climate adaptability

In this classification, the fruits trees are categorized into three recognized groups.

i. **Temperate fruits**: Temperate fruit plants are exacting in their climate requirement. They are grown only in place where winter is distinctly cold, require as exposure of specific chilling temperature for certain period without which they do not flower. These fruit plants are generally deciduous and stand frost e.g. apple, almond, peach, pear, plum, strawberry, apricot, persimmon, cherimoya, walnut, peanut, hassle nut, cherry, pistachios and kiwifruits etc.

ii. **Tropical fruits**: Tropical fruit plants are generally evergreen and are extremely sensitive to cold. The plants are generally grown in climatic conditions prevailing in the region between the tropic of cancer (23^0(27') N latitude) and the tropic of capricorn (23^0(27') S latitude). They do well under lesser fluctuations of diurnal temperature, light and dark periods they require a moist warm climate but are capable of withstanding dry weather in some cases e.g. mango, banana, papaya, sapota, etc.,

iii. **Sub-tropical fruits:** The fruit crops grown under a climatic condition between temperate and the tropical are known as subtropical fruit crops. They may be either deciduous or evergreen and are usually able to withstand a low temperature but not the frost. They are also quite adoptive to fluctuations of light and dark period during day and night. Some subtropical fruit plants require chilling for flower bud differentiation e.g. grape, citrus, durian, jackfruit, etc.,

B. Based on bearing habit

On the basis of bearing habit, fruit trees are classified in to six categories to facilitate cultural operation like pruning, skiffing, heading back etc.

a. Fruit buds born terminally and giving rise to inflorescence without leaves e.g. mango, cherry, etc.

b. Fruit buds born terminally and unfolding to produce leafy shoots which terminate in flower clusters e.g. apple.

c. Fruit buds born terminally and unfolding to produce leafy shoots with flower or flower clusters e.g. guava.

d. Fruit bud born laterally containing flower parts only and giving rise to inflorescence without leaves or leaves present, they are reduced in size e.g. citrus.

e. Fruit bud born laterally and unfolding to produce leafy shoots terminally in flower clusters this type of flowering is noticed in grapes and cashewnut.

f. Fruit buds born laterally and unfolding to produce leafy shoots with flower clusters in leafy axils e.g. fig.

C. Based on fruit morphology

a. Simple fruit

1. **Berry :** Banana, Papaya, Grape, Sapota, Avocado, Guava
2. **Modified berry**
   i. **Balausta :** Pomegranate
   ii. **Amphisarca :** Woodapple, Bael

3. **Pepo :** Melon, Water melon
4. **Pome :** Apple, Pear, Loquat, Quince
5. **Drupe (Stone) :** Mango, Pear, Plum, Ber
6. **Hesperidium :** Citrus
7. **Nut fruit :** Cashew, Litchi, Walnut, Rambutan
8. **Capsule :** Aonla, Carambola

b. Aggregate fruits

1. **Etario of berries :** Custard apple, Raspberry
2. **Etario of druplets :** Blackberry, Longanberry
3. **Etario of achenes :** Strawberry

c. Multiple fruit

1. **Syconus :** Fig
2. **Sorosis :** Jackfruit, Pineapple, Breadfruit, Mulberry

D. Based on plant part used

Juicy placental hairs- Citrus
Mesocarp and endocarp- Banana
Endocarp- Coconut
Fleshy pericarp of individual berries- Custard apple
Fleshy receptacle- Fig
Thalamus and pericarp- Guava
Fleshy thalamus- Apple
Pericarp and placenta- Grape
Mesocarp- Mango
Aril- Litchi
Juicy covering of seed- Pomegranate
Stalk of fruit and thalamus- Pear
Seed- Almond and Walnut
Fleshy axis, bracts, perianth and seed- Pineapple
Fleshy layer of pericarp- Bael
Pericarp and thalamus- Jamun

E. Based on rate of respiration

Climacteric	Non-climacteric
Mango, Banana, Sapota, Guava,Papaya, Apple, Fig, Peach, Pear, Plum, Annona, etc.	Citrus, Grape, Pomegranate, Pineapple, Litchi, Ber, Jamun, Cashew, Cherry, Strawberry etc.
(Climacteric fruits produce much larger amount of ethylene than non climacteric fruits)	

F. Based on photoperiodic responses

Long day	Short day	Day neutral plants
Passion fruit, Apple	Strawberry, Pineapple, Coffee	Papaya, Guava, Banana

G. Based on relative salt tolerance

Highly tolerant	Medium tolerant	Highly sensitive
Datepalm, Ber, Amla, Guava,Coconut, Khirni	Pomegranate, Cashew, Fig, Jamun, Phalsa	Mango, Apple, Citrus, Pear, Straw berry

H. Based on relative acid tolerance

Highly tolerant	Medium tolerant	Highly sensitive
Strawberry, Raspberry, Fig, Bael, Plum	Pineapple, Avocado, Litchi	-

I. Based on growth pattern

Growth pattern	Examples
Single sigmoid growth curve	Mango, Apple, Datepalm, Pear, Sweet orange, Lemon, Strawberry etc.
Double sigmoid growth curve	Stone fruit (Peach, Plum, Nectarine, Apricot), Grapes, Papaya, Sweet cherries, Fig, Raspberry, Almond, Pineapple, Annona etc.
Triple sigmoid growth curve	Kiwi fruit

J. Based on longevity

a. Very long longevity → More than 100yrs - Date palm, coconut, arecanut

b. Long longevity → 50 - 100yrs - Mango, tamarind

c. Medium longevity → 10 - 50yrs - Litchi, guava, pomegranate

d. Short longevity → Less than 10yrs - Pineapple, banana

K. Based on continuation of growth

a. **Evergreen** - Mango, Citrus, Litchi, Sapota

b. **Deciduous** - Apple, Pear, Peach, Plum, Apricot

L. Based on type of inflorescence

a. **Racemose**

i. **Solitary-** Guava, peach, quince, almond, apricot, trifoliate orange

ii. **Raceme-** Blackberry, gooseberry, raspberry

iii. **Catkins-** Peacanut, walnut, chestnut, mulbery

iv. **Corymbose-** Pear

b. **Cymose**

i. **Panicle-** Grape, litchi, mango, loquat, pistachio nut

ii. **Solitary-** Papaya, sapota, citrus, phalsa, persimmon, strawberry

iii. **Fasicle-** Sweet orange, ber, plum, cherry

c. **Spadix**: Banana, arecanut, coconut, datepalm

d. **Hyphanthodium**: Fig, pomegranate

M. Based on botanical relationship with genomes

Family	Crops	Scientific name	Fruit type	Chromo-some No.	Origin
Monocotyledoneae					
Musaceae	Banana	*Musa paradisiaca, Musa balbisiana*	Berry	22,33,44	Indo-Malayan
	Plantain	*Musa acuminata*	Berry	22,33,44	Indo-Burma
Bromeliaceae	Pineapple	*Ananas comosus*	Sorosis	50,75,100	Brazil
Palmae/Aracaceae	Peach plum	*Guillielma gasipes*	Drupe		West Asia
	Date palm	*Phoenix dactylifera*	Drupe	36	West Asia
Dicotyledoneae					
Actinidiaceae	Kiwi fruit	*Actinidia deliciosa*	Berry	58	Central America
Anacardiaceae	Mango	*Mangifera indica*	Drupe	40	South East-Asia
	Pistachionut	*Pistacia vera*	Nut	30	Iran/Iraq
	Cashewnut	*Anacardium occidentale*	Nut	42	Brazil
	Indian hog plum	*Spondias pinnata*	Drupe		
	Hog plum	*Spondias mombin*	Drupe		

Annonaceae	Custard apple/ Seetaphal	*Annona squamosa*	Aggregate berries	14	West Indies
	Bullock heart/ Hanumanphal	*Annona reticulata*	Aggregate berries	14	
	Sour sop/ Lakshmanphal	*Annona muricata*	Aggregate berries	14	South America
	Cherimoya/ Ramphal	*Annona cherimoya*	Aggregate berries	14	Bovilia
	Atemoya	*Annona atemoya*	Aggregate berries	14	Man made hybrid
Apocynaceae	Karonda	*Carissa carandus*	Berry	22	
	Natal plum	*Carissa grandiflora*	Berry	22	
Bombaceaceae	Durian	*Durio zibetinus*	Berry	56	Malayan region (Borneo)
Actinidaceae	Kiwi fruit	*Actinidia chinensis*	Berry	56	
Caricaceae	Papaya	*Carica papaya*	Berry	18	Tropical America
Corylaceae/ Betulaceae	Filbert/ Hazelnut	*Corylus avellana*	Nut		
Dilleniaceae	Elephant apple	*Dillenia indica*	Fleshy calyx		South East Asia
Ebenaceae	American persimmon	*Diospyros vixgiana*	Berry		China
	Persimmon	*Diospyros kaki*	Berry	90 (6x)	China
Boraginaceae	Lasoda	*Cordiya mixa*	Berry		
Euphorbiaceae	Aonla/Nelli	*Emblica officinalis*	Capsule (Drupe)	28	Madagascar
	Star gooseberry	*Phyllanthus acidus*	Berry		
Fagaceae	Chinese chest nut	*Chestua mollissima*	Nut		
	European/ sweet chest nut	*Chestua sativa*	Nut		
Flacourtiaceae	Governor's plum	*Flacourtia indica*	Berry		
Guttiferae/ clusiaceae	Cowphal	*Garcinia cowa*	Berry		
	Malabar tamarind	*Garcinia cambogia*	Berry		

	Mangosteen	*Garcinia mangostana*	Berry	28	Malayan Archipelago
Lauraceae	Avocado	*Persea americana*	Berry	24	Central America
Malphighiaceae	Barbados cherry/ West Indian cherry	*Malphigia puncifolia*	Drupe	40	Trinidad and Tobago
Moraceae	Aini	*Artocarpus hirsuta*	Sorosis	56	
	Jack fruit	*Atrocarpus heterophyllus*	Sorosis	56	India
	Bread fruit	*Artocarpus altilis*	Sorosis	56	Indo-Malayan
	Monkey jack	*Artocarpus lakoocha*	Sorosis	56	Western Ghats
	Fig	*Ficus carica*	Synconus	26	
	Mulberry	*Morus alba*	Sorosis	308	
Myrtaceae	Guava	*Psidium guajava*	Berry	22	Tropical America
	Jamun	*Syzygium cuminii*	Drupe	40	India
	Rose apple	*Syzygium jambos*	Drupe	20	
	Malayan apple	*Syzygium malacense*	Berry		
	Pineapple guava	*Feijoa sellowiana*	Berry		
	Watery rose apple	*Syzygium aqueum*	Berry		
Oleaceae	Indian olive	*Olea ferruginea*	Drupe		
	Olive	*Olea europaea*	Drupe	46	Mediterran ean region
Oxalidaceae	Bilimbi	*Averrhoa bilimbi*	Berry	24	
	Carambola	*Averrhoa carambola*	Berry	24	Sri Lanka
Passifloraceae	Passion fruit	*Passiflora edulis*	Berry	18	Brazil
Proteaceae	Macadamia nut	*Macadamia ternifolia*	Nut	48	Australia (East)
Punicaceae	Pomegranate	*Punica granatum*	Balusta	18	Iran (Persia)
Rhamnaceae	Ber (Chinese jujube)	*Ziziphus jujube*	Drupe	48	China
	Indian jujube	*Ziziphus mauritiana*	Drupe	48	India

Rosaceae	Almond	*Prunus communis*	Drupe	16	Central Asia
	Apple	*Malus x domestica*	Pome	34	South Western Asia
	Apricot	*Prunus armeniaca*	Drupe	16	North Eastern China
	Loquat	*Eriobotrya japonica*	Pome	34	Central East China
	Quince	*Cydonia oblonga*	Pome	34	Caucasus region
	Peach	*Prunus persica*	Drupe	16	China
	Pear	*Pyrus communis*	Pome	34	Western China
	Plum	*Prunus domestica*	Drupe	32	China
	Sour cherry	*Prunus cerasus*	Drupe	16	South East Europe
	Sweet cherry	*Prunus avium*	Drupe	16	Asia minor
	Strawberry	*Fragaria x annanasa*	Etaerio of achenes	56 (8x)	France
Rutaceae	Bael	*Aegle marmelos*	Amphisarca	18	India
	Mandarin	*Citrus reticulata*	Hesperidium	18	South Eastern Asia
	Satsuma mandarin	*Citrus unshiu*	Hesperidium	18	South Asia
	Sweet orange	*Citrus sinensis*	Hesperidium	18	Indo-China
	Acid lime	*Citrus aurantifolia*	Hesperidium	18	Iran (Persian)
	Grape fruit	*Citrus paradisi*	Hesperidium	18	West Indies
	Rough lemon	*Citrus jambheri*	Hesperidium	18	South East Asia
	Lemon	*Citrus limon*	Hesperidium	18	South East Asia
	Wood apple	*Feronia limonica*	Amphisarca	18	India
Vitaceae	Grape	*Vitis vinifera*	Berry	38	Western Asia and Central Europe

Tiliaceae	Phalsa	*Grewia subenaequalis*	Drupe	36	India
Sapindaceae	Litchi	*Litchi chinensis*	Nut	30	South China
	Rumbutan	*Nephelium lappaceum*	Berry	22	Malayan Archipelago
Sapotaceae	Sapota	*Achras zapota Manilkara hexendra*	Berry	26	South Mexico
Juglandaceae	Walnut	*Juglans regia*	Nut	32	Central Asia
	Peacanut	*Carya illinoensis*	Nut	32	North America
Leguminosae	Tamarind	*Tamarindus indica*	Pod	24	India

B. CLASSIFICATION OF VEGETABLES

All vegetable belong to family to sub community spermophyte which include two division gymnosperm and angiosperm. Vegetable crop belong to division angiosperm. Most of vegetable belonging to dicot family and few are monocot e.g. Amarylidaceae, Araceae, Dioscoreaceae, Liliaceae and Poaceae.

Type of classification

Different authors have suggested various type of classification of vegetable crops. Classification based on method of culture still remains the best method for vegetable classification from farmers growers and commercial point of view. Botanical classification is more academics and taxonomic importance.

1. Based on botanical classification

Family	Crops	Scientific name	Edible part	Chromosome No.
Monocotyledoneae				
Amarylida-ceae/ Alliaceae	Onion	*Allium cepa*	Bulb	16
	Multiplier onion	*Allium cepa var. aggregatum*	Small bulbs	16
	Top onion	*Allium cepavar. viviparum*	Roots and bulbils	16
	Garlic	*Allium sativum*	Cloves	16
	Leek	*Allium porrum*	Blanched stem and leaves	32 (4x)
	Welsh onion	*Allium fistulosum*	Enlarged stem and leaves	16
	Shallot	*Allium ascalonicum*	Young bulb and green leaves	16
	Chive	*Allium schoenoprasum*	Enlarged stem and leaves	16,24,32
	Kurrat	*Allium kurrat*	Green leaves	32 (4x)

Araceae	Taro	*Colocasia esculenta*	Corm and cormel	
	Eddoe type	*Colocasia esculenta var. antiquorum*	Corm and cormel	24 (2x), 42 (3x)
	Dasheen type	*Colocasia esculenta var. globulifera*	Corm and cormel	42 (3x)
	Giant taro	*Alocasia macrorrhiza*	Corm	26, 28
	Swamp taro	*Cyrtosperma chamisonis*	Corm	26, 28
	Tannia	*Xanthosoma sagittifolium*		26
	Elephant foot yam	*Amorphophallus campanulatus*	Corm	26,28
Dioscoraceae	Yam	*Dioscorea spp.*	Underground stem tuber	30-80
	Greater yam	*Dioscorea alata*	Underground stem tuber	40 (4x)
	Lesser yam	*Dioscorea esculenta*	Underground stem tuber	40 (4x)
	White yam	*Dioscorea rotundata*	Underground stem	40 (4x)
Poaceae	Sweet corn	*Zea mays var. rugosa*	Soft immature kernel	20
Liliaceae	Asparagus	*Asparagus officinalis*	Spears	20
Dicotyledoneae				
Aizoaceae	New Zealand spinach	*Tetragonia tetragonioides*	Tender leaves and tops	22
Amaranthaceae	Amaranthus	*Amaranthus spp.*	Leaves and stems	32
Basellaceae	Malabar spinach	*Basella rubra var. alba*	Fleshy stem and leaves	24
Apiaceae	Carrot	*Daucus carota*	Enlarged and fleshy taproot	18
	Celery	*Apium graveolens*	Leaf stalk and leaves	22
	Celeriac	*Apium graveolens var. rapaceum*	Thick, tuberous root	22
	Leafy celery	*Apium graveolens var. secalinum*	Leaves	22
	Parsley	*Petroselinum crispum*	Leaves	22
	Turnip rooted parsley	*Petroselinum crispum var. tuberosum*	Swollen roots	22
	Parsnip	*Pastinaca sativa*	Large and fleshy taproot	22
	Turnip rooted chervil	*Chaerophyllum bulbosum*	Short swollen roots	
	Skirret	*Sium sisarum*	Bunch of roots that is produces from crown leaves	22
	Coriander	*Coriandrum sativum*	Young leaves	22
Chenopodiaceae	Beet root	*Beta vulgaris*	Fleshy tap root	18
	Palak	*Beta vulgaris var. bengalensis*	Leaves	18
	Chard	*Beta vulgaris var. cicla*	Large leaves and fleshy leafstalk	18

	Spinach	*Spinacia oleracea*	Rosette leaves	12
	French spinach	*Atriplex hortensis*	Leaves and immature shoots	12
	Pigweed	*Chenopodium album*	Leaves and tender twig	
Compositae	Lettuce	*Lactuca sativa*	Leaves	18
	Chicory	*Cichorium intybus*	Leaves	18
	Endive	*Cichorium endivia*	Leaves	18
	Globe artichoke	*Cynara scolymus*	Flower head	34
	Jerusalem artichoke	*Helianthus tuberosus*	Root tuber	102 (6x)
Convolvulaceae	Sweet potato	*Ipomea batatus*	Root tuber	90 (6x)
	Water spinach	*Ipomea aquatica*	Young terminal shoots and leaves	
Cruciferae / Brassicaceae	Cabbage	*Brassica oleracea var. capitata*	Head	18
	Cauliflower	*Brassica oleracea var. sabuda*	Pre-floral apical meristem	18
	Brussels sprout	*Brassica oleracea var. gemmifera*	Immature heads	18
	Sprouting broccoli	*Brassica oleracea var. italic*	Fleshy flower stalk	18
	Knol-khol	*Brassica oleracea var. gongylodes*	Enlarged stem portion	18
	Kale/collard	*Brassica oleracea var. acephala*	Rosette leaves	18
	Chinese cabbage (Pak-choi)	*Brassica campestris spp. chinensis*	Long leafy, elongated and compact head, fleshy petiole and leaf	20
	Chinese cabbage (Pe-tsai)	*Brassica campestris spp. pekinensis*	Loose leafy heads	20
	Chinese kale	*Brassica alboglobra*	Tender leaves and petioles	20
	Turnip	*Brassica campestris spp. rapifera*	Swollen root	20
	Rutabaga	*Brassica napobrassica*	Enlarged and elongated tap root	38
	Radish	*Raphanus sativus*	Fleshy swollen primary root	18
	Water cress (brahmi sag)	*Nasturtium officinale*	Tender mustard flavoured top and leaves	32
	Garden cress	*Lepidium sativum*	Leaves	16, 32
	Sea kale	*Crambe maritima*	Blanched, tender leaves and shoots	
Cucurbitaceae	Cucumber	*Cucumis sativus*	Immature fruit	14
	Musk melon	*Cucumis melo*	Ripe fruit	24
	Gherkin	*Cucumis anguria*	Young fruit	24

	Watermelon	*Citrullus lanatus*	Ripe fruit	22
	Round melon	*Citrullus lanatus var. fistulosus*	Immature fruit	22
	Pumpkin	*Cucurbita moschata*	Ripe fruit	40
	Summer squash	*Cucurbita pepo*	Immature fruit	40
	Winter squash	*Cucurbita maxima*	Ripe fruit	40
	Buffalogourd	*Cucurbita ficifolia*	Fruit	40
	Bottle gourd	*Lagenaria siceraria*	Immature fruit	22
	Bitter gourd	*Momordica charantia*	Immature fruit	22
	Balsam apple	*Momordica balsamina*	Immature fruit	22
	Giant spine gourd	*Momordica cochinchinensis*	Immature fruit	28
	Ridge gourd	*Luffa acutangula*	Immature fruit	26
	Sponge gourd	*Luffa cylindrica*	Immature fruit	26
	Pointed gourd	*Trichosanthes dioica*	Immature fruit	22
	Snake gourd	*Trichosanthes anguina*	Immature fruit	22
	Wax gourd	*Benincasa hispida*	Immature fruit	24
	Ivy gourd	*Coccinia grandis*	Immature fruit	24
	Chow-chow	*Sechium edule*	Single seeded fruit	28
	Mitha karela	*Cyclanthera pedata*	Immature fruit	32
Euphorbiaceae	Cassava	*Manihot esculenta*	Tuberous roots	36
	Chekkurmanis	*Souropus androgynus*	Green leaves	
Labiateae	Chinese potato	*Coleus parviflorus*	Adventitious tuberous roots	
	Chinese artichoke	*Stachys siebeldi*	Long, slender tuberous roots	
Leguminoceae	Garden pea	*Pisum sativum var. hortense*	Tender seeds	14
	French bean	*Phaseolus vulgaris*	Tender pod and seeds	22
	Lima bean	*Phaseolus lunatus*	Tender pods	22
	Lab-lab bean	*Lablab purpureus*	Tender pod and seeds	22
	Cluster bean	*Cyamopsis tetragonolobus*	Tender pod and seeds	14
	Winged bean	*Psophocarpus tetragonolobus*	Green pods and seeds, flowers, roots	22
	Broad bean	*Vicia faba*	Green pod and seeds	12
	Cow pea	*Vigna unguiculata*	Tender pod immature seed and mature seeds	22
	Soy bean	*Glycine max*	Tender and dry seeds	40
	Yam bean	*Pachyrrhizus erosus*	Root tuber	22
	Fenugreek	*Trigonella foenumgraceum*	Tender leaves	16
Malvaceae	Okra	*Abelmoschus esculentus*	Tender fruit	130
Moringaceae	Drumstick	*Moringa oliefera*	Green pod and leaves	28

Polygonaceae	Rhubarb	*Rheum rhaponticum*	Thick leaf stalk	44 (4x)
	Buck wheat	*Fagopyrum tataricum*	Tender tops	16
Portulacaceae	Ceylon spinach	*Talinum triangulare*	Leaf and tender stem	
Rutaceae	Curry leaf	*Murraya koenigii*	Leaves	18
Solanaceae	Potato	*Solanum tuberosum*	Stem tuber	48 (4x)
	Brinjal	*Solanum melongena*	Fruit	24
	Tomato	*Solanum lycopersicum*	Fruit	24
	Currant tomato	*Solanum pimpinellifolium*	Fruit	24
	Chilli	*Capsicum annuum*	Fruit	24

2. On the basis of plant part used

i. **Flower** – Agathi, male flower of Pumpkin.

ii. **Flower head-** Broccoli, Globe artichoke.

iii. **Prefloral apical meristem-** Cauliflower.

iv. **Modified above ground stem-** Knol-khol, Asparagus.

v. **Modified stem-** Potato, Jerusalem arctichoke, Yam, Elephant Foot Yam, Taro, Onion, Garlic.

vi. **Modified root-** Radish, Carrot, Beetroot, Turnip, Sweet potato.

vii. **Modified tap root-** Chinese artichoke.

viii. **Modified adventitious root-** Chinese potato.

ix. **Fruits-** Brinjal, Tomato, Chilli, Peas and Beans, all Cucurbits, Okra.

x. **Corm-** Colocasia, Elephant Foot Yam.

3. On the basis of edible portion

i. **Placentae-** Cucumber, Watermelon.

ii. **Endocarp-** Ridge gourd, Sponge gourd, Ash gourd.

iii. **Mesocarp and pericarp-** Pumpkin and Musk melon.

4. On the basis of climacteric pattern

i. **Climacteric** – Muskmelon, Water melon, Tomato, Brinjal.

ii. **Non climacteric-** Cucumber, Pumpkin, Pointed gourd, Chilli, Capsicum and Tamarillo.

5. On the basis of photoperiodism

i. **Long day plants (LDP)** – Potato, Onion, Cabbage, Cauliflower, Radish, Lettuce, Spinach, Palak, Turnip, Carrot and Beet root.

ii. **Short day plants (SDP)** – Sweet potato, Indian spinach, Dolichos bean, Cluster bean and Winged bean.

iii. **Day neutral plants (DNP)** - Tomato, Brinjal, Chilli, Okra, Cucurbits, Amaranthus and French bean.

6. On the basis of acid present

i. **Citric acid** – Tomato, Beet root, Leafy vegetable, Legumes and Potato.

ii. **Malic acid** – Carrot, Celery, Lettuce, Onion and Broccoli.

7. On the basis of aroma containing compound

Cucumber – Non adrenal.

Cabbage – (Raw) Allyl isothio cynate

(Cooked) Dimethyle disulphide

Potato – Dimethyle pyrazine

Radish – Isothio cynate

Onion – Allyl propyl disulphide

Garlic – Diallyle disulphide

8. On the basis of inflorescence

i. **Raceme-** Cole crops, Cucurbits, Radish.

ii. **Cyme-** Spinach, Sweet potato, Broccoli, Brinjal, Tomato, Potato.

iii. **Panicle-** Moringa, Palak.

iv. **Spike-** Beet root.

v. **Compound umbel-** Carrot, Coriander.

vi. **Capitulum-** Lettuce.

9. On the basis of tolerance to soil pH

i. **Long tolerance (6.8-6.00)** - Cole crop, Okra, Muskamelon and Onion.

ii. **Medium tolerance (6.8-5.5)** - Brinjal, Chilli and Tomato.

iii. **High tolerance (6.8-5.00)** - Potato, Rhubarb, Sweet potato and Water melon.

10. On the basis of water requirement

i. **High** – Cole crops, Sweet pepper, Radish, Ridge gourd, Turnip, Beetroot and Leafy vegetable.

ii. **Moderate** – Brinjal, Chilli, Tomato, Onion, Carrot and Potato.

iii. **Low** – Bean and Pea.

iv. **Very low** – Water melon, Musk melon, Pumpkin and Ash gourd.

11. On the basis of toxic substance

i. **Apiin-** Celery.

ii. **Calcium oxalate-** Colocasia and Elephant foot yam.

iii. **CN glycosiden-** Cassava.

iv. **Cucurbitacins-** Cucurbits.

v. **Dioscorine-** Yam.

vi. **Heameglutine** - French bean.

vii. **Oxalic acid and oxalates-** Amaranthus, Partulaca, Celosia, Basella and Colocasia.

viii. **Saponine-** Spinach, Tomato and Asparagus.

ix. **Sinigrin-** Cole crop.

x. **Solasodine-** Brinjal.

xi. **Trypsin inhibitor-** Soybean.

xii. **Phytic acid (Inositol hexaphosphoric acid)-** Pea and Beans (Mature seed).

xiii. **Tomatine-** Tomato.

12. On the basis of photosynthesis

i. **C_4 plant-** Amaranthus and Glove artichoke.

ii. **C_3 plant-** Lettuce, Carrot, Potato, Sweet potato, Tomato and Sugar beet.

13. On the basis of pollination

i. **Self pollinated crops -** All bean (except Dalichos bean, Lima bean), Garden Pea, Lettuce, Tomato, Globe artichoke, Fenugreek.

ii. **Cross pollinated crops -** Amaranthus, Cabbage, Cauliflower, all gourd, Chow-chow, Knol-khol, Dalichos bean, Musk melon, Onion, Pointed gourd, Pumpkin, Radish, Round and Ridge gourd, Sprouting broccolis, Spinach, Sweet potato, Snack gourd, Turnip, Water melon, Winter squash.

iii. **Often cross pollinated crops -** Okra, Chilli, Lima bean, Brinjal.

14. On the basis of sex form

Maturity pattern of sex organs opening of flower (anther) are the basic mechanism that fevor the cross pollination.

i. **Monoecious –** Cucurbits, Amaranthus, Sweet corn and Cassava.

ii. **Dioecious –** Pointed gourd, Scarlet gourd, Spine gourd, Asparagus, Spinach, Yam and Beet root.

iii. **Hermophrodite** – Ridge gourd and Cucumber.

iv. **Andromonoecious-** Muskmelon.

v. **Gynoecious** – Cucumber (seamy line).

vi. **Trimonoecious** – Cucumber, Muskmelon and Ridge gourd

C. CLASSIFICATION OF FLOWERS

1. Based on season of growing

i. **Summer season annuals-** Zinnia, Kochia, Portulaca, Gailardia, Gomphrena, Sunflower, Tithonia.

ii. **Rainy season annuals-** Balasam, Cock's Comb, Amaranthus, Gailardia.

iii. **Winter season annuals-** Aster, Corn flower, Lark spur, Sweet Sultan, Phlox, Candytuft, Petunia, Nigella.

2. Based on colour of flower

i. **White flowering-** Dianthus, China Aster, Zinnia

ii. **Purple, Lavender or Blue flowering-** Ageratum, Anchusa, Clitoria, Delphinium, Petunia, Verbena, Statice.

iii. **Yellow or Orange flowering-** Calendula, Zinnia.

3. Based on purpose of growing

i. **For rockery-** Ageratum, Alyssum, Phlox, Portulaca, Linum, Saponaria, Euphorbia.

ii. **For hanging basket-** Dwarf Ageratum, Petunia, Portulaca, Verbena, Begonia, Sansevieria.

iii. **For edging of bed or path-** Dwarf Ageratum, Alyssum, Dianthus, Nigella, Portulaca, Saponaria, Iresine.

iv. **For fragrant flowers-** Sweet Alyssum, Sweet Sultan, Sweet Pea, Stock, Phlox, Carnation, Rose, Jasmine, Tuberose.

v. **For bedding purpose-** Dahlia, Marigold, Phlox, Verbena, Carnation, Petunia, Ice-plant, Candytuft, Balsam, Portulaca.

vi. **For aromatics-** Rose, Jasmine, Tuberose.

vii. **For pots-** Carnation, Antirrhinum, Petunia, Aglaonema, Alocasia, Anthuriums, Aralia, Begonia, Chlorophytum, Dracaena.

viii. **For dry flowers-** Statice, Acrolinum, Nigella, Lady's lace.

ix. **For loose flowers-** Marigold, Chrysanthemum, Aster, Sunflower, Zinnia, Gailardia.

x. **For hedge purpose-** Lawsonia, Duranta, Tecoma, Bougainvillea, Hibiscus, Murraya.

4. Based on nature of growth

i. **Annuals-** Ice-plant, Nasturtium, Hollyhock, Sweet pea, Chrysanthemum, Carnation, Corn flower, Sweet Alyssum, Dahlia, Marigold, Verbena, Phlox.

ii. **Perennials-** Rose, Jasmine, Chrysanthemum.

5. Based on mode of reproduction

i. **Bulbous plant-** Lily, Narcissus, Tulip.

ii. **Cormellous plant-** Gladiolus, Crocus.

iii. **Rhizomatous plant-** Canna, Iris.

iv. **Tuberiferious plant-** Dahlia.

6. Based on growth behavior

i. **Herbs-** Linum, Anchusa, Browalia, Verbena, Viola.

ii. **Shrubs-** Rose, Jasmine, Bougainvillea, Tecoma, Chandani.

iii. **Trees-** Champa, Amaltas, Dhak, Kadamb, Pride of India, Gulmohar.

7. Based on photoperiodic requirement

i. **Short day plants-** Salvia, Poinsettia, Primerose.

ii. **Long day plants-** Aster, Calendula, Gardenia, Delphinium, Stock.

iii. **Day neutral plants-** Carnation, Hibiscus.

8. Based on ability to grow

i. **Climber-** Plants capable to grow over a support. These plants possess tendrils, rootless, thorns as climbing structure. For example Antigonan, *Ficus repens*, Wild rose etc.

ii. **Twiner-** Plants devoid of climbing structure, but still able to climb over the support. For example Asparagus, Madhulata (*Hiptage benghalensis*) etc.

iii. **Rambler-** Plants unable to climb, but somehow manage to support themselves over the stem or branches. For example Rangoon creeper (*Quisqualis indica*).

iv. **Creeper-** Plants unable to climb vertically but grow horizontally over the ground surface. For example Potato vine (*Solanum jasminoides*).

D. CLASSIFICATION OF SPICES

1. Based on completion of life cycle

i. **Annual-** Cumin, Fennel, Coriander, Fenugreek.

ii. **Biennial-** Onion, Garlic, Seed crops of- Radish, Carrot, Turnip.

iii. **Perennial-** Cardamom, Cinnamon, Clove, Saffron, Bay leaf.

2. Based on growth behavior

i. **Herbaceous spices-** Cumin, Coriander, Fenugreek, Onion, Garlic, Turmeric, Ginger.

ii. **Shrubaceous spices-** Black pepper, Cardamom.

iii. **Tree spices-** Cinnamon, Bay leaf, Nutmeg, Clove.

3. Based on importance

i. **Primary spices-** Chilli, Cardamom, Ginger, Turmeric.

ii. **Secondary spices-** Cumin, Fennel, Coriander, Fenugreek, Clove, Nutmeg, Cinnamon.

4. Based on part used

i. **Seed spices-** Fenugreek, Ajwain, Cumin, Coriander, Fennel, Dil seed.

ii. **Fruit spices-** Cumin, Coriander, Fennel, Black pepper, Chilli, Dil seeed.

iii. **Flower spices-** Saffron.

iv. **Bud spices-** Clove.

v. **Underground rhizome-** Turmeric, Ginger, Onion, Garlic.

vi. **Bark spices-** Cinnamon, Bay leaf.

vii. **Leafy spices-** Mentha, Coriander, Bay leaf, Fenugreek.

5. Based on utility

i. **Taste imparting spices-** Cardamom, Ginger, Coriander, Cumin, Garlic, Onion, Tamarind, Black pepper, Chilli.

ii. **Flavour imparting spices-** Clove, Cardamom, Coriander leaf, Curry leaves, Cinnamon, Asafoetida, Garlic.

6. Based on cultural management

i. **Horticultural spices-** Spices grown on small scale are counted under this group, e.g. Ginger, Turmeric, Chilli, Onion, Garlic, Mentha, Ocimum, Curry leaves, Fennel.

ii. **Plantation spices-** The spices which are planted permanentally and remain dedicated to the soil for many years are termed as plantation spices, e.g. Cardamom, Clove, Nutmeg, Cinnamon, Bay leaf, All spice.

iii. **Agronomic spices-** The spices which are planted on large areas are called agronomic spices, e.g. Coriander, Cumin, Ajwain, Chilli, Fennel.

7. Based on botanical relationship

Monocot

i. **Zingiberaceae-** Ginger, Turmeric, Cardamom.

Dicot

i. **Piperaceae-** Black pepper, Piplamool.
ii. **Umbeliferae-** Cumin, Coriander, Fennel, Ajwain, Asafoetida, Black cumin, Dill seed, Celery, Parsley.
iii. **Labiateae-** Ocimum.
iv. **Solanaceae-** Chilli.
v. **Alliaceae-** Onion, Garlic.
vi. **Myrtaceae-** Clove.
vii. **Myristicaceae-** Nutmeg, Mace.
viii. **Lauraceae-** Cinnamon, Tejpat.
ix. **Papaveraceae-** Khas-khas.
x. **Rutaceae-** Curry leaves.
xi. **Crucifereae-** Mustard.
xii. **Iridaceae-** Saffron.
xiii. **Orchidaceae-** Vanilla.
xiv. **Guttifereae-** Kokam.
xv. **Araceae-** Buchh.
xvi. **Papilionaceae-** Fenugreek.

8. Based on photoperiodic requirement

i. **Short day plants-** Onion.
ii. **Long day plants-** Nutmeg, Garlic, Chilli, Fennel, Dill seed, Henbane.
iii. **Day neutral plants-** Capsicum, Basil.

E. CLASSIFICATION OF PLANTATION CROPS

1. Based on botanical relationship

Monocot

i. **Arecaceae-** Coconut, Arecanut.

Dicot

i. **Theaceae-** Tea.
ii. **Rubiaceae-** Coffee.
iii. **Moraceae-** Rubber.
iv. **Sterculiaceae-** Cocoa.
v. **Piperaceae-** Black pepper.
vi. **Lauraceae-** Cinnamon.
vii. **Myrtaceae-** Clove.
viii. **Myrtisticaceae-** Nutmeg.
ix. **Anacardiaceae-** Cashewnut.

2. Based on growth behavior

i. **Vine-** Vanilla, Black pepper.
ii. **Shrub-** Tea.
iii. **Tree-** Cashewnut.

3. Based on utility

i. **Food-** Coconut, Cashewnut.
ii. **Industrial-** Rubber, Arecanut, Oil palm.

4. Based on extent of growing

i. **Homestead plantation-** Coconut, Black pepper.
ii. **Estate plantation-** Tea, Coffee, Rubber.

5. Based on intensity of cultivation

i. **Single storeyed-** Clove, Nutmeg.
ii. **Multi storeyed-** Coconut.

F. CLASSIFICATION OF MEDICINAL PLANT

1. Based on plant part used

i. **Leaves-** Belladonna, Foxglove, Henbane, Senna, Periwinkle or vinca, Aloe, Neem,
ii. **Seed-** Dill or sowa, Isabgol (psyllium),
iii. **Root-** Ashwagandha (winter cherry and Indian ginseng), Sarpagandha, Safed musali, Liquorice or mulathi, Periwinkle or vinca, Medicinal yam, Ipecac, Long pepper,
iv. **Fruit-** Opium (poppy), Medicinal solanum, Neem
v. **Bark-** Cinchona,
vi. **Herb-** Datura.

2. Based on chemical content and uses

Common name	Chemical content	Uses
Belladonna	Atropine	Neurologic pain, ampholinergic property
	Hyoscyamine	Hyoscyamine used as truth confessor in criminological investigations
Foxglove	Digitoxin	Cardiotonic property. Used in cure heart diseases
Henbane	Hyoscyamine	Used to cure Asthama and whooping cough. Antispasmodic and Anticholingenic property
Senna	Sennosides A,B,C,D	Laxative property, constipetion
Dill or sowa	Carvone	Oil is used to make gripe water
Ashwagandha	Withanine, somniferine	Used to make general tonic
Sarpagandha	Serpentine, Reserpine, Saponins	Used as treatment for hypertension as a sedative (reduce nervous exitement)
Safed musali	Saponins	To make vital tonics, to cure general diabeties. IInd silajeet
Liquorice or mulathi	Glycyrrhizin	Used to cure intestinal and peptic ulcers 150 times sweeter than sugar
Periwinkle or vinca	Amacline, vincristine, vinblastine	Used as tranquilizer (blood pressure control), cancer theraphy
Opium (poppy)	Morphine, codine, narcotine	God of sleep, painkiller, analgesies (reduces pain) and hypotonic effect, used to cure leukemia and found linaleic acid
Isabgol (psyllium)	Mucilage	Laxative, soothing and cooling agent, used against irritation in gastrointestinal tract
Medicinal solanum	Solasodine	Major source of steroid in India
Aloe	Aloin oil	Skin tonic and herbal cosmetics
Medicinal yam	Diosgenin	Production of sex hormones and contraceptic pills
Neem	Azadiractin	Diabeties treatment
Cinchona	Quinine	Treatment to malaria
Datura	Hyoscine tropane	Preanasthetic in surgery, in relief of withdrawal symtomps in morphine
Ipecac	Cephaline, emetin	To reduce vomiting, use against amoebeiosis
Long pepper	Piperine	Improve appetiti, laxative
Guggal	Guggulipids	Treatment of obesity, anthritis

3. Based on botanical classification

Common name	Botanical name	Family
Belladonna	*Atropa belladona*	Solanaceae
Foxglove	*Digitalis purpurea*	Scrophularia
Henbane	*Hyoscyamus niger*	Solanaceae
Senna	*Cassia angustifolia*	Leguminoceae
Dill or sowa	*Anethum graveolens*	Apiaceae
Ashwagandha	*Withania somnifera*	Solanaceae
Sarpagandha	*Rauvolfia serpentina*	Apocynaceae
Safed musali	*Chlorophytum boribilianum*	Liliaceae
Liquorice or mulathi	*Glycyrhiza glabra*	Leguminoceae
Periwinkle or vinca	*Catharanthus roseus*	Apocynaceae
Opium (poppy)	*Papaver sominiferum*	Papavaraceae
Isabgol (psyllium)	*Pantago ovata* (stemless)	Plantagonaceae
Medicinal solanum	*Solanum khasianum*	Solanaceae
Aloe	*Aloe vera, A. barbadensis*	Liliaceae
Medicinal yam	*Dioscorea floribunda*	Dioscoreaceae
Neem	*Azadirachta indica*	Meliaceae
Cinchona	*Cinchona spp.*	Rubiaceae
Datura	*Datura innoxia*	Solanaceae
Ipecac	*Cephaelis ipecacuna*	Rubiaceae
Long pepper	*Piper longum*	Piperaceae
Guggal	*Balsamodendrum mukul*	Burseraceae

G. CLASSIFICATION OF AROMATIC PLANT

1. Based on plant part used

i. **Leaves-** Davana, Rose geranium, Japanese mint, Bergamot mint, Lemon grass, Patchouli, Java citronella, Palmarosa grass, Indian basil.

ii. **Flower-** Rose geranium, Oil bearing rose, Kewda, Hops.

iii. **Seed-** Ambrette or muskdana, Celery.

iv. **Root-** Vitever grass.

v. **Fruit-** Jamalagota.

vi. **Herb-** Rosemary, Melissa.

2. Based on oil content and uses

Common name	Oil content	Uses
Davana	Hydrocarbons	Delicate fragrance for floral decoration. Bouquets, cosmetics
Rose geranium	Geraniol rhodinol	Perfumes, powder, creams, body lotions
Japanese mint	Menthol, carvone, linalool	Scenting in the supari
Bergamot mint	Carvone	
Oil bearing rose	Citronellal, geraniol	Auto of rose, ruha gulab , rose oil
Lemon grass	Citral, farnesol	Starting material for ionones and Vitamin A manufacturing
Patchouli	Patchouliol	Fixative property
Vitever grass	Viteverol	Carminative property
Java citronella	Citronellal	Mosquito repellents, deodorants, scented soaps
Palmarosa grass	Geraniol	Soaps, perfumery
Kewda	Lupilin	Keweda water (rooh or attar)
Hops		
Ambrette or muskdana	Fernesol	Musk odour used in incense stickes, panmasala, perfumery, cosmetics, scent
Jamalagota		Violent purgative
Celery	Limonine	Seeds: spice seed oil seasoning, flavouring sauces, purees
Indian basil	Methyl chavicol	Flavouring foods
Rosemary	Camphene, cineol	Anticancer and antioxidant property
Melissa	Citrol, nerol	Perfumery, cosmetics

3. Based on botanical classification

Common name	Botanical name	Family
Davana	*Artimesia pallens*	Asteraceae
Rose geranium	*Pelargonium graveolens*	Geraniaceae
Japanese mint	*Mentha arvensis*	Labiatae
Bergamot mint	*Mentha citrate*	Labiatae
Oil bearing rose	*Rosa damascena*	Rosaceae
Lemon grass (koachin oil)	*Cymbopogon flexuosus*	Gramineae
Patchouli	*Pogostimon patchouli*	Laminaceae
Vitever grass	*Vetevaria zizanoides*	Viteveraceae
Java citronella	*Cymbopogon winterianus*	Gramineae
Palmarosa grass	*Cymbopogon martini*	Gramineae
Kewda (serimpine)	*Pandanas fassicularis*	Pandanaceae
Hops	*Humulus lupulus*	Cannabinaceae
Ambrette or muskdana	*Abelomoschus moschatus*	Malvaceae
Jamalagota	*Croton tiglium*	Euphorbiaceae
Celery	*Apium graveolens*	Umbellifereae
Indian basil	*Occimum basilium*	Lamiaceae
Rosemary	*Rosemarius officinalis*	Lamiaceae
Melissa	*Melissa officinalis*	Lamiaceae

Chapter 5

Soil and Climate

Soil- Soil is the upper most crust of earth surface which supports plant growth. It is defined as a three phase system in which plants grow. These phases are solid, liquid and gas and are essential. Solid part is frame which provides space for other two. This consists of minerals, clay minerals and organic matter. The soil is also a living system with millions of microbes that breakdown organic matter and builds it again.

Some points are following

- Microbes are essential and survive only when soil is well aerated and rich in organic matter and devoid of waterlogged conditions.
- Texture of soil depends on the size of solid particles and classified as gravel, coarse and fine sand, silt and clay.
- Soils are classified according to relative distribution of these particles and there are 12 textural classes.
- Likewise, arrangement of these particles is referred as structure, and both texture and structure lend soil physical properties like water holding capacity, aeration and bulk density.
- Generally loamy soils and crumb structure are most preferred for fruit crops.
- According to level of organic matter, soils are classified as mineral soil or organic soil and soil having more than 20% organic matter is organic soil like peat and muck.
- Minerals and salts lend chemical properties to the soil like pH, alkalinity, solidity, salinity and cation exchange capacity which influence the availability of nutrients in soil.
- Therefore, for making choice for soil, soil analysis in terms of following criteria is essential to decide on land capability.

Criteria for land capability class

i. Slope and erosion hazard.

ii. Soil depth.

iii. Drainage.
iv. Workability.
v. Stoniness and rockiness.
vi. Water holding capacity.
vii. Permeability.
viii. Nutrient availability.
ix. Fertility status.
x. Salinity, alkalinity and acidity hazards.

- Based on these criteria there are 8 capability classes, of which (i) to (iv) are suitable for cultivation and (v) to (viii) are not suitable for cultivation.
- The soil provides support for the plant and act as store house of nutrients and water as well as oxygen for root growth.
- The ability of the soil to support plant growth is often referred to as its productive capacity which depends on fertility and physical condition. Therefore, the soil has to be a good soil.
- A good soil is one which has the capacity to nourish and sustain plant growth by providing mineral particles (nutrients) in an available form to plants by their interaction with soil air, moisture, microbes and humus.
- Generally a loam soil is considered to be a good soil.
- Generally fruit crops need porous, aerated, deep (2m) uniformly textured soils and the pH of soil should be within range of 6-8.
- Soil with hardpan within 120 cm from surface, soil with high clay content at surface and very less at subsurface or vice-versa are not suitable for fruit crops.
- Fruit crops are susceptible to waterlogged condition and growth is adversely affected by salinity, solidity and alkalinity.
- It is, therefore, important that soil be analyzed for its quality and then choice of the crop is made for sustainable production.
- If the soils are problematic like poor aeration or drainage, solidity, alkalinity, acidity and salinity, they require improvement or reclamation before taking up crop production or the venture would fail.
- Alternatively tolerant or resistant crops can be chosen for different problems.

Salinity tolerant crops: Kair, Khirni, Woodapple, Date palm, Ber, Aonla, Fig, Sapota etc.

Sodicity tolerant crops: Ber, Tamarind, Woodapple, Date palm, Aonla, Karonda, Fig, Phalsa, Pomegranate, Guava, Bael and Almond.

Drought tolerant crops: Ber, Aonla, Phalsa, Lasoda, Kair, Custard apple, Karonda, Fig, Guava etc.

Grouping of fruits according to their tolerance to salinity

a. **High salt tolerance :** Date palm, Ber and Aonla.

b. **Medium salt tolerance :** Pomegranate, Fig and Grape.

c. **Low salt tolerance :** Apple, Orange, Almond, Lemon and Avocado.

- In making choice of soil for fruit crops physical properties should he emphasized, more as chemicals can be added from outside to improve nutrient status and chemical properties of the soil.
- Generally the depth and the drainage-ability are very important for crop production.
- To upkeep soils for sustainable production following things are to be done before and after planting a crop:

Soil Analysis in Terms of Its Physical and Chemical Attributes

- Bring the soil to its optimum potential by applying organic matter, chemical fertilizers, micronutrient and amendments depending on soil analysis report.
- Adoption of soil conservation technique like green manuring on regular basis.
- Use of improved water management techniques like drip irrigation and check basin or furrows.
- Incorporation of large quantity of bulky organic matter each year.
- Creation of appropriate drainage around the plot.
- Scrapping of salts and reclamation of soil by application of gypsum, iron pyrites, press mud etc., on regular basis in case of salinity problem.
- Replenishment of nutrients harvested by the crop on regular basis by preparing a balance sheet for nutrients.
- Recycling of organic waste.
- Soil is the most important natural resource for horticultural crops and it needs to be protected and improved.

Climate: Climate is the most important factor on which choice of the crop for a region depends and therefore, understanding about soil and climate and their requirement for different crops for optimum production on sustainable basis is important for horticulturists.

Climate is defined as the whole of average atmospheric phenomena for a certain region calculated for a period of thirty years. These phenomena are light, heat, water and air.

Light

- Electromagnetic radiation to which the organs of plant react ranging in wavelength from 4000 to 7700 angstrom units and is propagated at a speed of about 540 kilometers per second.
- It is essential for the process of photosynthesis and therefore, for growth and development of plants.
- There are two aspects of light, its intensity and duration which are important for plant development.
- The light intensity can be estimated from the number of hours of bright sunlight or from the cloudiness of sky.
- Generally horticultural crops need a lot of light and must be grown in sunny climate, but there are some crops which can tolerate shade e.g. Turmeric and ginger.
- The duration of light for the time elapsing between dawn and dusk referred as photoperiod or day length. This exerts considerable influence on flowering.

Based on the response by plants the major classes are following. However, fruit crops for such categories are not known.

1. **Long day plants:** Passion fruit, Apple, etc.
2. **Short day plants:** Strawberry, Pineapple, Pear, Peach, Plum, etc.
3. **Day neutral plants:** Papaya, Guava, Banana, etc.

Heat

- Heat is a non-mechanical energy transfer with reference to a temperature difference between a system and its environmental surrounding.
- It is measured as temperature by thermometers.
- The growth of the plants depends primarily on temperature.
- Availability of heat units decide the crop for a given place and the average temperature of a place gives an idea about heat units available on the basis of which crop can be decided.
- Temperate fruit crops like Apple, Pear, Peach, Plum and Almond become dormant due to short day conditions in the region and need chilling of various lengths to break dormancy.
- Frost and chilling are harmful for tropical and subtropical plants.
- On the other hand extremely high temperatures found in arid region cause Wilting, Sunscald, Necrotic spot and even death of plants.

Therefore, under such conditions appropriate choice of plants and provision of protection become important.

Based on temperature variations on the surface of the earth we have the following climates.

1. **Tropical:** Tropical equable climate with no distinct winter, e.g. Mango, Banana, Papaya, Sapota, Pineapple, Coconut, Cashew, Arecanut, Breadfruit, Jackfruit and Avocado.
2. **Subtropical:** Subtropical climate with distinct winter and summer, e.g. Guava, Grape, Citrus, Date palm, Phalsa, Pomegranate, Litchi and Loquat.
3. **Temperate:** Distinct winter, summer and autumn with temperature below freezing during winter is common, e.g. Apple, Pear, Peach, Plum, Quince, Apricot, Walnut, Almond, Strawberry and Cherry.

Water

- Water is a transparent, colourless and tasteless liquid compound of hydrogen and oxygen (H_2O) with 11.91% hydrogen and 88.81% oxygen.
- It is essential for plant growth and development as a substrate in photosynthesis, regulation of plant temperature, distribution of metabolites and nutrients.
- It comes through precipitation of rain and snow.
- Near equator the total rainfall is 2000 mm per year and away from it, which reduces but again influenced by a number of factors like mountain ranges.
- Water requirement of plant is dependent on soil type and evapo-transpiration rate.
- For crop production it is not the total rainfall but its distribution is more important and in Indian subcontinent we have rains mainly confined to June to September, thereby fruit culture in India had to be supported by irrigation or one has to select crop where fruiting is confined to water availability periods and trees remain dormant during stress.
- Water is also present in the atmosphere as vapour and we call it as humidity.
- This atmospheric humidity also influences growth and development of plants.
- Low humidity has drying effects and enhances water requirement.
- Whereas high humidity favors fungal diseases. Plants liking for high humidity and low humidity are there:
- **High humidity:** Sapota, Banana, Mangosteen, Jackfruit and Breadfruit.
- **Low humidity (Dry)**: Ber, Grape, Date palm, Pomegranate, Citrus, Aonla and Guava.

Air

- A mixture of oxygen, nitrogen and other gases that surrounds the earth and forms its atmosphere.
- It is also one of the climatic factors influencing plant growth.
- If its quality is polluted by the accumulation of gasses like hydrocarbons, SO_2, CO_2, NO_2 ethylene and methane the plant growth adversely affected but we are more concerned with the movement of air (wind) causing great damage to crops in deserts. Coastal areas, valleys for which provision of windbreaks and shelterbelts are suggested and such situations sometimes have to be avoided for plantation.
- Storm has a wind speed of 50km/hr whereas, hurricane has a wind speed of more than 100 km/hr.

Chapter 6

Water Management

Water

Water is one of the most important inputs essential for the production of crops. Plants need it continuously during their life and in huge quantities. It profoundly influences photosynthesis, respiration, absorption, translocation and utilization of mineral nutrients etc. Both its shortage and excess affects the growth and development of a plant directly and consequently its yield and quality.

Soil needs the application of water to:

- Remove stress condition.
- Release nutrients in the soil solution for absorption by plants.
- Leach or wash out injurious salts from the soil.
- Preparation of land for raising crops.
- To maintain the temperature and humidity of the soil micro-climate and the activity of soil microbes at optimum level.
- For the normal aeration and functioning of roots and shoots of the plants.
- Excess water needs to be removed for the normal aeration and functioning of roots and shoots of the plants
- Excess water creates unworkable soil condition.

Irrigation

It is defined as the artificial application of water to the plants in the event of shortage of natural rains in order to obtain rapid growth and increased yields . It is an essential item in the cultivation of crops. Success in gardening depends on how efficiently irrigation is provided to gardens because it is governed by many factors such as frequency, duration, intensity, source and method of supply.

Factors affecting the supply of irrigation water to plants

- Topography and soil characteristics.
- Kind of plant (Root depth, Water absorption capacity, Growth habit, etc.).
- Weather condition.

When to irrigate?

- The time when a plant needs irrigation can only be judged by a keen observing eye.
- The plants need water when their new leaves begin to show a wilting appearance. A little before the trees show the sign of wilting.
- The shedding of broad leaves in orchard shows distress symptoms.

How much to irrigate?

- If water supply is limited, only a light irrigation can be given at a time with higher frequency of irrigation.
- If water is available in plenty, the irrigation may be heavy with longer intervals between successive irrigations.
- However, inadequate irrigation reduces the growth and fruiting of the trees while, over irrigation serves no useful purpose and it may even prove to be harmful.
- It may create water logging, the nutrients may get leached and fruits may become watery and develop poor quality.
- Plants which have suffered from drought should not be given liberal doses of irrigations all at once. That may result in the splitting of fruits and even the splitting of bark of the branches and trunk.

Systems of irrigations

- Different systems of irrigation are followed in different parts of the country. The best system is the one which meets the moisture seepage and evaporation.

Principally, irrigation systems can be divided under three broad headings

I. **Surface irrigation :** a. Flooding b. Basin type c. Furrow type d. Ring type

II. **Sub-surface irrigation :** a. Trench method b. Through underground pipelines c. Perforated pipelines.

III. **Overhead or aerial irrigation:** a. Sprinkler b. Revolving nozzles

IV. **Drip or trickle irrigation**

I. Surface Irrigation

a. Flooding

- When the land is flat, letting in water from one end floods the entire area.
- This system is commonly practiced in canal or tank bed areas.

- It is the easiest method and permits the use of bullock drawn implements in the orchards.
- But in this there is wastage of water and leads to soil erosion also.
- It encourages growth of weeds and spread of diseases like gummosis in citrus and collar rot in papaya.

b. Basin system

- In this system, circular basins are provided around the trunk of the tree.
- The basins are inter-connected in series and are fed through the main channel running perpendicular to the tree rows.
- When compared to flooding, this system minimizes the loss of water.
- In this system of irrigation, the water close to trunk may bring about certain diseases like gummosis and nutrients are likely to be carried over from one basin to the other.

c. Furrow system

- Unlike the flood system, here the entire land surface is not covered with irrigation water.
- The furrows are opened in the entire orchard at 4 or less apart, depending upon the age of the trees.
- Water is let in these furrows from the main channels.
- In orchards, two furrows on each side of the rows are generally made.
- It is suited to such lands, which have a moderate slope to the extent of 1-2% if the water is to run freely and reach the ends of the furrows.
- Where the slope is sharp, the furrows are made to follow the contour more or less closely.
- This method has disadvantage of excess of water penetration at the head than at the farther end, which may result in variation in vigour and growth of trees.

d. Ring system

- This is an improvement over the basin system.
- In this system, a ring is formed close and around the tree and water is let into the basin.
- This method is recommended for citrus trees thereby reducing the chances of collar rot to which these trees are often susceptible.
- The size of the ring will increase as the tree grows.
- In this system, the spread of diseases like collar rot, etc., are prevented.

- However, it involves more labour and capital and it does not permit uniform distribution of water throughout the bed or basin as in the basin system of irrigation.

II. Sub-Surface Irrigation

- This system consists of conducting water in number of furrows or ditches underground in perforated pipelines until sufficient water is taken into the soil so as to retain the water table near the root zone.
- In limited situation, this may be a very desirable system of irrigation.
- In general, however, it must be used with great caution because of the danger of water logging and salt accumulation.
- If the sub-strata are so slowly permeable that practically no water moves through, water added may stand in soil sufficiently for long time which results an injury to the plant root due to poor aeration.
- Where irrigation water or the sub-soil contains appreciable amount of salt, sub-soil irrigation is usually not advisable.
- Land must be carefully leveled for successful sub-soil irrigation so that raising the water table will wet all parts of the field equally.

III. Over Head or Aerial Irrigation

- In this system, water is applied in the form of spring, somewhat resembling rainfall.
- This is accomplished by pumping water from original source into the main supply line from where it is distributed to perforated pipes, which operate at low pressure (80 to 120 lb per square inch) and supply the water in a fairly uniform rectangular pattern.
- They have a high rate of application, usually 1 /hour or higher. Because of the high application rates, their use is restricted to soils with high infiltration rates, such as sandy or gravelly.
- Revolving nozzle is also at times used, which operated on either low or high pressure. Usually the rate of application followed in the rate of 0.2 to 0.3 per hour.

Sprinkler Irrigation

- May have definite economic advantages in developing new land that has never been irrigated, particularly where the land is rough or the soil is too much porous, shallow or highly erodible.

- It is quite useful where only small streams are available, such as irrigation wells of small capacity.
- It is helpful in irrigating at the seedling stage when the furrowing is difficult and flooding leads to crusting of soil.
- Fertilizer materials may be evenly applied by this method.
- This is usually done by drawing liquid fertilizer solutions slowly into the pipe.
- It has several disadvantages like
  - High initial cost,
  - Difficult to work in windy location,
  - Trouble from clogging of nozzle,
  - Interference in pollination process
  - Requirement of more labours while removing or resetting.
  - In general, this system is best adopted for areas where ordinary surface systems are inefficient.

IV. Drip or Trickle System

- This is the most recent system of irrigating the plants.
- It is usually practice for high value crops, especially in green houses and glass houses.
- There will be an installation of pipelines with nozzles very close to the soil.
- The nozzle is fitted in such a way that water is dripped almost in the root-zone of the plants.
- Water is allowed to move in pipes under very low or no pressure and it drop at regular interval.
- This system of irrigation has advantages like no disturbance of the soil; soil moisture is maintained, lesser leaching of nutrients from the soil.

Chapter 7

Nutrition of Plants

Nutrients

The nutrients are chemical elements which are absorbed by the plants in more or less quantity to transform light energy into chemical energy and to keep up plant metabolism for the synthesis of organic materials. These materials constitute among other things, foods for humans and animals and a range of raw materials for various industrial uses. Feeding of plants with nutrients is termed as nutrition. Successful growth and production of the plants in general requires a proper supply of the 17 elements. These elements are regarded as essential to life in higher plants.

Allen and Arnon (1955) laid out following criteria for categorising nutrients essentiality to plants:

1. Complete or partial lack of the element in question must make normal plant growth impossible
2. Deficiency symptoms must be reversibly by the addition of the elements in question
3. The element must play specific role in the plant metabolic symptom.

They are

1. **Basic elements (3) :** Carbon (C), Hydrogen (H) and Oxygen (O).
2. **Macro elements (6) :** Nitrogen (N), Phosphorus (P) Potash (K), Calcium (Ca), Magnesium (Mg) and Sulphur (S).
3. **Micro elements (8) :** Manganese (Mn), Molybdenum (Mo), Chlorine (Cl), Zinc (Zn), Boron (B), Copper (Cu), Iron (Fe) and Nickel (Ni).

Macro elements: The nutrients that are required in relatively large quantity are termed as macro elements.

Micro elements: The nutrients are those required in relatively less quantity are termed as micro nutrients.

- Besides some quasi essential elements like Aluminium (Al), Cobalt (Co), Sodium (Na), Silicon (Si) and Vanadium (V) are not considered necessary always because either their essential character has been proved only in some plants or in certain metabolic processes that are not always necessary.

Types of Fertilizers

Inorganic Fertilizers

- Industrially manufactured chemicals.
- Contains higher nutrient than organic manures.
- Nutrient input is lost through leaching, runoff, volatilization, fixation by soil or consumption by weeds etc.

Organic Fertilizers

- These are plant and animal wastes that are used as nutrients after decomposition.
- Improves the soil tilth, aeration, water holding capacity and activity of micro-organism.

Where to Apply the Manures?

- In fully grown trees, the manures and fertilizers should be given over the area, where their active roots are spread.
- Fertilizer should be given in restricted area i.e., in the surrounding area of about 1 to 1.5 m away from the trunk of the trees.

Time of Fertilizer Application

- It must be applied when the plants need it.
- Timing depends on the type of fertilizer and climate.
- Fruit trees require more nutrients at the emergence of new flushes and differentiations of floral buds.
- Utilized more during the course of fruit development.
- Nutrients should be available to them in February –March.
- So, it would be better to apply them in October-November to be available to the trees in February to March.

Nutrient Content of Organic Manures

Organic Manure	N %	P_2O_5%	K_2O%
Bulky Organic Manures			
1. Cattle dung	0.40	0.20	0.17
2. Poultry manure	3.03	0.63	1.40
3. Farmyard manure	0.50	0.25	0.50
4. Rural compost	0.75	0.20	0.50
5. Urban compost	1.75	1.00	1.50
6. Vermicompost	3.00	1.00	1.50

Concentrated Organic Manures			
1. Castor cake	4.37	1.85	1.39
2. Coconut cake	3.00	1.80	1.90
3. Neem cake	5.22	1.08	1.48
4. Blood meal	12.00	2.00	1.00
5. Groundnut cake	7.30	1.50	1.30
6. Pressmud	2.10	4.40	0.80

Composition of Inorganic Manures.

Fertilizers	Composition %		
	N	P_2O_5	K_2O
1. Sodium nitrate	16	-	-
2. Calcium nitrate	15.5	-	-
3. Potassium nitrate	13.8	-	-
4. Anhydrous ammonia	82	-	-
5. Urea	46	-	-
6. SSP	-	16	-
7. Double SP	-	32	-
8. Triple SP	-	46-48	-

Methods of fertilizer application

Broadcasting

- Fertilizer in solid state or granular or dust are spread uniformly over the entire field.
- Leaching loss may be more.

Disadvantages

- Some of the elements like phosphorous and potash do not readily move in the soil. Therefore, surface application may not be available to the trees especially in drier tracks.
- Leads to accumulation of potassium in surface soil beyond detrimental levels causing injury to plants.
- Surface application always stimulates weed growth.

Band placement

- Application of fertilizer on the sides of rows.
- Fertilizer in solid and liquid forms can be applied.
- Quantity of fertilizer may be economised.

Ring Placement

- Commonly followed in fruit trees.
- Fertilizers are applied in a ring encircling the trunk of the trees extending the entire canopy.
- It is more labour intensive and costly.

Foliar Application

- Fertilizers are applied in liquid form as foliar sprays.
- They are easily absorbed by leaves.
- Fertilizers are applied in a very low concentration tolerable to the leaves.
- Recommended when the nutrients are required in small quantity.

Starter Solution

- Liquid form of fertilizer application.
- Seedlings and propagules are kept emerged up to their root system for varying duration in starter solution.
- The starter solution is prepared either by dissolving concentrated fertilizer mixture at a concentration not exceeding 1%.

Fertigation

- Application of fertilizers in irrigation water in either open or closed systems.
- Nitrogen and sulphur are the principal nutrients applied.
- Phosphorous fertigation is less common because of formation of precipitates takes place with high Ca and Mg containing water.

Advantages

- Nutrients especially nitrogen can be applied in several split doses at the time of greatest need of the plant.
- Nutrient is mixed with water and applied directly near the root zone, as such higher use efficiency.
- Cost on labour is saved.
- Best results of fertigation are noticed when the fertilizer is applied towards the middle of the irrigation period and applied towards the middle of the irrigation period and their application terminated shortly before completion of irrigation. Use of soluble fertilizer improves use efficiency.

Note: The grower must consider the economics and advantages before deciding for using fertigation.

Tree Injection

- Direct injection of essential nutrients into the tree trunk.
- Iron salts are injected into chlorotic trees that are known to suffer from iron deficiency.

Feeding Needles

- Several types of feeding needles or guns are available.
- With these fertilizers either in dry form or in water solution placed in holes.

Factors favouring nutrients absorption and transport

- High humidity, proper temperature and incident radiation.
- Good CHO supply and vigorous growth.
- Chemical and physical properties of nutrient spray solution.
- Leaf characters like leaf thickness, hairyness and wax coating on the leaf.
- Generally more vigorous plant and young growing leaves have good capacity to absorb nutrients.
- Nitrogen- applied in the form of urea (1%) is readily absorbed.
- Sodium and potassium - readily absorbed by leaves and they are among the highly mobile elements.

Note

- Foliar application proves to be most effective where problems of nutrient fixation in soil exits. So far the most important use of foliar sprays is in application of micronutrients.
- Foliar sprays should be applied either with pressure sprayer or with specially designed spray guns. The trees should be sprayed until the nutrient solution begins to drip from the leaves.
- Foliar application of urea has been found effective in many fruit crops like Citrus, Guava, Apple, etc.
- Potassium spray (3-5g/lit) - Papaya, Pineapple, Citrus and Guava.

Precaution

- While applying foliar sprays, care should be taken to ensure correct concentration of spray solution.
- Apply in the morning or evening hours on a clear sky day.

Organic Farming:

- Green revolution has brought spectacular increase in production as well as productivity of crops in our country.
- But after the initial success, it had shown the symptoms of fatigue evident from the undesirable side effects on natural resources, such as soil, water and biodiversity and thus human health.
- The vast areas of soils once fertilizer was degraded due to soil erosion, stalinization or general loss of soil fertility.
- Water resources have been over-exploited and polluted due to excessive requirement of irrigation water for high yielding varieties and intensive use of agro-chemicals.
- Many plants and animal species were wiped out and are endangered.
- Residues of harmful pesticide in food and drinking water endangered both farmers and consumer health point of view and thus excessive use of external inputs consumes a lot of energy from non-renewable resources.
- Organic farming is a way of conserving the soil and maintaining the fertility, protect soil flora and fauna/diversity.
- It has lesser effect on pollution either of ground water, lakes and rivers.
- Organic agriculture does not utilize non-renewable external input and energy.
- Since no chemical or pesticide is used in crop production, there is very low chance of pesticide residues in food.
- At the same time the organic products are healthier and have better product quality like taste, aroma and storability.
- Input cost is drastically reduced in organic cultivation but the market price leading to higher income for farmers.

Aims of organic production and processing

- To produce sufficient quantities of high quality food, fibre and other products.
- To work compatibly with natural cycles and living systems through the soil, plants and animals in the entire production system.
- To recognize the wider social and ecological impact of and within the organic production and processing systems.
- To maintain and increase long-term fertility and biological activity of soils using locally adopted cultural, biological and mechanical methods as opposed to reliance on chemical inputs.
- To maintain and encourage agricultural and natural biodiversity on the farm and surroundings through the use of sustainable production systems and protection of plant and wildlife habitats.

- To maintain and conserve genetic diversity through attention to on-farm management of genetic resources.
- To promote the responsible use and conservation of water and all life therein.
- To use, as far as possible, renewable resources in production and processing systems and avoid pollution and wastes.
- To foster local and regional production and distribution.
- To create a harmonious balance between crop production and animal husbandry.
- To provide living conditions that allows animals to express the basic aspects of their innate behaviour.
- To utilise biodegradable, recyclable and cycled packaging materials.
- To provide everyone involved in organic farming and processing with a quality of life that satisfies their basic needs within a safe, secure and healthy working environment.
- To support the establishment of an entire production, processing and distribution chain which is both socially and ecologically responsible.
- To recognise the importance of, and protect and learn from, indigenous knowledge and traditional farming systems.

Organic food products exported from India

- **Organic cereals:** Wheat, Rice and Maize or Corn.
- **Pulses:** Red gram and Black gram.
- **Fruits:** Banana, Mango, Orange, Pineapple, Passion fruits, Cashew nut and Walnut.
- **Oilseeds and oils:** Soybean, Sunflower, Mustard, Cotton seed, Groundnut and Castor.
- **Vegetables:** Brinjal, Garlic, Potato, Tomato and Onion.
- **Herbs and spices:** Chilli, Peppermint, Cardamom, Turmeric, Black pepper, White pepper, Amla, Tamarind, Ginger, Vanilla, Cloves, Cinnamon, Nutmeg and Mace.
- **Others:** Juggery, Sugar, Tea, Coffee, Cotton and Textiles.

Chapter 8

Weed Management

Weed

Weed in orchards reduce crop yields by competing for moisture, nutrients, light and space. They also harbour insect pests and diseases. When they are large they interfere with orchard operation.

Common annual weeds which are found in orchards

- There are more than 30,000 species
- Around 1,800 … and cause serious losses
- Around 250 species are causing seriously

i. **Monocot weeds (Narrow leaf/Grasses)**

Rye grass, Oats grass etc.

ii. **Dicot weeds (Broad leaf weeds)**

Parthenium, Solanum etc.

Methods of weed control in orchard

1. Cultural methods
2. Biological methods
3. Chemical methods
4. Integrated weed control
5. Soil solarisation

Losses caused by weeds (Harmful effects)

1. Weeds compete with fruit crops for nutrients.
2. They increase the cost of production.
3. Reduction in crop yield
4. They impair the quality of crop.
5. Weeds harbour pests and diseases.
6. They bring problems in irrigation, drainage.
7. Weeds reduce human efficiency through

Chapter 8

Weed Management

Weed

Weed in orchards reduce crop yields by competing for moisture, nutrients, light and space. They also harbour insect pests and diseases. When they become large they interfere with orchard operations. Some of weeds climb on the trees and shade the foliage. There are some weeds which are parasitic partially or completely on the host tree e.g. Striga and loranthes on mango.

Commonly noticed weed species in fruit orchards

- There are more than 30,000 species of weeds distributed world over, out of which 18,000 are noxious and cause serious losses.
- Around 250 species are causing serious economic losses.

i. **Monocot weeds (Narrow leaf/Grasses):** Cyprus, Cynodon, Poagrass, Rye grass, Quackgrass etc.

ii. **Dicot weeds (Broad leaf weeds):** *Dandelion, Chenopodium* spp., Parthenium, *Solanum, Euphrobia spp*., Ground ivy etc.

Methods of weed control in orchards: Broadly classified as

1. Cultural methods
2. Biological methods
3. Chemical methods
4. Integrated weed control
5. Soil solarisation

Losses caused by weeds (Harmful effects)

1. Weeds compete with fruit crops for nutrients, moisture, air and light.
2. They increase the cost of production.
3. Reduction in crop yield.
4. They impair the quality of crop.
5. Weeds harbour pests and diseases.
6. They bring problems in irrigation, drainage etc.
7. Weeds reduce human efficiency through allergism and poisoning.

Cultural or mechanical control includes

1. Hand weeding
2. Tillage operation
3. Growing of intercrops
4. Use of mulching

Biological methods

It involves the use of natural enemies of the weeds which includes fungus, bacteria, insects, fish, animals and plants (through competitive replacement eg: *Cassia* spp. replacing parthenium).

Characters of successful bioagents

1. Host specific.
2. Easily adjustable to new environment.
3. Rapid destroyer of the target weed.
4. Easy to multiply.
5. Effective against several kinds of weeds.
6. Should not affect other cultivated species.

Insects as bio-agents

Weed	Bioagent	Kind of bio-agent
Cyprus rotundus	*Bactra verutana*	Insect (shoot boring moth)
Echinochola spp.	*Emalocera;Tripos* spp.	Insect (stem boring moth)
Parthenium	*Zygogramma bicolarata, Epiblema strenuana, Conotrachelus spp.*	Leaf eating insect Stem girdling insect
Orabanche	*Sclerotinia spp. (Fungus)*	Plant pathogen
Rumese spp.	*Uromycis rumicis (Fungus)*	Plant pathogen
Mycoherbicides products	**Content**	**Weeds controlled**
De-vine	Liquid suspension of *Phytopthora palmivora (*Rootrot of weed)	*Merrenia odorata* in citrus plantations
Bipolaris	Suspension of fungal spores of *Biopolaris sorghicola*	*Sorghum halepense*
Biolophos	Microbial toxin produced as fermentation products of *Streptomyces hygroscopicus*	Non-specific can be usedon general vegetation

Chemical control

- It refers to use of herbicide to suppress or kill weeds.
- Herbicide is any chemical that has phytotoxic properties.
- Herbicides include wide variety of compounds classified on the basis of :

1. Chemical structure.
2. Selectivity (selective and non-selective).
3. Contact or translocated (systemic).

i. **Selective herbicides**: Are those which kill certain kind of specific weed without causing any significant injury to others.

   For example: 2, 4-D (controls herbaceous dicot weeds), MCDA (controls *Cyperus rotundus, Plantago spp.* etc.),

ii. **Non-selective herbicide:** Will indiscriminately kill all the plants that come in contact.

   For example : Glyphosate, paraquat (destroy green tissue only).

iii. **Systemic herbicides:** They are also referred as translocated herbicides; they are absorbed by leaves, stems or roots of treated plants. Herbicides are translocated through either phloem or xylem.

   For example: Atrazine, Simazine, Diuron, Alachlor.

Guidelines for use of herbicides

1. Use correct recommended concentration.
2. Sprayers should be properly calibrated; nozzles should be directed towards the target weeds away from the fruit tree trunk.
3. Young weeds are killed easily than older ones or established ones.
4. Application should be avoided during raining or windy situations.
5. Wetting agent should be added to facilitate spreading of herbicide more uniformly on leaf surface.
6. If the leaves of fruit trees are accidentally sprayed the sprayed portion should be immediately be cut off.

Note: The efficiency of weedicide is good, when it is used on weeds with new sprout/growth.

Integrated weed management

This is a weed management system that suppresses weeds by combining two or more weed control methods. IWM seems to be best suited for control of weeds in tropics or in fruit orchards.

Practices

1. Deep ploughing during summer.
2. Repeated tillage and hand weeding/use of chemicals.

3. Intercultivation/cover cropping, intercropping etc.
4. Organic mulching in basins.
5. Use of herbicides – 2-3 times per year.
6. Use of bioagents whenever possible.
7. Proper regulation of irrigation.
8. Use of drip irrigation.

Chapter 9

Mulching

Mulching

It means covering of soil surface by some organic or inorganic materials for conserving the soil moisture besides covering on the soil moisture several other advantage of mulching. The materials which are used in mulching called mulch.

Advantages

1. **Direct or indirect conservation of moisture -**
   a. By reduce the evaporation.
   b. Less weed population.
   c. Saving in soil water.
2. **Temperature regulation** - Mulches are regulating the temperature in regulation of temperature two important factors that is.
   a. Effect of season.
   b. Material which are used.
      i. During winter mulches are raised the temperature and during summer it give cooling effect.
      ii. Organic mulch show both the effect either raised the temperature are cooling the temperature.
3. **Weed control -** Mulches are create the hindrances in germination of weed seed that is why weed are control. For controlling the weed labour saving ultimately the cost of cultivation is economical.
4. **To check the soil erosion -** The heavy rain cause soil erosion mulches are create some optical for erosion as soil and other advantage by mulch regarding soil erosion air circulation are minimize.
5. **To improve the soil texture -** The cover soils have been fine texture in compare to bare land by incorporation of organic matter.
6. **To improve the soil fertility -** By addition of organic matter.

7. **Improvement of beneficial organism population-** Mulching is the helpful to increase the population of earthworm, actinomycetes and bacteria.
8. **Better quality of vegetable-** In Tomato, Brinjal, Cucumber mulching are avoid the direct contact of vegetable from the soil.
9. **Mulching can improve the fruit size and colour-** By providing better micro climate.

Disadvantage

1. It requires extra labour during application and removal.
2. Some time due to ignorance of removal mulching crops are suffer from over moisture resulting plant will die.
3. Premature application of mulching should be disturb the crop stability therefore mulching should be done when crop are properly stables.
   a. After first weeding.
   b. After completion of top dressing.
4. Early mulching soon after transplanting cause harmful effect of seedling growth are ultimately it's may be die during warm season this harmful effect is much more.
5. Due to decomposition soft organic material causes deficiency of nitrogen in soil. Although to fulfill the nitrogen requirement foliar application should be done.
6. Termite attack in woody mulch find haggard.

Type of mulching

Any crop in use generally two types of mulch.

1. Organic mulch
2. Inorganic mulch (plastic mulch)

Organic mulch- In organic mulch generally used saw dust, orchard leaves, shell of cobs etc.

Inorganic mulch- Inorganic mulch generally straw, paddy straw, wheat straw, French bean and soybean straw are generally used. It is found in the two types.

1. Transparent polythene sheet.
2. Coloured polythene sheet.

In coloured polythene sheet blue, black and milky white should be use.

Mulching by organic manures like compost and sugarcane baggas etc.

Stone mulch- It is more common in the ornamental potted plants.

Aluminium foil- It is not more common in horticulture crops.

Paper mulch- It is not more common in horticulture crops.

Mulching material- Ideal mulch is that which are available easily and cheaply with easy handling.

1. It should be thin polythene.
2. Crop residue like straw which are not commercially used and not appreciated by animal.
3. Rice husk, it is earlier use but now a day they are show many organic mulches are available e.g. Organic waste, Sugarcane leaves, Orchard leaves, Straw, Soybean and cacti etc.
4. Even stone mulch is potted.
5. Plastic sheet in general the transparent polythene.
6. Black sheet has been found most superior.

Note- Mulching is done two stage that is nursery stage and in field stage. Most suitable crop for mulching is tomato, potato, chilli, brinjal, onion, okra, carrot, french bean, lettuce etc.

Depth of mulching

It's vary depend upon the duration of crops and type of mulch. In long duration crop mulch is about 10 m and in short duration crop mulch is about 5 m. In annual crop thin mulch is sufficient and in perennial crop mulch should be thick. Regarding plastic mulch in earlier days 200 to 300 guage thick plastic are apply but now a day advancement and adoptability the thickness of plastic is show now 50 to 150 guage.

Out of the low density polythene sheet (LDPE) is more common. It is most suitable for most of the crop due to its durability. In case of LDPE it is more common thin that is why after one season it is damage.

Effect of mulching

Mulching is the most common practices in the crop production where on the different effect of mulch are found on the crops.

1. **Soil environment**

a. **Soil moisture-** Different mulch effect differentiable for example organic mulch (soft mulch) saw dust, fine straw as they have more absorbing the water, wheat and pea straw are considered as hard mulch. It have water absorbing capacity relatively poor if soil is not uniformly leveled they cause water stagnation.

b. **Temperature regulation-**Organic mulch show buffering effect of temperature means narrow down or minimizing the gap between day and night temperatures. The dark colour plastic mulch generally maintain high temperature than transparent. Black absorbed more radiation. Its believe that due to effect on temperature, moisture and other micro environment. They may be favourable effect of micronutrient in the soil to the plant (there is known proof in support of this stock).

c. **Biotic population-** The beneficial micro-organism such as aerobic bacteria, fungi, and actenomycetes amount with earthworm are reported that they increase under decomposition mulch. The crop residue used as mulch proof that the beneficial farm these organism when incorporated in the soil mulching causes softness of the top soil show increase earthworm in the soil.

   Wheat straw mulch fevour the growth as these organisms and also favour legume bacteria growth under presents of growth factor like protein and vitamins. The relationship between earthworm and mulch is appear to fruitful residue mulch provide readily available as food to earthworm and they protein farm cold and excessive hot desiccating wind. The earthworm also accelerated the humification of organic material on mulch and they create a use amount of humus zone.

d. **Corbon dioxide concentration-**It is require for photosynthesis but its present in soil is also important for proper root growth activity decomposing compost or manure. The soft mulch material release CO_2 and such release was observe that it's beneficial in cauliflower it triangle earliness.

e. **Soil structure-**Soil under mulches remains soft and friable compare to bared soil. Which remain hard and compact after rainfall / irrigation. However, it is temporary effect but in long term effect the structure do not change easily.

2. **Effect of mulch in crop production**

   On seed germination-Use of mulch is nursery has become compulsary because it is enhancing germination enlarge in its more common in tuber crops. Indirect season crop or closely space crop it is not so common.

3. **Effect on vegetative growth-**In mulch the soil vegetative growth is in general so good.

4. **On crop maturity-**In respect of plastic mulch the more work has been done. In use of plastic mulch it is reported that crop mature early.

5. **On the crop field-** In a study it is absorbed that solanaceous and cucurbitaceous crops have more yield.

6. **Quality of produce-** It is beneficial in vegetable production because due to better soil, environment underground process is bound to be higher quality and ground produces is also found superior.

7. **On the plant protection**

a. **Weed control-** After mulching the soil less production weed has been reported.

b. **Insect and disease control-** In a field taste mulch play an important role in reduce the population of aphid and reduce the incidence or attack of cucumber mosaic virus.

Economics

Ultimately organic mulch are more beneficial but not much study has been conducted regarding economics of mulch.

Chapter 10

Nursery Management of Fruit Crops

Nursery and its Importance

Nursery is a place where seedling, saplings or any other planting materials are raised, propagated, multiplied and sold out for planting. The prerequisites of a successful and remunerative fruit production are the availability of healthy and good quality planting materials. [illegible] has been [illegible] from the investment [illegible]

Importance of a Nursery

1. The young seedling requires special care [illegible] after germination [illegible] permanent [illegible]
2. [illegible] ready, specialization and [illegible] in a controlled condition [illegible] skilled labours.
3. Cutting and best period [illegible] nursery.
4. [illegible] method [illegible] of seedling raised in nursery.
5. Nursery hardened plants are preferred [illegible]
6. Besides these, [illegible] of seedling or sapling [illegible] preplanting preparations.
7. Seasoning of seedling against natural odds.

Chapter 10

Nursery Management of Fruit Crops

Nursery

Nursery is a place where seedling, saplings or any other planting materials are raised, propagated, multiplied and sold out for planting. The prerequisites of a successful and remunerative fruit production are the availability of true-to-type, healthy and good quality planting materials. Setting up of a fruit nursery is a long term venture and requires careful planning and expertise, because mistakes committed initially cannot be rectified easily and may adversely affect the return from the investment. Thus, one should pay due attention on every aspects when nursery is to be established.

Importance of a Nursery

1. The young seedling requires special attention during the first few weeks after germination. It is easier and economical to look after the young and tender seedling growing in nursery bed in a small area than in the large permanent site.
2. Majority of fruit crops are propagated by vegetative means. The propagules require special skill and after care before transferring them in the main field in a controlled condition in nursery, all these can be provided successfully by skilled labours.
3. Cutting are best rooted in mist-chamber which is an integrated part of a nursery
4. Direct sowing method is not successful when compared with transplanting of seedling raised in nursery.
5. Nursery hardened plants are preferred for causality replacement in orchards.
6. Besides these, raising of seedling or sapling in nursery provides more time for replanting preparations.
7. Seasoning of seeding against natural odds is only possible in nursery.

Classification

Nursery may broadly be grouped into two on the basis of its size:

1. Home Nursery
2. Commercial Nursery

Home Nursery: Home nursery is the area where planting materials are specifically grown only to eater the needs of the grower's garden. The area is small and the primary consideration is the raising of quality materials. Costly methods of nursery practices are adopted.

Commercial Nursery: The commercial nursery is mainly concerned with economic return from the investment and, therefore, very expensive nursery practices are avoided without affecting the quality of the products. This type of nursery can be subdivided into two groups which are as follows:

a. **Rural Nursery**: Rural nursery is situated in a village near the highway road or railway station. In general, the size of rural nursery may be large as the land and labour charges are cheaper. The products are also sold at a cheaper rate.

b. **Urban Nursery**: The nurseries which are located inside the city or close to it are known as urban nurseries. As the land is very costly and not easily available, the size of this type of nursery is usually small. The labour charges, transport cost etc. are also very high, but these are compensated by the higher price of products and volume of sale. Sometimes they act as middlemen i.e., procure planting materials from rural nursery and resale to the customers.

Factors Affecting the Establishment of a Nursery

1. Location and Site

a. **Topography**: The land for the nursery should be as flat as possible with a gradual slope in one direction. This helps in quick draining out the excess water during the heavy down pour. The area should be somewhat elevated than the adjoining area to avoid water logging and congestion.

b. **Climate:** It is of prime importance to select only those species and varieties which thrive well in the region.

c. **Reputation of locality for nursery business**: The locality where a nursery is intended to be established should have the reputation for the business. This means that the nurseries should be established in the known locality. Since such a place is known to the customers, the fledgling nursery gets the advantage of publicity. Apart from this, skilled labours and various inputs are also readily available.

d. **Transport facility**: Adequate transport facilities are of prime importance for successful nursery business. A nursery should be located near a metal road, or close to a railway station to deliver the plant materials to the customers in a short time. It should be easily accessible to the customers, but totally free from pilferage.

2. Selection of Soil

Type of soil, drainage and soil fertility are the three basic components to be considered while selecting the soil for establishing a nursery. Almost all the fruit crops do well in friable, loamy soil, rich in organic matter with the soil reaction varying from slightly acidic to near neutral (pH 5.5 to 6.5). However, a clay-loam soil is advantageous as in this type of soil, it is easy to lift the evergreen plants with earth balls intact. Shallow soil with hard and compact subsoil's should be avoided as it creates hindrance in proper root growth of mother-plants. A depth of 75.0 cm is sufficient for nursery practices but for the progeny block a soil depth of 1-1.5 m is desired. Presence of calcium carbonate layers affects permeability and aeration, and results stagnation of water which is detrimental to root respiration.

3. Water Supply

Nursery stocks require frequent light irrigation. A regular water supply must be assured in a nursery. The water for irrigation should be free from any dissolved salts and pH should be near neutral. A surface well may be dug or a tube-well may be installed for this purpose. In canal-irrigated areas, it is advisable to construct a water reservoir, so that the requirements may be met with the stored water during the dry period.

4. Manures

For nursery work, plenty of organic manures viz. farm yard manure, compost, leaf mould, sludge etc. are required. These should be available in sufficient quantities.

Parts of a Nursery

A nursery should consist of the following parts

1. Building structures

The building structures include office, Sale counter, Packing shade, Potting shade, Store, Implement shade, Bullock shade and Residential quarters etc.

Office-The office is the most important among all the building structures because all the business transactions are done from the office. The size of office depends on the size of business.

Sale counter-The sale counter should be attached to the office.

Packing shed-Before delivering the material to the customers they are to be packed and labeled properly. Packing materials like baskets or boxes are kept in this shed. It should be located near the sale counter.

Potting shed-Pot of varying sizes and shapes and the potting mixture (eg., loamy soil, leaf mould, well rotten cow dung, fine river silt, sand) are kept in the shade. Potting operations are executed under shade where all the materials are easily available in right condition throughout the year. Only the plants are brought from the nursery beds. Potting under shade also minimises desiccation of plant, saves time and helps to keep other areas of the orchard clean.

Store-A store is needed to keep the fertilizers, sprayers, insecticides, fungicides etc. This should be located inside the nursery and away from the main office.

Implement shade-A shade is required for keeping the garden implements.

Bullock shed-Many bullock drawn implements are generally used in a small nursery. In such case, a shed is necessary and should be located in the rear side of the nursery to maintain the bullock shed of the nursery.

Residential quarters-Sometimes the owner desires to live in the nursery premises with his family. In such case, the house should be constructed according to the choice of the owner. In large enterprises, residential arrangements are also made for the skilled labours and other staff members.

In general, the placement of structures or quarters should be on the northern border of the nursery which does not obstruct the emission of light and flow of wind inside the nursery. Further movement of workers becomes easy if these are placed on the border.

2. Progeny tree block

The correct choice of kind and variety of fruit crops and collection of true-to-type mother plants has strong bearing on the success and goodwill of a nursery industry. Suitable fruit crops should be selected to meet the demand of the customers. There should be a collection of good number of promising varieties of popular crops to make a wide choice. The progeny trees should be healthy, disease free, genetically true-to-type and free from insect-pests attack. The pedigree of these plants should also be known to the nursery man.

3. Propagation structures

The outdoor conditions may not be always congenial for successful multiplication and raising of plants. The freezing cold atmosphere in winter and hot desiccating wind in summer preclude the outdoor cultivation of propagules. Different types of propagation structures green house (glass house), hotbed, cold frame, lath house, net house and mist chamber are in commercial use to create propitious conditions in respect of light, temperature and humidity for facilitating germination of seed, rooting of cutting and also for hardening of young seedling before transplanting them to main field.

The green house and hotbed are structures with temperature control and ample light, and mainly used for seed germination and rooting of cutting. The lath house and cold-frame are structures for hardening the young and tender plantlets before planting them in outdoor conditions.

Green house-A green house is a structure covered with glass for protection against adverse climatic conditions to cultivate plants. Plants are grown or cuttings are rooted in a green house when the atmospheric condition does not permit for raising them in outdoor condition. Modern green houses are equipped with regulatory mechanism for controlling temperature, light intensity, air flow and humidity. To minimise the high cost of glass, it may be replaced by polyethylene films of various thickness. Polyethylene of 0.10 to 0.15 mm (0.004 to 0.006 inch) thickness, resistant to ultraviolet ray is found most suitable for green house. For controlling the temperature and humidity inside the green house, arrangement should be made for proper air movement. Conservation of heat is essential in the green houses. In general, green houses are heated by steam or hot water passing through pipes fitted suitably from a central boiler. In large green houses, heated air is often blown into large (30 to 60 cm) polyethylene tubes having small (5 to 7.5 cm) holes spaced throughout the length to release the hot air inside, which are hung overhead along the length of green house. The heat loss in green house can be reduced by providing a double layered, sealed polyethylene sheet outside the glass.

Plants, in green house, are grown in the ground bed or bench type raised beds. The size of the green houses and the dimensions of beds vary according to the needs of the propagules.

Hotbed- It is a small fixed structure having three components namely, frame, cover and heating unit. It is also used for growing small tender seedling and rooting of cuttings. The cover is made of glass or transparent polyethene sheet. The soil of bed is dug out and replaced with 30-50 cm thick layer of raw cowdung, preferably horse manure and covered with 15-20 cm thick rooting medium. Decomposition of raw dung generates heat and the temperature of the rooting medium is raised. In large size modern nursery, improved heating arrangements like steam piping, hot water piping, electric cable etc. are used for heating the bed. The frame can be made of wood or any light metal.

Cold-frame-It is a small and movable structure of glass which encloses a ground bed. It is used for hardening or conditioning of rooted cutting and young seedlings before transferring them out. There is no bottom beating arrangement and heat is tapped from the solar energy. It should, therefore, be located in a sunny place. For assured success, care has to be taken in respect of proper ventilation, shade, watering and winter protection. The sash is removed during day time for quick raising of temperature of growing medium.

Lath house-Lath house is a structure which is made with the object of providing shade and thereby protecting the young tender seedlings or rooted cuttings which are sensitive to strong sunlight and high temperature. The transpiration and evaporation loss of moisture are directly related with temperature. So, in lath house the loss of moisture from leaf as well as from soil surface is greatly reduced, due to low temperature and light intensity, resulting into less water requirements of plants. Seedlings are transferred for hardening from green house or hotbed to lath house. The structure and size of lath house vary widely. Different kinds of shading materials are used (e.g. wood strips, polypropylene fabrics etc.) for the roof.

Net house-A net house resembles to a green house where the roof as well as sides are made of wire nets fixed on iron or wooden frame. The roof may be covered by polyethylene sheet, leaves or some climbers may be allowed to grow and cover the roof to provide shade. A net house is used for growing shade loving plants, orchids, cactus and also for raising seedlings. The inside atmosphere remains cool in summer and warm during winter.

Mist propagation chamber- Mist propagation technique has made a breakthrough in the rooting of cuttings of difficult-to-root plants. In this system, an intermittent water mist is provided during day time over the cuttings and to the rooting media which increases the relative humidity surrounding the leaf and lowers the air and leaf surface temperature, thus reduces the rates of transpiration and respiration. The intermittent mist is controlled by an electrically operated timer mechanism, regulating a solenoid valve, spraying water for 5 seconds and then cut-off till the leaves starts drying and again turned on. Electronic leaf having two terminals may be placed under the mist along with the cuttings to control the mist. Mist technique is ideal for rooting of leafy cuttings. There may be some losses of minerals by leaching, which can be replenished by adding nutrients to the mist.

4. Nursery beds

A nursery bed should be prepared by repeated ploughing and pulverizing the soils to obtain a fine tilth. Adequate amount of organic manure and compost should be incorporated into the soils. Nitrogen at the rate of 25 kg per hectare may be added for quick growth of seedling at the initial stage. Addition of wood ash makes the soil loose and acts as a source of potassium which is required for better growth. A loose, friable, clay loam soil, rich in organic matter is ideal for the young tender seedling. Proper drainage system must be assured because the young seedlings are sensitive to water logging condition. Nursery beds may be little raised during rainy.

Raising of Rootstocks

Rootstock is that part of the plant onto which a scion buds or bud stick is placed. It provides the root system to the grafted or budded plant. It is well documented that root stocks have strong influences on the growth, flowering, and precocity of bearing, fruit quality of the grafted or budded plant. They also impart resistance to various pest and diseases and adverse soil and climatic conditions. The desired performance of the scion cultivar depends on the correct choice of the rootstock. The nursery should raise its rootstocks. The information available on the standardization of rootstock of tropical and subtropical fruit crops are scanty, barring citrus and grapes. In general, the rootstocks are raised from seeds. The polyembryonic varieties have been reported to produce uniform nucellar seedlings. The techniques of mound layering may be successfully employed for raising uniform rootstocks in some fruit crops like guava and jackfruit.

The seeds should be collected from the healthy, disease free tree. The seeds are to be washed thoroughly and dried in shade prior to sowing. Some seeds need immediate sowing. The spacing and depth of sowing vary with the size of seeds, viz citrus seeds are sown 2 cm apart in rows at a depth of 1 cm whereas mango stones are placed at a depth of 3 to 6 cm with a spacing of 15 to 20 cm between stone. The germination of seeds normally commences about 3 weeks after sowing. The young seedlings are susceptible to extremes of climate. They should be protected against frost in winter and hot desiccating wind during summer. Light dressing with nitrogenous fertilizers after one month helps in rapid growth of seedling at the initial stage. The beds should be kept free from weeds. Irrigation should be given at an interval of 7-10 days during summer months. Seedlings become ready for grafting or budding at the age of one year when they attain a size of pencil thickness at about 15 to 20 cm above the ground level.

Management of young nursery plants

a. **Irrigation:** The young tender seedlings are exacting in their water requirement. Over watering is as harmful as under watering. To maintain the turgor pressure in the cell for maximum photosynthetic activity, light irrigation should be given at an interval of 7 to 10 days during summer and 15 days in winter. Proper care has to be taken to avoid subsoil congestion.

b. **Nutrition**: Proper nutrition has profound influence on the growth of nursery plants. Liberal manuring with well decomposed organic matter is a prerequisite for achieving success in nursery business. A light and frequent does of nitrogenous fertilizer @25 kg per hectare may be applied to obtain quick growth of seedling.

c. **Weed control:** Weeds poses severe threat to the young seedlings in the nursery bed. Weeds being wild in nature grow vigorously and get established earlier than the crop plant. Often the seedlings are crowded over by the weeds if they are not controlled initially. The nursery bed should be kept free from weeds by shallow hoeing. This also helps in better aeration of the soils. The roads and irrigation channels also should be made free from weeds to avoid the chances of spread of weed seeds.

d. **Plant protection**

i. **Protection against adverse climatic condition:** During the daytime in summer season, temperature shoots up in tropical regions resulting into striking rise of transpiration and evaporation rates. If high temperature in accompanied by flew of hot wind, the problem is further aggravated and the tender seedling soon losses its vitality. The tolerance limit of fruit plants to high temperature varies with species.

Seedlings can be protected from scorching sun by providing some shades during day time. Thatches may be erected over the seed bed. Shade crops may also be grown. Windbreaks on the eastern and southern sides of the nursery can reduce the wind velocity, and thereby, minimise the moisture losses from leaf and soil surfaces as well. Recuperation of soils with frequent light irrigation during summer months greatly helps to overcome this problem.

The tissues of young seedlings are highly susceptible to frost. Occurrence of early and late frost may affect the plants severely. Generation of smokes by slow burning of dry grasses or plant debris helps to ward off frost from nursery. Irrigation during cold period keeps off the condensation of frost from the nursery. Erection of thatches and planting of wind breaks also provide substantial protection against frost.

ii. **Protection against pests and diseases:** The reputation of a nursery depends on the supply of genuine, healthy and disease free plants. Once the seedlings are affected by pests and / or diseases, their growth is arrested and they turn pale and weak. The tender seedlings are susceptible to various pests and diseases but the degree of susceptibility varies with species and age of seedlings.

Lifting and packing of seedling: It is desirable to lift the plants with balls of earth intact while the deciduous plants can be lifted bare rooted during dormant condition. Light irrigation should be given, if required, before lifting the seedlings.

The type of packing depends on the size of stock and type of plant. The transplants lifted bare rooted are packed with their roots wrapped in moist sphagnum moss and moist paper. The ball of earth may be wrapped with coconut leaves or rice straw and packed in basket.

Storage: Low temperature (0.5 to 1.5°C) in association with high humidity (80-90%) in the atmosphere of storage reduces the respiration and transpiration rates. The store house should be well ventilated to drive out the carbon dioxide and heat of respiration.

Chapter 11

Plant Propagation

Propagation

Plant propagation means multiplication of plant by sexual or asexual method. The success in plant propagation depends on a thorough knowledge of the growth of plants, choice of suitable method and technical skill. The propagation of plants may be done either by the gametes or from the somatic cell, tissues or organs. In other words, propagation may be done by sexual methods or by asexual methods. The details of the methods are presented below.

There are two type of plant propagation

1. Sexual propagation
2. Asexual propagation

A. Sexual propagation

Sexual propagation means multiplication of the plant by seed. It is also known as seed propagation. Sexual propagation is the raising of plants by means of seeds which are formed due to the fusion of male and female gametes within the ovule of a flower. A seed is a miniature packed plant ready for sowing with nourshing tissues and a protective cover. A seed consists of three basic parts namely (i) embryo, (ii) the food reserves (endosperm, cotyledon) and (ii) the seed coat (testa). The embryo is a minute plant, carries all the genetic information and is capable of giving rise to a new individual in a congenial condition. An embryo may also be developed from the somatic tissues in some species without meiosis which is known as apomixis.

Advantages of sexual propagation

1. This is the easily and cheaper method.
2. Some of the plant does not response well by asexual method (Papaya) this type of plant only propagated by sexual propagation.
3. Sexually raised plant are long lived have extensive root system and bear heavily as compare to asexually propagated plants.
4. Hybrid can develop only by seed propagation.
5. Seed can be store for longer duration.

Disadvantages of sexual propagation

1. Most of the fruits plants are heterozygous in nature.
2. Seedling raised plants are generally tall and spreading type causing hazard for carrying out various management practices.
3. Sexually raised plant take longer duration to come bearing.
4. Seeds of the many fruits are to be shown immediately after extraction, because they loss their viability soon e.g. Phalsa, Jackfruit and Mango etc.

B. Asexual propagation

Asexual propagation means propagation of plant by vegetative part like stem, root, leaf etc.

Advantages of asexual propagation

1. Most of the fruit crops are heterozygous in nature. Genetic architecture can only be maintained true-to-type by asexual mean.
2. Some of the fruit plants do not produce viable seed (Banana, Pineapple), multiplication of then is only possible through asexual means.
3. Vegetativelly propagated plants are early bearing.
4. Height of plant can be regulated and resistance of biotic and abiotic stress can be developed by use of suitable rootstock.
5. Bridge grafting-repairing of the plants.

Disadvantages of asexual propagation

1. Vegetative propagation does not involve in new varieties.
2. Some time it is expensive and it require special technique.
3. Vegetativelly raised plants are short lived.

Methods of asexual propagations

A. Apomictic Seed- Citrus, Mango etc.

B. Specialized vegetative structure- Bulb, Corm, Rhizome, Tubers, Suckers, Runner and Crown.

C. On the own root system-

i. **Cutting-** Herbaceous, Soft wood, Semi hard wood and Hard wood.

ii. **Layering-** Simple, Tip, Trench, Air layering, Mound layering and Serpentine layering.

D. On the root system of other plant-

i. **Budding** – T-budding, Ring budding, Forkert budding, Chip budding, Patch budding, Flute budding, I- budding etc.

ii. **Grafting-** a. Attached method of grafting-Inarching

b. Detached method of grafting- Veneer grafting, Toung grafting, Splice grafting, Whip grafting, Epicotyle grafting etc.

i. Cutting

Cutting is piece of plant which produce adventitious root (in case of stem and leaf cutting) and a new shoot system (in case of root cutting) when produce in rooting media keeping all other condition are favourable. It gives rise to a new plant almost true to mother plant.

Advantages of cutting

1. It is very easy to perform and economical.
2. Rapid multiplication is possible with in a short time.
3. Does not require much space.
4. Complicated stionic relationship can be avoided.
5. Cutting can be transported to any place because the stem or root piece remain fresh for 5-7 days if packed properly.

Disadvantages of cutting

1. All the plant does not root very easily.
2. The benefit of root-stock cannot be exploited.

Classification of cutting

1. **Stem cutting-** Herbaceous cutting, soft wood stem cutting, semi hard wood stem cutting and hard wood stem cutting.
2. **Leaf cutting**. Not common in fruit crops.
3. **Leaf bud cutting-** Not common in fruit crops.
4. **Root cutting-**It is more common in forestry crop.

   Length of cutting- 8-15 cm with 2-3 nodes and diameter of cutting 1-2 cm.

Time of cutting

i. Deciduous plant- March-April

ii. Evergreen plant -May-September

Climate of cutting

Average temperature- 20-25^{0}C, day temperature-21-27^{0}C, night temperature-15-16^{0}C and humidity- 80% and rooting period-15-30 days.

i. **Stem cutting**: Stem cuttings are of four different types-herbaceous, softwood, semi-hardwood and hardwood cuttings.

Herbaceous cuttings: Herbaceous cuttings are the tender succulent special leafy parts of the stems of herbaceous plants. The terminal 7.0 to 12.0 cm of a healthy shoot is cut and the basal leaves are removed leaving the upper leaves undisturbed. The cuttings once detached should not desiccate at the cut end. Though cuttings root easily yet application of auxins promots the regeneration of adventitious roots.

Softwood cuttings: Softwood cuttings are those prepared from the soft succulent terminal portions of woody perennials. It is desirable to retain some leaves on the cuttings for photosynthesis, but more leaves are undesirable which may cause moisture loss due to transpiration. Care has to be taken to maintain high humidity to prevent from drying due to excessive moisture loss by transpiration. Softwood cuttings are 8.0 to 15.0 cm long with two to three nodes. The basal cut is given just below the node and the adjacent leaves are removed. Cuttings should be taken from slightly mature but flexible, moderately vigorous shoots in March-April (deciduous) and May-September (evergreen) months. Extremely vigorous or slow growing, soft, thin shoots collapse quite soon before producing roots. Cuttings put forth roots within 15 to 30 days if both temperature (20-26^{0}C) and humidity (80%) are conducive. Softwood cutting responses well to exogenous auxin application.

Semi-hardwood cuttings: Semi-hardwood cuttings are prepared from partially mature but tender woody shoots. The terminal shoot is detached as previous. Cuttings should be taken in the early morning when the cells are fully turgid. Intermittent mist sprays of water and treatment with auxins have been reported to be beneficial.

Hardwood cuttings: These cuttings are taken from the lignified mature woody shoots. The length of hardwood cuttings varies widely from 20 to 50 cm having diameter of 1.0 to 2.0 cm or more. Each cutting should consist of at least 2 to 3 nodes. The apical 2.0 cm portion is discarded as it is low in food reserves. The cuttings should contain sufficient stored food materials. Usually, cuttings are made from the previous season's growth in the dormant season i.e. late fall or early spring. Cuttings root easily in the mist chamber with exogenous application of auxins. Various fruit crops are multiplied commercially by hardwood cuttings.

ii. **Leaf cutting**: The fleshy leaf or leaf blade and petiole of many plants are used as propagating materials. The original leaf does not form any part of the new plant and it dries up when the new plant is well developed. New plants arise at the point where the veins are cut. High humid condition is essential to obtain better success in leaf cutting. In general, the root promoting hormones are not used in leaf cuttings. The method has very little application on fruit crops.

iii. **Leaf-bud cutting**: A leaf-bud cutting is made from a leaf blade, petiole and a short piece of the stem with a dormant axillary bud. This technique is practiced in blackberry, lemon etc. Fully expanded physiologically active leaves from current season's growth are taken for preparing leaf bud cutting. The adventitious roots are formed at the base while the dormant bud develops into new shoot system.

iv. **Root cutting**: In root cutting a new shoot system is regenerated from a piece of root. Maintenance of correct polarity is of prime importance in root cutting as the new shoot develops from the proximal end i.e., from the part close to the crown. So it is advisable to keep the proximal end above the ground surface. Root cuttings are generally taken in late winter or early spring when roots are well developed and rich in stored food materials. This method is followed in Apple, Pear, Cherry, Guava, Wood apple etc.

Factors Affecting Rooting of Cutting

A. External Factors

1. **Water**: When a cutting is detached from the mother plant its natural water supply is stopped but transpiration continues resulting into severe water loss from leaf surface. For rapid and better regeneration of roots it is necessary to maintain the turgidity of the cells. The transpiration rate can be minimised effectively by maintaining a high humidity around the cuttings. Intermittent mist spray of water is ideal for reducing the water loss and maintaining the turgor pressure of cells. But, excess water is detrimental as it may lead to fungal attack causing death of the cuttings.
2. **Temperature**: Temperature has a strong influence on the regeneration of adventitious roots. High temperature results into excessive moisture loss from the cuttings. Apart from this, high temperature encourages shoot development prior to root development. It has been observed that a day temperature of 21^0-27^{0}C and night temperature of 15^0-16^{0}C are most congenial for rooting of cuttings of most species. However, some species root better at s lower temperature. Perceptible successes have been achieved in some difficult-to-root plant with bottom heat technique which keeps the rooting medium warm.
3. **Light**: The regeneration of adventitious roots in cutting is also influenced by the presence of light. The rooting of cutting varies widely from species to

species depending upon the intensity of light. In general, illumination on herbaceous and softwood cuttings promotes the root initiation, while it has little or no effect on hardwood cuttings. The promotion of rooting of cutting due to illumination may be ascribed to increased synthesis of carbohydrate in herbaceous and softwood cuttings which are poor in carbohydrate reserve. Hardwood cuttings being rich in stored food material may not be influenced by the situation.

Long day has been found to favour the regeneration of roots due to more accumulation of carbohydrates. The light and dark conditions for regeneration of shoot and root respectively are directly correlated. Etiolation as a means of root regeneration is based on this principle.

4. **Rooting medium**: Rooting medium has four basic roles to play (i) It holds the cutting in place, (ii) It absorbs high amount of moisture and supplies to the newly emerged roots, (iii) It creates a condition congenial for root respiration (iv) It maintains adequate temperature for the process.

An ideal rooting medium should be loose, porus with high water holding capacity. The nature of roots arising from the cuttings is also influenced by the type of rooting medium. For example, cuttings when planted in pure sand produce long, unbranched and in coarse brittle roots but those planted in a mixture of sand and soil or sand and peat, produce well developed, branched, flexible root system suitable for transplanting. The pH of the rooting medium should be towards neutral (6.5-7.0).

B. Internal Factors

1. **Juvenility (age of the stock plant)**: The age of the stock plant has a striking influence on the regeneration of roots. Cuttings taken from the young plants produce roots promptly as compared to the cuttings obtained from aged plants. In general, the ability to root decreases with increasing age of plant which may be due to increase in concentration of rooting inhibitors and decrease in levels of rooting co-factors. Reduced rooting potential of aged plants may be ascribed to lowering of phenolic levels which are postulated as auxin co-factors or synergists in root initiation. Juvenility can be induced to aged plants by drastic pruning which encourages new vegetative flushes.

2. **Types of wood**: Cuttings made from lateral shoots root more efficiently than those taken from terminal ones which seem to be due to higher carbohydrate content of lateral shoots.

   The antagonistic relationship between vegetative and reproductive growth in plants is most evident in difficult to root species where roots do not grow even after removal of flowers, indicating the physiological harrier may be associated with flower bud differentiation. The phenomenon also holds well in easy-to-root plant species where levels of auxin induce rooting at the cost of flowering.

In woody plants variations in the rooting ability of the different positions of a same shoot has been reported and the best rooting is obtained in the cutting made from the basal part of a shoot. This might be due to more accumulation of carbohydrate and presence of root promoting substances towards the basal part of a shoot.

3. **Effect of leaves and buds:** In most species removal of all leaves and buds causes severe set back in rooting of cuttings. Retention of some leaves in cutting, therefore, helps synthesis of carbohydrates and other metabolites which, in turn, accelerate the initiation of adventitious roots. However, retention of all the leaves may be harmful as it will increase the water loss through transpiration. Hardwood cuttings being well mature retain root promoting substances and root even without leaves.

4. **Position of the basal cut**: The rootability of cuttings varies with the position of the basal cut with reference to node. In some species it is promoted when the cut is given slightly above or below the node and in some when the cut is made at node. However, cuttings of some species produce roots irrespective of the position of the basal cut.

5. **Nutrition:** In general, high carbohydrate and moderate nitrogen levels favour rooting of cutting. It has been found that cuttings with high carbohydrate and low nitrogen put forth many roots but meagre shoots. On the other hand, very low carbohydrate and high nitrogen status does not encourage the production of either roots or shoots. Shoots making luxuriant growth and having high nitrogen content are not suitable for cuttings because they are generally low in carbohydrate content. The carbohydrate content of the shoot can be increased by girdling (removal of the bark or phloem tissue in the form of a ring) which causes accumulation of carbohydrate above the girdled portion of the shoot. The nitrogen fertilization of stock plant should be reduced to check the shoot growth before propagation which in turn enhances the accumulation of carbohydrate.

   High phosphorus also promotes the regeneration of roots in cutting. The favourable effect of zinc on root initiation seems to be associated with its role in tryptophan synthesis which is a precursor of indole acetic acid. Root initiation is inhibited by the increased concentration of manganese which is known to be an activator of indole acetic acid oxidase, an enzyme that degenerated the natural auxins.

6. **Hormone**: Among the various growth hormones auxins have profound influence on adventitious root formation. It has been confirmed that application of auxin, naturally or artificially, is essential for initiation of adventitious roots on stems and indeed, it has been shown that the initial division of the first root cells is dependent on either applied or endogenous auxin. Synthetic auxins like indole-3-butyric acid and naphthalene acetic acid are more effective than the naturally occurring indole acetic acid for this purpose. The enhanced rooting in cutting following auxin treatment has been considered to be partly due to enhanced hydrolysis of nutritional reserves under the influence of auxins. The interaction between rooting cofactors and auxins has been reported to trigger the processes of adventitious root formation.

Application of cytokinin to leaf cuttings have been found to promote rooting while, GA_3 in general, has inhibitory effect on rooting. Lowering the natural levels of gibberellin in the tissue stimulates adventitious root formation in plant parts. Auxin synergists are found effective for root regeneration in difficult-to-root plant species.

ii. Layering

Layering involves the regeneration of adventitious root from a shoot when it is still attach with the mother plant. The exogenous application of auxin has been found to hasten the initiation of root, increase percentage of rooting and number of roots per layers. This is more common in guava, litchi, citrus etc.

Advantages

1. It is easy method does not require much care and arrangement like cutting.
2. Mother plant supplies nutrient and it remain attached while rooting.
3. Some of plant species which do not root by cutting can be propagated by layering.

Disadvantages

1. The number of new plant can produce from any given mother plant by layering is low as compare with cutting.
2. Costly method where labour charged is very high.
3. Layered plants are generally shallow rooted.
4. Benefit of root stock cannot be exploited.

Type of layering

1. **Simple layering**: Low flexible shoot which bend freely is selected for simple layering. All the leaves and side shoots are trimmed off leaving 15.0 to 20.0

cm from the tip. The shoot is then bent slowly to the ground level and buried into the soil (5.0-7.0 m) leaving the tip of the shoot exposed. The shoot is held in position with the help of peg. Making a notch or girdling in the buried part of the shoot interrupts the downward movements of food materials synthesized by the leaves and causes profuse rooting. The soil surrounding the buried shoots should be kept moist to avoid the drying up of newly emerged roots. Rooting will be completed within 5 to 7 weeks. The ideal time for simple layering is early spring or rainy season.

2. **Tip layering**: For tip layering the current season's shoots are selected. The apical parts or tips of the selected shoots are buried into soil to a depth of 5.0 to 7.0 cm. In the absence of light and other conditions favourable for root growth, the buried shoot tips soon (16-20 days) get flattened and produce adventitious root and new shoot system developed on the above ground level. These shoots are then gradually detached from mother plant and transplanted in nursery beds. Tip layering is followed in blackberries, raspberries etc.
3. **Trench layering**: In trench layering, the entire branch of a plant (or sometimes the tree as a whole) is bent slowly, placed into a shallow trench, and covered with soil (5.0-7.0 cm) leaving the terminal part exposed. Bending of the branch forces the new shoots to emerge out throughout its length. As the shoots grow, more soil is placed to cover the basal parts of newly emerged shoots for exclusion of light (etiolation). The soil surrounding the trench is kept moist. When rooting is complete, the soil is removed and rooted shoots are separated carefully from the mother plant and transplanted in the nursery beds.

   This method may be practiced in apple, pear and in some ornamental shrubs. The advantage of the type of layering is that many plants can be produced from each branch.
4. **Air layering**: Air layering (Syn. gootee, potlayerage. marcottage) is a common means of propagation of many tropical and subtropical fruit crops (e.g. guava. litchi, citrus, jackfruit, pomegranate etc.)

   Fairly long, partially hardened, one to two year old shoots having pencil thickness are selected for air layering. Fully mature shoots should be avoided as they do not strike roots freely. The basal leaves of the selected shoots are removed. The bark (1.5 to 2.5 cm in length) at the base should be stripped off in the form of a ring to check the downward translocation of food materials from the leaves. The cambium layer should be scrapped off from the exposed part, without causing any injury to the wood, to prevent from healing. Application of auxins (in lanoline base) to the upper part of the girdled portion hastens the initiation of roots and causes profuse rooting.

A ball of sphagnum moss or moist soil is placed around the ringed or girdled section and wrapped carefully with transparent polyethylene sheet. The two ends of the sheet is then twisted and tied tightly. The advantages of using transparent polyethylene sheet are (i) It retains the inside moisture, (ii) It allows the gaseous exchange and (iii) The growth of adventitious roots becomes visible from outside.

Rooting takes place within 30 to 45 days. The rooted layers are then severed from the mother plant and transplanted in the nursery bed. It has been found that separation of the layered shoots in two to three stages gives higher percentage of survivability. In that case first a V-shaped notch is made on the layered shoot 2.0 cm below the earth ball which is deepened after 5 to 7 days and finally detached from the mother plant 4 to 5 days after the second cut. The ideal time for air layering is early spring or the onset of monsoon.

5. **Mound or Stool layering:** In mound layering the stem is cut back to a height of 10 cm above the ground level during the dormant season. New shoots start emerging out from the stool with the onset of spring. When these shoots have grown 10 to 15 cm in height, they are earthed up with soil mixed with farm yard manure around the stool. As the shoots grow, more soil is drawn up around the stump. A final earthling up is done when the shoots attain a height of 35 to 45 cm and the base of each shoot is then covered with soil up to 15 to 20 cm from the ground level. The soil surrounding the stump is kept moist to encourage rooting. Covering the base of shoots with soil serves the purpose of etiolation. In the beginning of winter season the soil around the stump is removed without causing injury to the new shoots which have already produced roots. They are separated from the mother plants and transplanted in the nursery bed.

   After detaching the layers, the mother stool remains exposed until they put forth another vegetative flush in the following spring. With proper management a stool can be used for 15 to 20 years. Mound layering can be practiced with varying degree of success for clonal propagation in mango, guava, jackfruit, apple, pear etc. Girdling and treatment with auxin have been found to promote more rooting in mound layering.

6. **Compound layering:** It is also known as serpentine layering. This method is practised in plants having long soft shoots which bend easily. The shoots are covered and exposed alternately along its length. A slanting cut is given just below a node where it is to root. Adventitious roots are formed from the node buried into the soil and new shoot develops from the node above the ground. When the shoots have attained considerable size they are severed and planted in nursery.

iii. Grafting

Grafting is the art of uniting or joining the parts of two independent plants in such a manner that they unite together and develop into a single independent plant. The part of graft which is to become the shoot system is termed as scion. The part which is to become the root system is called as root stock.

Types of grafting

- Approach grafting
- Inarching
- Bark grafting
- Cleft grafting
- Splice grafting
- Root grafting
- Bridge grafting
- Side grafting
- Veneer grafting
- Epicotyl grafting (Stone grafting)
- Soft wood grafting

iv. Budding

Budding is also method of grafting where only one bud with a piece of bark, and with or without wood, is used as scion material. It is also called as bud grafting. The plant successful union of the stock and bud is also known as budding.

Methods of budding

T-budding (shield budding), inverted T-budding, patch budding, flute budding, ring budding, chip budding.

Advantages

1. Benefit of root stock can be successfully utilized.
2. An inferior variety can be changed into superior type by top working.
3. Growing number of variety in one plant is possible.
4. Difficult to root can be successfully multiplied.
5. Early new of flowering and fruiting can be obtained.
6. The damaged plant part can be repair by grafting.

Disadvantages

1. All plants are not compatible to each other.
2. The method are confined only indicates plant having continue cambium, monocot and dicot have vascular cambium.

Different between cutting and layering

Cutting	Layering
In cutting the cut portion are remove from the mother plant initiation of roots take place when all condition are favourable.	In layering the initiation of roots in the plant parts when it is still attached with the mother plant when all condition are favourable

Different between budding and grafting

Budding	Grafting
In budding single bud is taken as a scion shoot	In grafting the length of stick is taken as a scion shoot which have more than one bud

Different between attach method of grafting and detach method of grafting

Attach method of grafting	Detach method of grafting
In attach method of grafting rootstock and scion shoot should be attached and after getting union scion shoot are detached with the mother plant	In detach method of grafting scion shoot are detached from the mother plant then union of rootstock and scion shoot occur

Formation of Union between Stock and Scion

The success in grafting and budding depends on the earliness to union. The stock and scion are placed in such a way that the cambium layers of both the components remain in close contact with each other and hold tightly till the union formation is complete. It is the cambium tissues of stock and scion which start dividing rapidly forming callus tissue consisting of parenchyma cells. The parenchyma cells soon get united with each other and differentiated to form new cambium layer. The new cambium cells are then redifferentiated into xylem and phloem establishing a new vascular connection between stock and scion to facilitate upward movement of nutrients and moisture from soil and downward translocation of metabolites.

Incompatibility

Incompatibility refers to the failure in formation of successful union between two components (stock and scion) and develops into one plant. The degree of compatibility among plants is a natural phenomenon. In general, the distantly related plants are incompatible while plants of the same species are compatible to each other.

Symptoms of Incompatibility

The following symptoms may be seen in relation of incompatibility:

1. Failure to form a successful union between the graft components.
2. Differential growth rate and time of occurrence of vegetative flushes between stock and scion.
3. Leaves turn pale yellow and drop down early.
4. The union is formed, the tree grows for one or two years but eventually dies.
5. Over or under growth at, above or below the point of attachment.
6. The tree splits clearly at the point of union.

Types of Incompatibility

Graft incompatibility is of two types (i) Localized incompatibility and (ii) Translocated incompatibility. Localized incompatibility involves the condition when it is resulted from the actual contact between stock and scion. It can be overcome by inserting a mutually compatible interstock in between them. The influence of translocated incompatibility involves phloem degeneration and cannot be checked by inserting a mutually compatible interstock.

Causes of Incompatibility

The exact causes of incompatibility are yet to be discovered. However, the failure in formation of a successful union may be due to anatomical causes, physiological reasons and pathogenic attack or a combination of all. Sometimes the vascular connection between stock and scion is interrupted due to the formation of soft parenchyma cells at the joint. Accumulation of excess callus tissues between the graft components may result into weak unions. For a successful union formation, proper lignification of the cell walls is much essential. Degeneration of the phloem tissues may lead to accumulation of assimilates in scions and disturbs the water conductivity resulting into starvation of root system and death of scion. Production of substances by one of the graft components (eg. prunacin-a cyanogentic glucoside in pear-quince combination) toxic to other may impair the formation of successful union.

Stock-Scion Relationship

A. Effect of Stock on Scion

1. **Tree height and nature of growth**: The size and vigour of tree can be manipulated by the use of specific stock plants. Several rootstocks have been identified and released by East Malling Research Station, U.K. which have striking influences on the size of the apple tree as for example, M-

XXVII (extremely dwarfing), M-IX (very dwarfing), M-XXV (dwarfing), M-VII (semi dwarfing). M-II (invigorating) etc. have been developed. The effect of stock on the size and growth habit of tree have been reported in other fruit crops like citrus, pear, peach, sweet cherry etc.

2. **Fruiting**: Use of dwarfing rootstock causes marked reduction of tree height resulting into decrease in yield per tree but the per unit area yield is increased significantly as more number of trees can be accommodated. On the other hand, vigorous rootstocks increase the tree height and volume resulting into higher accumulated yield in the long run.
3. **Size and quality of fruits**: The effect of rootstocks on the size and quality of fruits varies which species and varieties. In Washington Novel orange, the fruit size is larger on sour orange stocks and smaller on the Palestine sweet lime. Use of sour orange as rootstock results into smooth, thin skinned, juicy fruit in sweet orange, tangerine and grapefruit.
4. **Winter hardiness and disease resistance**: In apple, the rootstock like M-XI and M-XVI have been reported to impart winter hardiness, while rootstocks like MM-104, MM-106, MM-109 etc. are found to be resistant to wooly aphids.
5. **Adaptability to soil conditions**: Almond and Myrobalan plum rootstocks can tolerate fairly large concentration of boron better than Mariana' plum rootstock.

B. Effect of Scion on Rootstock

Like the rootstock, the scion cultivar also influences the growth habit of stock plant. When a vigorously growing scion is grafted on a relatively weak stock, the growth of the rootstock is also stimulated as compared with its normal growth rate and vice-versa. The scion cultivar has a strong bearing on the root growth pattern of stock plant. For example, budding of 'Red Astrachan' on apple seedling results into a fibrous root system with few tap roots, while budding on 'Oldenburg' or 'Fameuse' causes development of two to three strong tap roots and no fibrous roots. It has been found that in some species the scion cultivar influence the winter-hardiness of stock plant by prolonging the period of root growth.

Grafting Method

1. **Approach grafting**: In approach grafting two independent plants growing on their own root systems are grafted together. In this method, generally, the rootstocks are grown in pots and taken to the mother plain (scion) for grafting. After union the top of the rootstock is removed while the scion shoot is cut below the graft union. It is a popular method of grafting in mango. However, this method is being replaced by other easy techniques.

a) **Splice approach grafting**: In this method a thin splice of bark and wood (4.0 to 5.0 cm long) is removed from the stock plant at a height of 30 to 35 cm above the ground level. Similar cut is also made on a smooth surface between nodes of scion plants. Both the cut surfaces should be as smooth as possible to obtain higher percentage of contact. The two cut surfaces are then held together and tied with jute string or rubber tape. It is important to note that the thickness of both the graft components should be same so as to match the cambium layers on each other. Union completes after 50 to 60 days depending on the species, atmospheric condition and the conditions of the graft components. The top of the stock and bottom of scion are then removed in two to three stages.

b) **Tongue approach grafting**: In tongue approach grafting the stock and scion are prepared first as described in splice approach grafting. Subsequently, tongues are made on both the cut surfaces to provide rigidity and to increase the cambium area for contact at the graft union. For this purpose a downward and inward cut is given in stock while a tongue is made in scion by giving an upward and inward cut. The scion is then fitted into the stock and tied with string to cover with grafting wax. Plum is commonly propagated by this method.

2. **Inarching:** The method of inarching is similar to approach grafting but the only difference is the top of the stock never extends above the graft union. It is mainly used for replacing the damaged root system of an established plant. In this method, seedlings are planted near the base of the damaged plant and inarched into the trunk during the active growing season. When the union is formed the seedling provides the damaged tree with nutrients and moisture.

3. **Side grafting**: In side grafting, a slanting downward and inward cut is made on a smooth surface of the stock plant at a height of 20 cm above the soil surface. The scion shoot is collected from 1 year old shoot having 2 to 3 buds. The scion shoot is sometimes defoliated to induce the dormant buds in axils of the leaves to sprout. Two slanting cuts of 2.0 to 3.0 cm in one side and slightly shorter in other side are made at the base of scion stick. The stock plant is then bent slightly to the opposite direction of the cut and the wedge shaped scion is inserted into the cut keeping the longer side towards centre and tied as usual. When both the components join together (after 45 to 55 days) the top of the stock is cut back to the graft union.

4. **Veneer grafting**: Veneer grafting differs from the side grafting in that the vertical flap of the stock is completely removed and a slanting cut is given on one side of the scion. For this purpose, a shallow downward cut (3 to 4 cm) is given on a smooth surface of stock plant. A shorter downward and

inward cut is made at the base to remove the piece of bark and wood from stock plant. A long slanting cut of similar length is given on one side of the scion shoot (having at least three nodes) and a small wedge shaped cut is made at the opposite side. All the cut surfaces should be as smooth as possible so that no gap remains in between stock and scion when they are grafted. The grafted scion and stock are tied together tightly with a string or tape. The rootstock is cut when the scion resumes its growth.

The merits of veneer grafting are that the scion shoots may be stored and transported for grafting in situ. It is a popular method for propagation of mango.

5. **Whip or Splice grafting**: A slanting cut of 2.0 to 4.0 cm is given on the stock and a cut of similar length is made on the scion, so as to match both the cut surfaces perfectly. The cut surfaces are placed together and tied tightly. Splice grafting is done in early spring.
6. **Cleft grafting**: The branches or main stem of the stock having a diameter of 3.0 to 10.0 cm are first sawn off horizontally. A vertical split (5 to 8 cm) is made at the centre of the cut end with a heavy knife. The split is kept open by inserting a chisel like material. The scion (preferably 3 budded shoot) is prepared by giving two slanting cut of 5.0 cm each on opposite sides. The chiesel like instrument is then taken out are the scion is inserted. Any gap on the surface of union is waxed to prevent rain water to enter inside. Cleft grafting is mainly done in the end of dormant season or before the tree resumes active growth for the purpose of top working. Sometimes, opposite cuts are also provided to the stock and scion, i.e. the wedge or tongue is made on the stock while cleft on the scion. The method is known as saddle grafting.
7. **Bark grafting**: There are various modifications of bark grafting. The common method is that the branch is sawn at first and the bark is split downward up to 4.0 to 5.0 cm. The scion (three budded) is prepared by giving one long slanting cut on one side and a short cut on the opposite side. The scion is then inserted into the split of bark keeping the longer cut surface inside and tied to hold in position tightly. It gives higher percentage of success when the bark slips well.
8. **Root grafting**: In root grafting a piece of root is used as stock for the operation. Slanting cuts are made at the base of the scion and top of the root in such a manner so as to fit well. Scion is then placed onto the root and tied properly woodapple and elephant apples are commonly propagated by this method.
9. **Epicotyl or stone grafting:** This method is commonly practised in mango. Stones are sown in moist sand bed and covered with 5.0 to 7.0 cm layer of

leaf mould for germination. When the seedlings are of 15 days old they are taken out and grafted indoor. The top of the seedling is removed by a slanting cut at a height of 6.0 cm from the stone. A current season's scion shoot (8.0 to 10.0 cm long) is prepared by a similar slanting cut at the base in one side so as to match with the cut end of stock. It is then placed on the stock and tied with polyethylene tape. The grafted seedling is then planted in a poly-bag containing sand, soil and farm yard manure at a ratio of 1:1:1 and watered immediately. The poly bags are kept in a partial shade condition and watered daily. When the scion produces 4 true leaves, they are transplanted in the nursery bed.

10. **Bridge grafting:** Bridge grafting is done with the object of repairing a damaged plant. The scions are prepared by slanting cuts on the same side of both the top and the base. These scions are inserted above and below the injured portion of the plant and tied properly.

Budding Methods

1. **Shield budding or T-budding**: When a 'T' shaped cut is made on the smooth surface of the stock at a height of 15 to 20 cm from the ground level for bud insersion, it is known as "T" or shield budding. To achieve this, first a vertical cut of 2.5 cm is given with the help of a budding knife followed by a right angle horizontal cut at the top. Cuts should be made in such a way so that the wood does not get injured. Two flaps at the junction of cuts are then loosened slightly. Desired scion buds are selected from current season's growth with dormant bud. The leaves are removed from the scion shoot leaving a petiole attached with it for easy handling. The shield shaped buds are taken by slicing 1.0 cm below and 1.0 cm above the leaf axil. The shield containing bud should be as thin as possible as and slightly greater in width than the bud. The bud may contain a piece of wood or it may be removed.

   The bud is then inserted by gentle push downward into the exposed flaps of the T-cut on the stock plant and tied with polyethylene strip leaving the bud and leaf stalk open. The polyethylene strip is removed when the bud resumes growth. The ideal time for carrying out the operation is during the active growth stage of stock plant i.e. when the bark slips well. During rainy season it is suggested to make cut resemble to inverted T to avoid seeping of water into the cut. This method is commonly practiced in citrus, rose etc.

2. **Patch budding:** A rootstock of 1 to 2 years old with a diameter of 1.0 to 2.5 cm is selected. Bark of the stock is removed in the form of a rectangle having a length of 25 cm and breadth of 1.5 cm. A patch of bark of similar in size containing a bud is removed from the scion plant. The bud is placed on the cut surface of the stock plant and tied with polyethylene strip leaving

the bud exposed. The optimum time for patch budding is when the bark slips well. It can be practiced in mango, citrus and guava. It has been reported that patch budding done from mid-May to mid-August in aonla (*Emblica officinalis*) gives highest percentage of success.

3. **Chip budding**: A long slanting downward and inward cut (2.0 to 3.0 cm) is given on a smooth surface of the stock plant. A second cut, at 45^0 angles, is made so as to intersect the first cut and to remove a 'chip' of bark along with wood. A chip of similar size containing a bud is placed on the cut surface of the stock so that it fits well and tied with polyethylene tape to hold the chip in position leaving the bud exposed. When the bud starts sprouting the stock is detopped. This method can be adopted even if the bark does not slip well.
4. **Ring budding:** A healthy 1 to 2 year old stock plant having 1.0 to 2.0 cm diameter is selected. A ring of bark, 2.0 to 3.0 cm in length, is removed from a smooth portion between nodes of the stock plant. A ring of bark of the same dimension containing a plumpy bud is taken from the scion plant and placed on the exposed surface of the stock plant and tied. This method is also practiced when the bark slips well.
5. **Forkert method:** In forkert method of budding, the piece of bark is not removed from the stock plant rather it is prepared in such a way so that it hangs. First two vertical cuts of 2.0 to 3.0 cm in length are made on a smooth surface of the stock which is then connected by a transverse cut (1.0 to 2.0 cm) above the vertical cuts and the bark is peeled off slowly. A rectangular piece of bark containing the bud is taken from scion plant which fits well in the cut surface of stock. The patch of bark (scion) is then placed on the stock and the flap is drawn over, followed by tying as usual. The vertical flap gives additional protection against adverse climatic condition. When the bud resumes growth, the flap is removed and the stock is detopped.
6. **I-budding**: In I-budding two transverse cuts are given on the bark of the stock which are connected by one vertical at their centres. The flaps are then loosened with the spatula of the budding knife. The scion bud is prepared correspondingly to be inserted into the I-cut, followed by tying. I-budding is practiced where the bark of stock plant is thicker than scion.
7. **Flute budding:** In flute budding a patch of bark (flute) encircling the stock is removed leaving a narrow strip attached thereon. A similar patch of bark containing the bud is taken from scion plant and placed on the cut surface of the rootstock followed by tying as usual when the bud exhibit the signs of growth the top of the stock is cut back.

Propogation through Specialized Vegetative Structures

Various modified plant organs like bulb, corm, tuber, rhizome etc. which are primarily storage organ for food are used as planting material. Aerial part of these plant has die at the end of season while the underground part remain in dormant condition and resume their activity and sprout when prevailing climatic condition are favourable. There are certain plant modifications which are used for vegetative propagation of plants. These modified plant parts may be stem, root, or leaves and are usually specialized for food storage. Two principal methods are used for propagation of plants by using these modifications.

a. **Separation** : Naturally detachable structures, such as bulbs or corms are separated and planted individually e.g. Bulb, Corm.

b. **Division**: The plants modification such as rhizomes, tubers etc., are cut into sections to obtain new plants from each section e.g. rhizome, tuber.

Bulbs: A bulb is a storage organ consistory of a short flattened stem bearing growing point at the apex enclosed fleshy scale leaves. When the bulb place in optimum condition adventitious roots are emerging out. Bulbs are produced by monocotyledonous plants in which the stem is modified for storage and reproduction. Bulb is a specialized underground organ consisting of a short freshly, usually vertical stem axis bearing at tip apex or growing points and enclosed by thick freshly scales. Bulb scales morphologically are the continuous sheathing leaf base. Growing points develop in the axils of these scales to produce miniature bulbs known as bulblets/daughter bulbs. These daughter bulbs can be separated from the mother plant at the end of growing season and used as propagating material eg. Tulip, Daffodils, Tuberose, Onion, Garlic, (cloves).

Tubers: Tubers are swollen underground modified stem containing food reserve and function an organ for vegetative propagation. Tuber consist all part of stem i.e. node, internodes, lateral and terminal buds. The eyes of tuber are arranged spirally representing nodes. A tuber is the short terminal portion of an underground stem which has become thickened because of accumulation preserved food material e.g. Potato. Propagation by tuber can be carried out either by planting the whole tuber or by cutting into sections each containing bud or eyes.

Tuberous roots: Fleshy modified root active an storage organ bearing growing point on the crown or stem end without node and internodes. Certain herbaceous perennials produce thickened roots which contain large amount of stored food. The tuberous roots differ from the tubers in that they lack nodes and internodes. Adventitious buds are present only at stem end or proximal end; fibrous roots are produced towards the distal end. These fleshy roots are separated and used for propagation e.g. Sweet potato, Dahlia, Tapioca (Cassava).

Rhizomes: Botanically rhizome is an elongated horizontal fleshy underground stem having node and internodes bearing bud in the axial of reduced scale leaves. Rhizome are cut into piece each with one or two viable bud and plated in favourable atmospheric condition. The horizontal, thick and fleshy or slender and elongated stem growing underground are known as rhizomes. Rhizomes have nodes and internodes and readily produce adventitious roots. The rhizomes are cut into pieces, each containing vegetative bud and transplanted e.g. Banana, Ginger, Ferns, Turmeric, and Cardamom.

Corms: Corm is short solid swollen underground base of stem axis having distant node & internodes and enclosed by dry scale like leaves. A corm is solid underground base of a stem having nodes and internodes and is enclosed by a dry scale like leaves. After flowering one or more corms may develop just above the old one, which disintegrates. In addition several new corms called caramels develop below each new corm. These may be separated and grown for 1-2 years to reach flowering stage eg. Gladiolus, Amor phophallus.

Cormels- Cormels are small corm develop in between old and new corm which require two year growth to come into flowering stage.

Runners: A long prostrate shoot arise from the leaf axils and give rise to a new plant at the end. The runner production is formed by long day & high temperature. Runners are specialized areal stems (stolones) arising in the leaf axils of plant having rosette crowns. New plants arise from nodes at interval along these runners. From these runners more new runners may arise thus developing natural clonal multiplication methods. The typical runner producing plant is straw berry which is photo sensitive with regard to its runner production. Long days favour runner production where as short days prevent runner formation eg. Strawberry.

Suckers: A shoot arising as an old stem or underground part of stem or on horizontal root system called sucker. Adventitious shoot from the underground portion of the stem or from their horizontal root systems are known as suckers and when these strike roots, they may be utilized as propagation materials. Well developed suckers are dugout and separated from the mother plant and planted in the nursery for further growth. Suckers are usually treated like rooted layers eg. Pineapple, Banana.

Crown-A crown is a very short condensed part of plant at the surface of ground which gives rise to new shoots, crown grown in top of the pineapple fruit. It is a vegetative growth attached to the central core of fruit which is use as planting material.

Offsets/offshoots: An offset is a shoot or thick stem of rosette like appearance arising from the base of the main stem of certain plant such as date Palm, Pineapple etc.,

- Date palm cultivars are propagated vegetative by separating away the offshoots and replanting them.
- However these are girdled and layered for about a year prior to separation, because offshoots do not root easily when directly separated from the mother plant and planted in the field.

Micro propagation- Multiplication of plant in septic condition and in artificial growth medium from very small plant part like meristem tip, callus, embryo, another etc. The German Plant Physiologist Haberlandt (1902) first described the biological principles of tissue and organ culture.

Merits

1. Tissue culture help in rapid multiplication of true to type plants throughout the year.
2. A new plant can be regenerated from a miniature plant part where as in conventional method a shoot of considerable length is required.
3. Large number of plant can be produce in culture to be in small space with uniform growth and productivity instead of growing them in large area in nursery.
4. Plant raised by tissue culture is free from disease.
5. Tissue culture coupled with somatic hybridization helping involving new cultivar in a short time.
6. Micro-propagation facilitates long distance transport of propagation material and long storage of clonal material.
7. Tissue culture method are particularly effective in plants that do not breed true from seed. Seeds are not viable (male sterile) or available easily.

Demerits

1. Cost involves in setting and maintenance of laboratory is very high and may not justify their use is all the horticultural plant ordinarily.
2. Tissue culture technique requires small manpower.
3. Slight infection may damage the entire leaf plants.
4. Seedling grown under artificial condition may not survive when placed under environmental condition.

Methods of Micro-propagation

1. **Meristem culture**: In meristem culture, the meristematic tissue dome and a few substending leaf primordia are placed into a suitable growing medium.

An elongated rooted plantlet is produced after some weeks which are transferred to soil when it has attained a considerable height. A disease free plant can be produced by this method even from an infected plant. Experimental results also suggest that this technique can be successfully utilised for rapid multiplication of various herbaceous fruit plants.

2. **Callus culture**: A callus is a mass of undifferentiated parenchymatous cells. When a living plant tissue is placed in an artificial growing medium, with other conditions favourable, callus is formed. The growth of callus varies with the endogenous levels of auxin and cytokinin and can be manipulated by exogenous supply of these growth regulators in the culture medium. The callus growth and its organogenesis or embryogenesis can be classified into three different stages:
   i. Rapid production of callus after placing the explant in culture medium.
   ii. The callus is transferred to other medium containing growth regulators for the induction of adventitious organs.
   iii. The new plantlet is then exposed gradually to the environmental condition.
3. **Cell culture**: A cell suspension culture refers to cells and/or groups of cells dispersed and growing in an aerated liquid culture medium. A piece of soft tissue is placed in a liquid medium and shoken vigorously so as to obtain a suspension of cells. The culture medium includes a complete range of ingredients like inorganic salts, sucrose, vitamins and balanced dose of hormones. The development of cytokinin induced adventitious buds in kiwi fruit in a suspension culture subcultured for about a week.
4. **Embryo culture**: In embryo culture, the embryo is excised and placed into a culture medium with proper nutrient in aseptic condition. To obtain a quick and optimum growth of the embryo, the culture medium is changed 2 to 3 times. When the embryo has grown into a plantlet, it is transferred to soil. It is particularly important for the production of inter-specific and inter-generic hybrids and to overcome the embryo abortion.
5. **Protoplast culture**: Protoplast of plant cell can be isolated with the help of cell wall degrading enzymes and grown in a suitable culture medium in a controlled condition for regeneration of plantlets. Under suitable condition the protoplasts develop a cell wall followed by an increase in cell division and differentiation and grow into a new plant. The protoplasts are first cultured in liquid medium at 25^0 to 28^0C with a light intensity of 100 to 500 lux or in dark and after undergoing substantial cell division they are transferred into solid medium congenial for morphogenesis. Many horticultural crop responses well to protoplast culture.

Chapter 12

Orchard Management

Orchard

Establishment of orchard is a long term investment. It is require a proper planning, any mistake during the selection of site, planting distance, choice of crop/variety, quality of nursery stock etc. reflect greatly on the orchard performance and efficiency.

Following points are keep in mind at time of orchard planning-

1. **Road-** Orchard should be well connected with the road for facilitate transportation of material to the orchard and produce of orchard to the market.
2. **Orchard structure-** In structure office, implement shed, godown come store etc. are required. Area under these structures is not more than 10% of total area.
3. **Fencing and wind break-** Before planting of plants, installation of fence is necessary for protecting the undesirable element. Fencing can be done by erecting a wall or by fixing iron angle or concrete cement pillar and tightening with running 4 to 5 times at a distance of 30-40 cm barbed wire.

   Fencing can be done by two ways-

   1. By barbed wire.
   2. By suitable hedge plant.

   Height of the hedge can be maintained with regular pruning. Pruning should be done twice in a year. The suitable plants are- *Carissa carandus, Lawsonia alba, Clerodendrum inerme, Durenta plumeri, Parkinsonia aculeata, Acacia spp., Zyziphus spp., Pithecellobium dulsis* etc.

   Wind break- Orchard tree should be protected from high velocity wind which could harm by uprooting tree, breaking branches, causing pre-maturing fruit drop, erosion of top soil and evaporation of soil moisture.

   Suitable plants are- *Casurina equisetifolia, Gravillea robusta, Polialthia longifolia, Acasia auriculiformis, Carissa carandus, Putranjiva roxburghii, Dalbergia sisso* etc.

4. **Irrigtion:** For irrigation source of water should be at the centre of the orchard.
5. **Demarcation of block-** Block should be demarcated according to nature of the plants. The water requirement of the plant, cultural requirement of the plants, training pruning requirement of the plant etc. are different i.e.why the specific nature of the plant should be demarcated in seperate block.
6. **Spacing-**Proper spacing should be keep provide favourable condition to root and shoot development. An optimum distance between row and within the row is most essential. Closely planted tree grows poorly and give poor yield and quality of fruits, suffer more with disease and pest. Planting distance varies with climatic condition, soil type, growth habit, root stock use etc. in general there are two type of growth habit i.e. spreading type and erect type. The spreading type plants required more spacing whereas, the erect type plant required less spacing. Some of the important fruit crops and there spacing are as follows:

Fruit Plants	Distance (m)
Mango, Jamun, Litchi, Ber	10×10 or 12×12
Jack fruit and Bread fruit	12×12
Date palm, Fig, Mandarin, Lime, Lemon	6×6
Pummelo, Grape fruit	6 ×6 or 7×7
Guava and Cashew nut	6 ×6 or 8× 8
Sapota, Loquat, Avacado	8× 8 or 9× 9
Custard apple	4.5 ×4.5

7. **Selection of planting material-** At the time of selection of planting material the following points are keep in mind.

- They should be true to type.
- They should not have been budded or grafted not more than 20-30 years old plant.
- Planting material should have to certify by competent authority.
- **Planting of fruit tree-** At the time of planting of fruit tree following points are keep in mind- i.e. growth behaviour, canopy development and fruiting habits. The fast growing tree should be planted in separate block whereas, the slow growing tree planted separately. In canopy development the erect type of plant and spreading type of plant are planted separately in separate block. Regarding fruiting habit there are two types of plant i.e. terminal bearing and axillary bearing each type of plants are planted separately.

Orchard Management

- Orchard is an area, often enclosed, devoted to the cultivation of fruit trees and as a unit it encompasses various resources like land, water, trees and external inputs.
- All these resources have to be well utilized to the best advantage for higher production per unit area on sustainable basis without adversely affecting the quality of environment.
- We should also understand that a good manager is one who gets maximum output of various inputs consistently without any loss of fertilizers and manure, plant, plant protection chemicals, produce etc.
- Therefore, one should understand the management of these qualities of both resource and output.

Resources for better comprehension of orchard management are;

1. Soil management
2. Water management
3. Nutrition management
4. Pruning and training (plant management)
5. Weed management
6. Plant protection against insect pests and diseases.
7. Bearing, fruitfulness and causes of unfruitfulness.
8. Maturity and harvest.
9. Post harvest handling, utilization and marketing.

Soil Management

- Soil management aims at maintaining soil in good condition, or improving the condition if necessary.
- This includes protection from direct sunlight and from the impact of rainfall and wind erosion.
- In annual crops like vegetables and flowers which do not leave vacant space.
- There is no such problem except that one has to replenish nutrients harvested by crops and leached out but in tree crops, wherein, it is usually several years after planting before a tree which form such an extensive canopy that it can provide adequate protection to the soil, the vacant space needs to be productively utilized and protected through different management practices like intercropping, cover cropping, cultivation, sod culture, mulching, crop rotation, high density planting.

Objectives of soil management

1. To create favourable conditions for moisture supply and proper drainage.
2. To maintain high fertility level and replenishment against losses.
3. To provide proper soil conditions for gaseous exchange and microbial activities through addition of organic matter.
4. To check or reduce soil erosion.
5. To ensure supply of nutrients for growth and development of plants.
6. To utilize vacant land for additional income because such a loss is inconceivable for small holders.
7. To reduce the cost of cultivation with high economic returns.
8. To suppress weed population.

Definitions of terms to be used in management of soil

1. **Intercrop:** Any crop other than main crop grown between the rows of perennial tree crops is known as intercrop and the cultivation there of is intercropping.
2. **Green manure crop:** The crop other than main crop grown for the purpose of enriching the soil for organic matter is called green manure crop.
3. **Cover crop:** The crop grown to provide a cover to soil to protect it from erosion. It may be green manure crop also.

Methods of soil management: Appropriate soil management method is important for the control of weeds, incorporation of organic and inorganic fertilizers and to facilitate absorption of water in soil.

The common soil management practices are,

1. Cultivation
2. Sod Culture
3. Mulching and
4. Crop rotation

Choice of the system is determined by many factors as mentioned below:

1. Type of crop.
2. Rooting depth of the crop.
3. Slope of the soil.
4. Rainfall of the area.
5. Climatic condition of the place.
6. Economic condition of the farmer.

Chapter 13

Planting System

Planting System

Main objective of layout is maximum number of plant accommodated in per unit area without affecting the efficiency of production. If more than one fruit is included in the orchard plan, each kind should be grouped into individual block. Similarly fruit ripened in particular season should be grouped to facilitate convenience in watch and ward, harvest and post harvest handling. Some kind of fruit trees need pollinators/pollinisers for improving the fruit set.

1. Square system
2. Rectangular system
3. Triangular system
4. Hexagonal system
5. Quincunx system
6. Contour system

The following are the important systems of planting generally followed on the basis of agro-climatic conditions to improve aesthetic view of the land.

1. Square System

It is the most commonly used method and easy to layout in the field. In this system, plant to plant and row to row distance is the same. The plants are at the right angle to each other, every unit of four plants forming a square. This system facilitates the interculture in two directions after the orchard is planted.

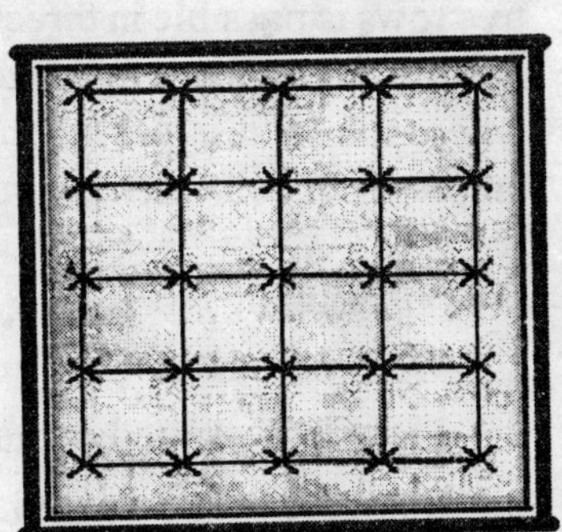

Advantage

1. Most easy and popular one.
2. In this row to row and plant to plant distance is kept similar.
3. Plants are exactly at right angle to each others.
4. Intercultural operations can be done in both the directions.
5. Adequate space for inter-cultivation of remunerative crops like vegetables.

2. Rectangular System

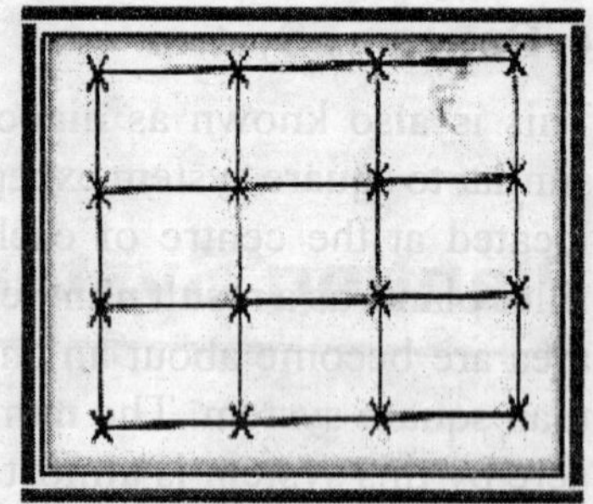

In this system, the plot is divided into rectangles instead of squares and trees are planted at the four corners of the rectangle in straight rows running at right angles. Like square system, this system also facilitates the interculture in two directions. The only difference is that in this system more plants can be accommodated in the row keeping more space between the rows.

Advantages

1. Lay out in rectangular shape.
2. More space between row to row.
3. Inter-cultural operations can be done in both the ways.
4. Plants get proper space and sunlight.

3. Hexagonal System

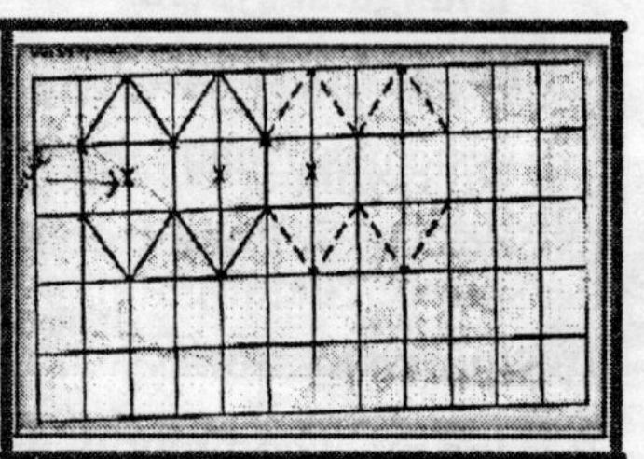

In hexagonal system, the trees are planted in the corners of equilateral triangles. Six trees thus from a hexagon with another tree at its centre. This system, through a little difficult for execution but accommodates 15 percent more plants than square system. Cultivation of land between the tree rows is possible in three directions with this system. This system is generally followed where the land is costly and very fertile with ample provision of irrigation water.

Advantages

1. Accommodates 15% more plants than the square system.
2. Plants are planted at the corner of equilateral triangle.
3. Six trees are planted making a hexagon.
4. The seventh tree is planted in the centre and called septule.
5. This requires fertile land.

Disadvantages

It is the complex nature of layout and more number of plants of plant population causing more competition for moisture and nutrient.

4. Quincunx System

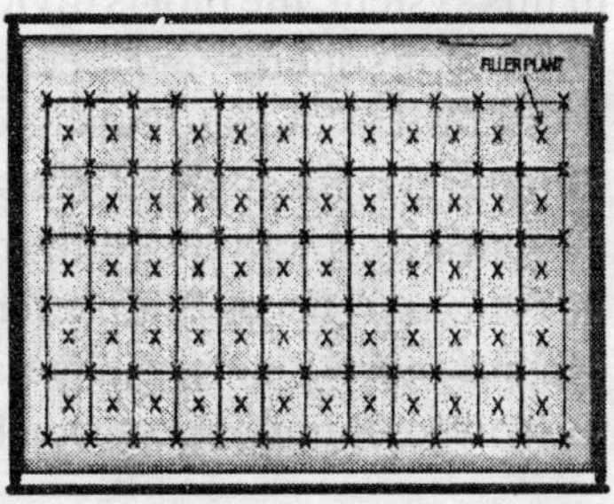

This is also known as diagonal system. It is similar to square system except that fifth plants located at the centre of each square term as filler plants as a result number of plant per unit area are become about an and half time more than square system. The number of plants per acre by this system is almost doubled than the square system. Fruit trees like papaya, kinnow, phalsa, guava, peach, plum etc. can be planted as fillers in the permanent trees provides an additional income to the grower in the early life of the orchard. The filler trees are uprooted when the main orchard trees start commercial fruiting.

Characteristics of filler plant

1. Short duration
2. Quick growing
3. Erect type
4. Early maturing-e.g.-Banana, Papaya, Pomegranate.

5. Contour System

Fig. 7.5. Contour System of planting

This system is usually followed in the hilly areas with high slopes but it is very much similar to the square/rectangular system. Under such circumstances, the trees may be well planted in lines following the contour of the soil with only a slight slope. Irrigation and cultivation are then practiced only across the slope of the land as this practice reduces the chances of soil erosion. In this system layout is done as in square/rectangular system, first by establishing the base line at the lowest level and then marking for the trees should be done from the base to the top. Bench terraces are used where the slope is greater than 10 per cent.

6. Triangular System

1. In this system, trees are planted as in the square system but the plants in the 2nd, 4th, 6th and such other alternate rows are planted midway between the 1st, 3rd, 5th and such other alternative rows. This system provides
2. Plants in alternate rows are offset half the space between plants in a row.
3. Result in 9 % fewer plants than square and rectangular system e.g. Amrapali – 1600 plants / ha.
4. More open space for trees and for intercrop.

Chapter 14

Training and Pruning

Horticultural plants are grown for their produce like fruit, vegetable, flower, medicinal component, spices etc. Therefore, these plants should be managed in such a way that human desires for the purpose of growing them are fully satisfied in terms of quality and quantity of produce. This demands direct manipulation of plant growth itself or plant environment through various inputs. In manipulation of plant development, training and pruning are important for which our knowledge about plant development and its phenology has to be complete. These practices are important in fruit crops.

Training

Physical techniques that control the shape, size and direction of plant growth are known as training or in other words training in effect is orientation of plant in space through techniques like tying, fastening, staking, supporting over a trellis or pergola in a certain fashion or pruning of some parts.

Objectives

- To improve appearance and usefulness of plant/tree through providing different shapes and securing balanced distribution.
- To ease cultural practices including inter-cultivation, plant protection and harvesting.
- To improve performance like planting at an angle of 45° and horizontal orientation of branches make them fruiting better.

Methods of training

Method of training of a plant is determined by the nature of plant, climate, purpose of growing, planting method, mechanization, etc. and therefore, intelligent choice is necessary.

Training in herbaceous annuals and biennials

These plants are usually grown without any attempt to alter their growth patterns because even if useful not practical being in large number in field. However, for some of ornamental value and creeping nature following types of training is affected.

1. Staking or supporting of vine like plants.
2. Training on pergola or trellis of vine type fruit plants or even indeterminate type tomatoes.
3. Nipping of apices for encouraging lateral growth to give bushy appearance or fulsome appearance in pot plants like aster, marigold and chrysanthemum.
4. De-shooting or removal of lateral buds for making single stem for large flowers as in chrysanthemum and Dahlia.
5. Staking with bamboo sticks and tying together various shoots in potted chrysanthemum.

Training of woody perennials

The woody perennials, which are widely spaced and remain on a place for a long duration, are trained for develop strong framework for sustainable production of quality produce and for ornamental beauty in different shapes (topiary). In these plants following types of training are followed.

i. Open centre system (Vase shaped)

- In this system the main stem is allowed to grow to a certain height and the leader is cut to encourage lateral scaffold from near the ground giving a vase shaped plant. This is common in peaches, apricots and ber (Fig. 14.1).

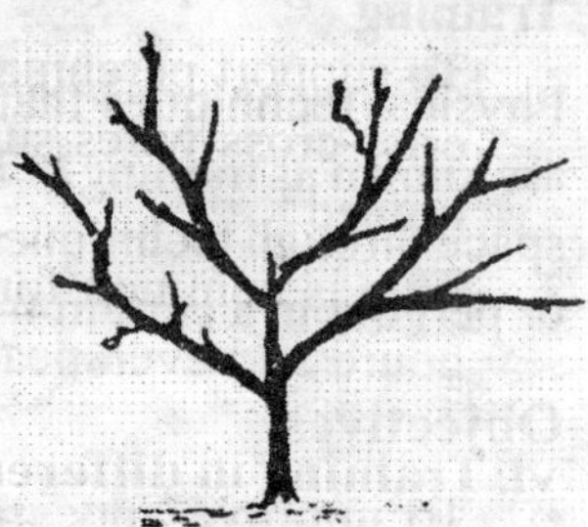

Fig. 14.1 : Open centre system

ii. Central leader system (closed centre)

- In this system the central axis of plant is allowed to grow unhindered permitting branches all around.
- This system is also known as **closed centre system** and common in use in apple, pear, mango and sapota (Fig. 14.2).

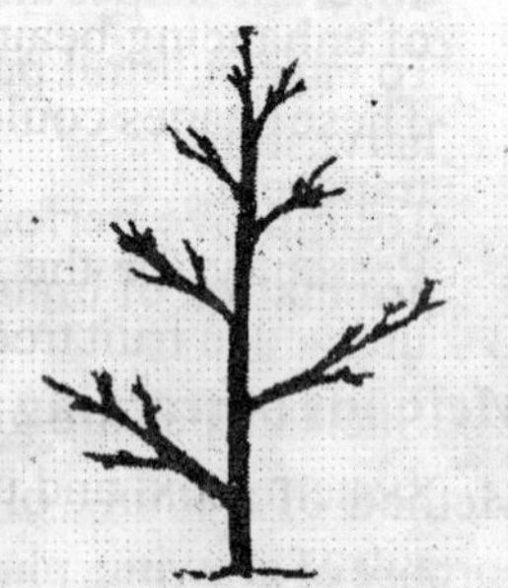

Fig. 14.2 : Central leader system

iii. Modified leader system

Fig. 14.3 : Modified leader system

- This system is in between open centre and central leader system wherein central axis is allowed to grow unhindered up-to 4-5 years and then the central stem is headed back and laterals are permitted.
- It is common in apple, pear, cherry, plum, guava (Fig. 14.3).

iv. Cordon system

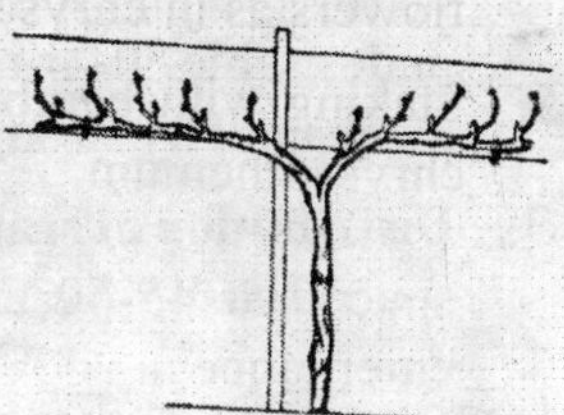
Fig. 14.4 : Cordon system

- This is a system wherein espalier is allowed with the help of training on wires.
- This system is followed in vines incapable of standing on their stem.
- This can be trained in single cordon or double cordon and commonly followed in crops like grape and passion fruit (Fig. 14.4).

v. Training on pergola

- To support perennial vine crops pergola is developed by a network of criss-cross wires supported by RCC/angle iron poles on which vines are trained.
- This is common for crops like grape, passion fruit, small gourd, pointed gourd and even peaches.

vi. Training in different shapes

- Generally ornamental bushes are trained in different shapes for the purpose of enhancing beauty of places.
- These shapes could be vase, cone, cylindrical and rectangular box, flat and trapezoid.
- Presently for the convenience of mechanization these shapes are being utilized in fruit trees.
- Such shapes are given to adjust the geometry of plantation like hedge row system, box, and unclipped natural in fruits like guava, mango, sapota and citrus.

Details of training

1. **Height of the head**: This is the height from ground to first branching or scaffolding.

Depending on the height the trees could be divided in three groups.

a. **Low head**: 0.7-0.9 m. This is common in windy areas. Such plants are easy to maintain.

b. **Medium head**: 0.9-1.2 m. This is the most common height which combines both effects, ability to stand against wind and easy management.

c. **High head:** More than 1.2 m. Common in tropics in wind free areas. Operations under the canopy are easy to perform.

2. **Number of scaffold branches**: It refers to allowing of number of scaffolds on the primary axis of the tree which vary from 2 to 15 but extremes are undesirable. In fruit trees 5 to 8 scaffolds are preferred to make the tree mechanically strong and open enough to facilitate cultural operations.

3. **Distribution of scaffolds**: Scaffolds should be distributed in all the directions spaced at 45-60 cm allowing strong crotches through wide angles of emergence.

A well trained tree is an asset to the farmer and therefore, efforts should be made for training trees appropriately in formative years for sustainable production. In fact the process should have begun from nursery itself.

Pruning

It is Judicious removal of plant part is known as pruning. It refers to removal of plant part like bud, shoot, root etc to strike a balance between vegetative growth and production. This may also be done to adjust fruit load on the tree.

Objectives

1. To maintain the growth and vigour of the trees and to have a balance between the vegetative vigour and fruitfulness, so as to be conductive for production of optimum crop of best quality.
2. To shape the tree to make the best use of the space between trees while allowing the necessary access.
3. To regulate the size and quality of the fruits by way of proper distribution of the fruiting area.
4. To regulate the succession of crop and to have the crop where it can be managed easily and cheaply.
5. To spread the trees for economic orchard management.
6. To remove the dead, diseased and over aged wood.
7. For effective spraying of pesticides to the crop.

8. To minimize biennial bearing and consequent risk of die back.
9. To get maximum plageiotrophic shoots/stems.
10. Establishment of transplant where leaves/shoots are pruned to strike a balance between roots and shoot so that plants lose less water against restricted root system lost during lifting of plants.
11. Elimination of non-productive vegetative growth like water sprouts, suckers, dead and diseased wood.
12. In case of forest trees production of knot free timber.

Types of pruning

Basically there are three types of pruning with definite purposes.

i. Frame pruning.
ii. Maintenance pruning.
iii. Renewal pruning.

1. **Frame pruning**: This pruning is done to provide shape and form to a plant in its formative years so that tree develops strong framework and a shape for ease of operations. This process begins from nursery itself and continues up to fruiting stage. This is done continuously irrespective of the season.
2. **Maintenance pruning**: To maintain status-in production level and for uniform performance this pruning is done. In some plants like Grapes, Apple, Pear, peach etc. (deciduous trees) it is an annual feature and in others (evergreen like mango, sapota) it is rare confining to removal of water sprouts and unproductive growth and opening of the tree.
3. **Renewal pruning**: This pruning is done in old trees like mangoes which shows decline. In this case severe pruning is required.

Factors to be considered in pruning

- In some of the tree species pruning as a regular feature in bearing trees is done to strike a balance between vegetative growth and production so that farmers get sustained production uniformly with optimum quality of produce.
- To achieve this one should consider the following factors.
- Time at which buds are differentiated in relation to blooming.
- The age of the wood that produces the most abundant and highest quality of fruit buds.
- In consideration of these factors our knowledge about bearing habit of the tree/plant should be complete.

- Bearing habit means relative position of a fruit with reference to its potential bud giving rise to flower or inflorescence in the shoot. This habit varies from plant to plant.

Principles of pruning

1. Excessive pruning should be avoided as it affects the growth of the plant by dwarfening and may induce more of water suckers, fasciations (union of a number of parts side by side in a flat plane) and thus affect the bearing potential.
2. In pruning, only that wood which is not necessary for the tree should be removed.
3. Pruning of larger limbs should be avoided as far as possible.
4. Pruning of young trees should be done more carefully than the yielding trees, since severe pruning of young trees delays the cropping and much more of yield area will be removed than what is desired.

Top Working

It is a technique or method of rejuvenation where in the objective is to upgrade seedling plantations of inferior varieties with superior commercial cultivars or hybrids suitable for domestic or export market or the desired variety of the grower. The technique involves grafting with procured scions of desired variety on shoots emerged on pruned branches by adopting softwood grafting during monsoon season (Season of top working slightly varies from species as it also depends on availability of good shoot and scions). The scion shoots and the emerged shoots should be of same thickness.

Advantages of top working

1. Increase the tree productivity /orchard productivity.
2. Conversion of old and senile orchards into productive orchards.
3. Conversion of seedling or inferior variety plantation /orchard into new orchard with desirable variety or varieties through top working.
4. Possibility of grafting several varieties on the same plant.
5. Increasing the fruit set of orchard by grafting few shoots with pollinate varieties.
6. Additional income by selling the pruned wood during non bearing season or period.

Disadvantages

1. Chances of death of plant if not done properly or on severe pruning.
2. Need good management post pruning period.
3. Loss of crop for 2-3 years
4. Chances of pest and disease occurrence (stem borer, anthracnose etc.).
5. Needs skilled labour for thinning of shoots, removal of side shoots etc.
6. Top working technique can be successfully followed in crops like Mango, Sapota, Aonla, Cashew, Guava, Tamarind, Jackfruit, etc.

Chapter 15

Bearing and Unfruitfulness in Fruit Plants

Bearing

Bearing is connotation of flowering and fruiting. When a fruit tree flowers and fruits, it is said in bearing condition. Different fruits have different bearing habits, inflorescences, types of flower, mode and medium of pollination, pollen viability and all these account a lot for the bearing of fruit plants.

Bearing habit

If one observes a mango tree, he/she may find it does produce the fruits terminally on a shoot and it citrus he/she finds the fruits always produced laterally in the leaf axils. The manner or patter in which a plant produces its fruit is known as bearing habit or fruiting habit. Bearing habits are specific to the kind of plant. In determining the bearing habit of any plant three points are to be considered.

1. The origin or position of the flower or fruit bud which may be either terminal or lateral on a shoot.
2. The nature of the bud, which may be either pure flower bud or a mixed bud.
3. Position of flowers or fruits on the flowering shoots especially in case of mixed bud. The flowering shoot may end with the fruits or carry fruits laterally on it.

Considering the above three points, the bearing habit of fruit plants are broadly classified into six groups.

Group I: Fruit bud terminal, pure flower bud producing only flower parts, e.g., Mango, Cashew.

Group II: Fruit bud terminal, mixed bud with flower parts situated terminally on the flowering shoot, e.g. Apple, Pear.

Group III: Fruit bud terminal, mixed bud, with flower parts situated laterally on the flowering shoot, e.g. Guava.

Group IV: Fruit bud lateral, pure bud producing only flower parts, e.g. Citrus, Coconut, Date, Gooseberry.

Group V: Fruit and lateral, mixed bud, with flower parts terminally on the flowering shoot, e.g. Grapes, Cashew and Annonaceous fruits.

Group VI: Fruit bud lateral, mixed bud, with flower parts laterally on the flowering shoot e.g. Fig, Mulberry, Ber, etc.

- Of these six groups, the first three come under terminal bears, through we see fruits laterally on the flowering shoot in Group III.
- The other three groups are lateral bearers through we see fruits terminally on the flowering shoot in group.
- In addition to these six main groups we do find some different bearing habits in some plants which cannot be conveniently classified under any of these six groups.
- These are therefore classified into separate groups.

Group VII: Flower buds borne sub terminally in the leaf axils, pure flower bud. This could be treated as a lateral bearer e.g. Papaya and Sapota.

Group VIII: Flower buds borne adventitiously on the main trunks or branches, pure flower bud, e.g. Jack fruit and Cacao.

Group IX: The growing apex (pseudostem) ending in a flower which could be treated as a terminal bearer e.g. Banana and Pineapple.

Group X: Fruit bud terminal or lateral, pure bud. These plants come under group I and IV and as such classified separately e.g. Pomegranate.

- In case of these groups occasionally the plants may bear in different pattern also deviating from its own characteristic pattern but majority of its bearing will be always as per the classification.
- The knowledge of bearing habits will be of much importance for regulating the bearing of any plant by means of pruning, terminal bearers are not normally pruned.
- Whereas in case of lateral bearers pruning certainly increase the bearing, as it encourages the sprouting of lateral buds.

Methods for Inducing Fruitfuleness

The fruitfulness of a tree is governed by various external and internal factors. The most important external factors are environment, insect pests, disease and nutrient supply to the plants. The important internal factors are sex distribution, heterostyly, dichogamy and aborted organs, non-viability of pollen, genetic incompatibility and nutritional status of the plant.

External factors: The environment comprises of temperature, rainfall, wind and light.

1. **Temperature** plays on important role in determining the fruitfulness.
  - Chilling is required for breaking dormancy and lack of it during winter is responsible for low yields of an apple at Connor.
  - Pollen of many deciduous fruit plants may germinate very freely at optimum temperature.
2. **Light intensity** also influence on fruit set to a certain extent
  - Interior branches of a tree, which bear fewer fruits.
  - In strawberry the flowers developed stamens when they are exposed to long daylight.
3. **Rainfall** also determines the extent of fruitfulness.
  - The period of water stress appears to be a most potential factor for influencing flowering in tropical fruit trees.
4. **Infestation of insect pests and diseases** also reduced the fruit set considerably.
  - The best examples are mango-hoppers, malformation of mango inflorescence and anthracnose in grapes.
  - By preventing the attack of these pests and diseases by suitable control measures in the beginning itself, one can actually increase the fruitfulness of these trees.

Internal factors

- In some of the fruit plants, individual plants are self-unfruitful as their flowers are unisexual i.e., flowers of one sex may be present in one plant as in case of papaya, strawberry, fig and date palm.
- The fruitfulness of these plants can be improved by inter planting of the plant bearing opposite sex flowers.
- Prevention of self pollination in perfect flowers may be due to the difference in the time of maturing of male and female sex organs and this is known as dichogamy, as found in Avocado.
- Genetic incompatibility is another cause of unfruitfulness. The pollen of some varieties are not capable of fertilizing the flowers of the same variety or certain other varieties as in the case of apple, sweet cherry, plum, pear, almond, mango, sapota etc, in such plants to improve the fruitfulness, certain suitable combination of varieties which would successfully cross pollinate each other should be planted.

- Fruitfulness of a tree is to a great extend determined by the nutrient supply and the nutritional status of the plant.
  - Application of manures and fertilizers a few days before blossom emergence is generally believed to increase the fruitfulness.
  - Relationship between C/N ratio and fruitfulness.
  - The fruit bud formation, setting of the fruit and its development mainly depends upon the requisite balance of nutrients in the branches of the trees at certain critical seasons.
  - Plants with plenty of nitrogen and high carbohydrate accumulation are found to make moderate growth and produce satisfactory crop. Whereas, plants with plenty of nitrogen and moderate carbohydrates are found to grow vegetative, the expense of fruit production. By adopting some of the horticultural practices like root exposure, root pruning, bending, girdling or ringing, notching and smudging, the plants can be made to accumulate more of carbohydrates at the desired positions of the plant and these make them more fruitful.

1. Root pruning

- This is a recognized practice in the dwarf fruit tree culture.
- Every year a trench is dug a few centimeters away from the trench of the previous year.
- The trench is then filled with manures liberally and watered.
- As a result of this, circular mass of fibrous roots increases very slowly from year to year and the tree becomes short but stocky and well matured shoots will be rich in their reserve food material and will be more fruitful.

2. Root exposure

This is commonly practiced to force flowering and fruiting of orange, guava and other citrus fruits in the desired season. It is called as Bahar Treatment.

- About two months before the bloom, the soil around the tee is removed near the main roots from an area of 60cm radius.
- The fibrous roots are removed and the main roots are exposed to the sun.
- The trees are allowed to go dry until the leaves wither or even some of them fall. Time taken for leaf fall is 3-4 weeks.
- After this stage, the exposed roots are covered with a mixture of soil and manure and watered immediately.
- During this period of root exposure, the trees are forced to take rest since the upward movement of water is adversely affected.

- Within three weeks of covering the roots and watering, the trees burst into heavier bloom, and set a much larger crop.
- This treatment can be practiced only in orchards planted in retentive soils which remain moist for a long time and do not allow plants to take a post harvest rest even though watering is stopped.
- Now a days this treatment is becoming up popular in view of the fear that it may adversely affect the performance of the trees in the long run.

3. Bending

- This is widely practiced for increasing the fruit production in guava, especially in the erect growing varieties.
- The large branches in their erect and upright position have a natural tendency to produce fruit bearing shoots near about their ends, while the lower branches remain more or less dormant.
- When such large branches are bent and tied and pegs fixed in the ground in an arch fashioned way, the fruiting area is considerably increased due to the increased number of side branches produced on the lower parts of the main limbs.
- This practice is not necessary in spreading varieties like Sardar Guava (Lucknow- 49).

4. Ringing or girdling

- This is one of the well known methods of increasing fruit bud formation.
- The operation consists of removing a strip of bark of a tree.
- It interrupts the downward movement of carbohydrates and thus causes them to accumulate above the ring or girdle.
- In India girdling is sometimes practices on mango to force flowering in over vegetative trees, which normally do not bear satisfactory crops.
- The branches of 15 to 20 cm thick are girdled by removing a strip of bark about 2 cm wide all around at the base of the branch or little above the point where it joins another branch.
- In santra, saw passed round the branches is just enough to cause the ring.
- It is usually done between 15th of April and 15th of May.
- The healing of the ring and complete restoration of new bark on the girdled portion is highly imperative after fruits have set.
- The ring of bark removed should be such as not to injure the cambium.

- It is recommended to practice the girdling on the trees which are vigorous in growth. The exhausted trees should be avoided.

5. Notching

- This is practiced in fig. This consists of removal of the small narrow strip of bark just above a dormant bud.

  Notching affects the sprouting in three ways.

  - Firstly, it prevents the inhibitory influence of certain compounds in the bud.
  - Secondly, it cuts off the supply of carbohydrates synthesized from the leaves above and increased the supply of nutrients from below.
  - Thirdly, the bud which was once one of the lower most of the branches becomes apparently the top most due to construction in the bark connection with the part of the branch above the notch. Notching can be given below bud also.

6. Smudging

- This is practiced for mango in Philippines to produce off season crop.
- This consists of burning trash wood on the ground and allowing the smoke to pass through the crown of the tree.
- To direct the smoke to different parts of the tree, a cone shaped enclosure with a tall chimney at the top is built with wooden stakes and thin bamboo strips woven together.
- The tree will be smoked heavily and continuously for a week and then mild fire are made at regular intervals for about a month or till the tree comes into bloom or till the terminal buds start swelling and show the symptoms of sprouting.
- Smoke is known to contain ethylene, which is a flowering hormone.

Alternate Bearing

Tendency of variety to bear heavy crop load in one year (on year) and reduce crop load in following year (off year) is known as alternate bearing.

Factors affecting the alternate bearing: The following factors are affecting the alternat bearing.

1. **General factors-** In general the North Indian varieties are biennial in nature whereas, South Indian verieties are regular bearing eg.-Neelam, Banglora and Rumani.

2. **Fruiting pattern-** Plant have the two types of fruiting pattern i.e. terminal bearing and axillary bearing. The terminal bearing plants are always alternate bearers because its flowers comes always in one year old branches whereas, the axillary bearing plants are always regular bearer because its flowers comes always in current season growth. The auxiliary bearing plants require regular pruning for pramoting current growth.

   Regarding fruiting patern the two terms are neccesory to understand i.e. Flower Bud Differentiation (FBD) and Flower Bud Initiation (FBI).

   F.B.D- It means the anatomical transition of vegetative primordia to reproductive primordia.

   F.B.I- It means emergence of flowering bud.

   When FBD process is completed then FBI started. In general the South Indian varieties flowers early in comparision to North Indian varieties. This is only due to the FBD process comes early in South Indian varieties as comparision to North Indian varieties.

3. **C:N ratio-** In general the C:N ratio is very important. The high carbohydrate and high nitrogen favours F.B.D whereas, low level of CHO reverse flowering and fruiting. In general there are four type of C:N ratio i.e. CCCC:N (Very high carbohydrate and very low nitrogen), CCC:NN (Moderate carbohydrate and low nitrogen), CC:NNN (Low carbohydrate and moderate nitrogen) and C:NNNN (Very low carbohydrate and very high nitrogen). Out of these the moderate carbohydrate and low nitrogen and the moderate nitrogen and low carbohydrate favours the flower bud differentiation.

4. **Hormonal factor-** Beside C:N ratio there are some indigenous substances are also responsible for alternate bearing. Thel level of auxin, GA_3 and ABA are also responsible for flowering and fruiting. The pants have high auxin and low GA_3 induce more flowering whereas, low auxin and high GA_3 reduce the flowering.

5. **Climatic factor-** The climate play an important role in alternat bearing. When temperature is high plant have more flowering because at the time of high temperature the level of ABA is high and the level of GA_3 is low, due to synergistic effect of ABA and ethylene the level of ethylene also high. Due to high concentration of ethylene the more flowering take place in the plant. At the same time if temperature is low reduces flowering and more number of male flowers. This is due to low temperature level of ABA is low due to antagonistic effect of ABA and GA_3 plant have increase the GA_3 concentation i.e. why vegetative growth takes place in the plant due to high concentration of GA_3 and flowering is low.

6. **Cultural factors-** If orchard is not properly managed then there is very less chance of flowering and fruiting.

Overcome of biennial bearing- For overcome of biennial bearing following point are commonly practices.

A. Proper management of orchard.

B. To maintain efficient C:N ratio.

C. By smudging-(Smudging is the procedure by which temporary inhance the temperature of orchard by fumigation for promoting the flower bud initiation).

D. Application of paclobutrazol@5ml/tree (Paclobutrazol is an antigibberalin chemical, by application of which plant have reduces the level of GA_3 and induce the level of ABA).

Always planting regular bearing variety like Mallika, Amrapali, Ratna, Sindhu, Arka Puneet etc.

Problem of Unfruitfulness

In an orchard all the fruit trees do not bear equally or regularly and sometimes fail to flower and fruit under similar conditions where another fruit tree bears heavily. This failure to set fruits may be attributed to unfruitfulness. To understand the problem of unfruitfulness in orchards a familiarity with following terms is necessary.

1. **Fruit setting:** It refers to initial growth of ovary and its associated parts after blossoming and taking it to maturity.
2. **Fruitfulness:** It is the state of plant when it is not only capable of flowering and fruit setting but also takes these fruits to maturity and inability to do so is unfruitfulness or barrenness.
3. **Infertility:** Ability of a plant not only to produce fruits but develop viable seeds and the inability to do so it referred as sterility or infertility. All fertile plants are fruitful but all fruitful plants are not fertile (Seedless fruits).
4. **Self fruitfulness:** Ability of a plant to mature fruits after self pollination.
5. **Self fertility:** Capacity of a plant for the production of viable seeds after self pollination.
   - The ability of a plant to produce optimum crop is Fruitfulness.
   - The inability to achieve this is referred to as Unfruitfulness.

This unfruitfulness is one of the serious problems of many orchards and its causes need to be understood properly for effective control and obtaining economically acceptable production level. The causes to this problem can be many and they have been broadly grouped into two categories

A. Internal factors
B. External factors.

A. Internal factors associated with unfruitfulness

There are a number of internal factors which are associated with unfruitfulness or sterility. They have further been categorized into three major categories, they are

1. Evolutionary tendencies.
2. Genetic influence.
3. Physiological factors.

1. Evolutionary Tendencies

In the process of evolution, a number of situations may lead to imperfect flowers or varied developmental periods leading to unfruitfulness unless suitable measures are adopted.

i. Monoecious and Dioecious nature

- A plant with stamens and carpels in different flowers on the same plant is monoecious e.g. Coconut, Arecanut, Pecan nut, Capri fig and Hazelnut.
- In monoecious fruit plants in general there is no or very little problem of pollination, fruit setting and fruitfulness. Nevertheless, pollinators need to be ensured.
- Plants which bear male and female flowers on different plants are known as dioecious e.g. Papaya, Date palm and Strawberry.
- Likewise a few varieties of plum produce too little pollen to call them bisexual.
- Profuse flowering without fruit set in ornamental pomegranate is a result of their being unisexual.
- A number of sex forms have been reported in papaya by different scientists.
- In case of fig two types of flower clusters are born namely staminate and pistillate flowers.
- In Capri fig staminate flowers are borne near the eye and pistillate flowers are borne near the end. To ensure good fruit set, retention of a few staminate trees (9:1) is essential as pollinizers.

ii. Heterostyly

- A condition in the flower where length of the style, relative to other parts of the flower, differs in the flowers of different plants.

- In this case in some flowers styles are short with long filaments and in some of the flowers of some species or varieties styles are long with short filaments.
- Styles and stigmas at different height prevent self pollination.
- In case of brinjal there are 4 types of flowers according to their length of style i.e. long, medium, pseudo short and true short. Out of these pseudo short and true short do not produce any fruit.
- Similarly in delicious group of apples extreme upright positions of the stamens accompanied by spreaded petals do not permit bees to do pollination while collecting nectar.
- When the pistils of heterostyled plants are pollinated with pollen from the same flowers or from other flowers containing stamens of an equal height the union may be fruitful but it is likely to be of varying degree of sterility. Here arrangement for cross pollination needs to be created.

iii. Dichogamy

- When stigmatic receptivity period does not coincides with pollen viability in monoecious plants it is known as dichogamy.
- In dichogamy self pollination is prevented in perfect flowered plants, due to maturity of two sex elements at different times.
- If the stamens ripe before the stigmas become receptive the flowers are known as **protandrous** and if stigmas become receptive before the stamens produce viable pollens it is known as **protogynous**. This results in low production of fruits.
- Protogyny is present in monoecious plants like walnuts, hazelnut, etc. whereas protandry is present in many coconut varieties.
- Majority of dioecious plants are also protogynous.

iv. Abortive flowers or aborted pistils or ovules

- This occurs in the developing flower's pistils and stigmas of many species and is responsible for failure in fruit setting.
- Abortion of partially developed flower buds is common. Setting and maturity of two sexes depend on the erosion of two properly formed sex cells.
- Any interference with their development and functioning may lead to sterility or unfruitfulness; such things can be observed in some grape varieties and tomato varieties.
- The late flowers of strawberry cluster are always abortive. This is more common in indeterminate type of plants.

- Degeneration of pistils takes the form of abortion and it is more common in ornamental pomegranate.
- Certain olive varieties have 10-60% abortive embryos.
- It is also common in some apple varieties. Embryo sac abortion becomes a cause of seedlessness in certain instances than fruitfulness.

v. Impotency of pollen

- Many varieties of grapes produce non viable or impotent pollens though they appear as perfect flowers.
- Sterility in grape varieties was the result of impotent pollens. Sterile pollen in the grape results from degeneration processes in the generative nucleus or arrested development prior to mitosis in the microspore nucleus.
- This is also common in J.H. Hale peach, Washington Navel orange and Tahiti lime.

2. Genetic influences

- Self sterility is a condition determined by the inheritance received but can develop in favourable environment. Self sterility affects it's off springs as well as hybrids.

i. Sterility and unfruitfulness due to hybridity

- Generally wider the crossing, greater is the degree of sterility encountered.
- The cross between peach and plum bears abundance of flowers but they are without pistils with malformed stamens.
- Flower characteristics were constant sterile and barren.
- A hybrid between the pear and the quince was seedless.
- Most of the citranges (cross between Sweet orange and *Citrus trifoliata*) produce no fertile female gametes.
- Seedlessness in most of the banana and pineapple varieties is due to hybrid nature of their ancestors.
- Most of the triploid apple varieties produce aborted pollen.
- A number of hybrids between *Vitis rotundifolia* and *Euvitis* are completely sterile.
- Similar was the case with hybridization of *Vitis vinifera* and *Vitis rotundifolia*.

ii. Incompatibility

- One of the most common causes of self unfruitfulness and self sterility is due to incompatibility between the pollen and ovules of the same plant or of the same variety.
- Pollen and ovules are fertile but they fail to affect conjugation.
- In apple, pear, plum and aonla self incompatible varieties require another pollinizer varieties for fruit setting.
- Self incompatibility has been reported in some of the mango varieties like Langra, Dashehari and Chausa.
- Self sterility and self unfruitfulness has been reported in apple, pears, plums, almond, apricot, the Clementine, mandarins, may be attributed to incompatibility where normal processes of fertilization fails somewhere between production of functional gametes and the fusion of sex cells.

3. Physiological Influences

i. Slow pollen tube growth

- Slow growth of the pollen tube results in unfruitfulness.
- Differences have been found in the rate of growth in selfed and crossed apples, pears, cherries and certain citrus fruits.
- This may be considered one type of incompatibility due to chemotropic or hormone influences.
- Besides this, fertilization should take place within a short time failing which abscission will take place at the base of the style, ovary pedicel or peduncle and fruit setting does not take place.

ii. Premature or delayed pollination

- Premature or delayed pollination leads to unfruitfulness.
- Tobacco flowers are very susceptible to injury from premature pollination.
- When mature pollen grains are applied to immature pistils they germinate, penetrate the style, enter the ovule and if the ovules are not ready for fertilization the flowers fall.
- However, in case of oranges premature pollination did not have any deleterious effect whereas some injury was noticed in tomato.
- Lower setting due to premature pollination was noticed in persimmon, Pear, plum and peach.
- Similarly, if pollination is delayed the flowers fall without setting.

- Delay in pollination for 1 or 2 days did not affect fruit set. However, further delaying may result into polyembryonic seeds in some species.

iii. Nutritive condition of plant

- Nutritive condition of plant just before or at or and just after the time of blossoming is an important factor determining the percentage of flowers carrying for setting and for maturity.
- It may affect the pollen viability or fertility of pistils.

Pollen viability : Pollen is said to be viable if it germinates over stigmatic surface effecting elongation of pollen tube sufficiently to fertilize egg cell. Bearing in fruit plants depends a lot upon pollination and subsequent fertilization of egg cell. The viability of pollen is adjudged by acetocarmine test. In this test, the pollen grains are placed over slide and 1-2 per cent acetocarmine solution is placed over it. The pollens which are viable are stained and nonviable types fail to get stained. The viable pollens are counted under microscope to ascertain viability percentage. The germination of viable pollen is further studied to know the fertilization of egg cells and ultimately the fruit set. For this purpose sugar solution of 10-25 per cent are used. Pollen grains are incubated in sugar solution for different periods of time and their germination percentage is studied under microscope. Agar and boron add in enhancing germination of pollen grains.

Growth curve: Growth curve of fruits are idealized as being S-shaped. The growth has three distinct phases; logarithmic, linear and senscence phases. In the logarithmic phase, size increases exponentially with time i.e. growth rate is slow at first but continuously increases at an increasing rate. In the linear phase, increase in size continues at a constant rate, usually maximum rate for some time. In senscence phase, the growth rate decreases.

Some fruits such as pineapple, grape, blueberry, currant, olive, peach, apricot, cherry and plum show double sigmoid growth curve. In it, the first senscence phase is followed by another lag-phase and then a second sigmoid phase follows.

a. **Effect on pollen viability** - There was significant difference in germination percentage of pollen collected from old apple trees and from strong young trees of the same variety.

b. **Effect on defectiveness of pistils -**

- Exhaustion of tree by over bearing, drought or poverty of soil leads to production of defective pistils.
- Over bearing weakens the fruit tree and in coming season production is adversely affected.

- Close correlation was reported between defective pistils and unfruitfulness in American plums.
- In case of *Vitis vinifera* carbohydrate deficiency is the common cause of flower drop.
- Due to carbohydrate deficiency flower abortion and ultimately unfruitfulness also occur in green house grown tomatoes.

iv. Fruit setting of flowers in different positions

- Fruits borne on terminal growth have more competition in many fruit crops and mature and set under normal nutritional conditions but percentage of set is small.
- This positional competition takes place between fruits and branch as well as between different fruits influencing fruitfulness.

Strong and weak spurs

- Nutritional condition of spurs has positive correlation with fruit setting in apple. Spurs on vigorous limbs with large leaves set more fruits than those borne on weak limbs.
- More flowers ultimately lead to more fruit set and more flowers are generally borne on strong limbs. Likewise flowers borne singly set fruits and mature as fruit and majority of those born in clusters drop down.
- Ringing or girdling also lead to accumulation of an extra store of food material leads to fruit set and develop parthenocarpically.
- In the process of fruitifications the embryo is more important for development *i.e.* if nutritive condition is favourable, it accompanies the development of the seed coat and fruit wall, if not, only the latter portions are in high degree retardation in development.
- Under insufficient nutrient supply the numbers of seed forming ovules are diminished and under extreme nutrition deficiency both fruit wall and large number of ovules are diminished leading to enabling to form seed.
- In case of green house cucumbers, nutritional deficiency leads to arrest of growth of growing fruits depending upon the position of the fruits and time of pollination. If a few of the cucumbers are harvested remaining fruits resume growth.
- In case of strawberries producing bisexual flowers may lead to produce pistillate flowers if nutritional deficiency was observed.
- However, nutritive condition has indirect influence on compatibility.

B. Unfruitfulness associated with external factors

1. **Nutrient supply**

- In certain families like Graminae, Cruciferae and Leguminaceae sterility normally occur due to over feeding.
- Jonathan apple self sterile in rich soil becomes self fertile in poor soils.
- High fertility level is generally associated with good pistil development and low level with poor pistils and good stamens in grapes.
- In olives low fertility leads to partial or complete degeneration of pistils.

2. **Pruning and training**: Pruning tends to produce more true hermophrodite condition in grape variety "Hope". If pruning is not done the variety tends to remain sterile and produces aborted pistils.
3. **Locality**: Jonathan apple which is sterile in one location is reported to be self fertile in another location.
4. **Season:** Hybrid grape Ideal is self impotent early in season but becomes self potent later on.
5. **Temperature**: High temperature at flowering dries up stigmatic secretion and prevents pollination. Tomato varieties grown at high temperature do not produce any fruit.
6. **Light**: Exposure of strawberry plants to long photoperiod results in development of stamens and pistils in strawberry flowers.
7. **Pests and diseases**: Mango hopper, powdery mildew, etc. adversely affect the fruit set and development in mango and grape.

- Spraying the trees when they are in bloom i.e. spraying at flowering reduces fruit set.
- Some of the fungicides gave inhibitory effect on pollen grains *i.e.* copper fungicides at 200 to 10000 ppm prevent the germination of pollen grains on the stigma.

Steps to Overcome the Problem of Unfruitfulness

- Having known that there could be many reasons for unfruitfulness, it is necessary to make necessary corrective measures which should begin from planning level and extend to an established orchard.
- Choice of the crop and variety should be made on the basis of climatic and edaphic conditions of the site of orcharding.
- Provision of windbreak and shelter belts for areas prone to wind damage.
- In case of problems of pollination due to heterostyly, dichogamy incompatibility, sterility, embryo abortion, hybridity, etc. a mixture of varieties

should be grown by introduction effective pollinizer varieties and pollinators (Honey bees).

- Unfruitfulness due to slow growth of pollen tube, premature and delayed pollination, use of plant regulators can be affected after standardization in terms of chemical concentration and timing of application.
- Problem due to overbearing can be managed through thinning at appropriate stage.
- Irrigation management would be key role in situations with drought and waterlogged conditions.
- Maintenance of critical nutrient status in tree leaves for optimum crop production by adopting correct nutritional programme based on plant and soil analysis.
- In crops requiring regular pruning standard practices will have to be adopted based on crop, variety and its phenology.
- Unfruitfulness due to pathogens should be managed through effective plant protection measures following integrated approach.
- Problem of unfruitfulness due to tendency of alternate bearing should be over come through replacement of regular bearing varieties and crop regulation.

Chapter 16

Plant Growth Regulators

The quantitative increase in plant body such as increase in the length of stem and root, the number of leaves etc., is referred to as plant growth whereas, the qualitative changes such as germination of seed, formation of leaves, flowers and fruits, falling of leaves and fruits is referred as development. Utilization of these substances for proper development of the plant is regulated by certain chemical messengers called plant growth substances or plant growth regulators, which in minute amounts increase or decrease or modifies the physiological process in plants. Plant growth substances are the chemical other than nutrient which required in very small amount but without which plant can not complete their physiology.

The two sets of internal factors, *viz*., nutrition and hormone control the growth and development of the plant. The raw material required for growth is supplied by nutritional factors which include the minerals, organic substances the protein, carbohydrates, etc.

Phytohormones: These are the hormones produced by plants which in low concentrations regulate plant physiological process. These usually move within the plants from a site of production to a site of action.

Plant growth regulators: These are organic compounds other than nutrients, which in small amounts promote, inhibit or otherwise modify any physiological process in plant.

It may be defined as any organic compounds which are active at low concentrations (1-10 ml) in promoting, inhibiting or modifying growth and development in plants. The naturally occurring (endogenous) growth substances are commonly known as plant hormones, while the synthetic ones are called growth regulators.

Plant hormones: It is an organic compound synthesized in one part of plant and translocated to other parts, wherein very low concentration causes a physiological response.

The plant hormones are identified as promoters (auxins, gibberellin, and cytokinins), inhibitors (abscisic acid and ethylene) and other hypothetical growth substances (Florigen, death hormone, etc.).

A. Auxins

- Auxin is a Greek word derived from Auxein which means to *increase.*
- It is a generic term for chemicals that typically stimulate cell elongation by loosening cell wall but auxins also influence a wide range of growth and development response.
- The chemical isolation and characterization was done by Kogi *et al.* (1934).
- Auxins are the first identified hormones of which IAA seems to be the major naturally occurring endogenous auxin in plants and crops.
- Besides IAA, plants contain three other compounds which are structurally similar and elicit many of the same response as that of IAA, Chloro indole acetic acid (CIAA), Phenylacetic acid (PAA), Indole butyric acid (IBA).

  Site of auxin synthesis: Auxins are synthesized in stem tips and in young tissues and move mainly down stem (Basipetal movement) i.e., from shoot tip to root.

Synthetic compounds are classified into five major categories

- Indole acids
- Napthalene acids
- Chlorophenoxy acid
- Picolinic acid.
- Derivatives.

Role of auxin

1. **Cell division and enlargement:** IAA + GA, example-cambial growth in diameter.
2. **Tissue culture:** Shoot multiplications (IBA and BAP), callus growth (2, 4-D), root multiplication IAA and IBA (1-2 mg).
3. **Breaking dormancy and apical dominance (inhibition of lateral buds):** NAA
4. **Shortening internodes:** Apple trees (NAA) dwarf branch fruit.
5. **Rooting of cutting:** 10-1000 ppm NAA, IAA, Phenyl acetic acid.
6. **Prevent lodging:** NAA develop woody and erect stem.
7. **Prevent abscission:** Premature leaf, fruit and flower fall (NAA, IAA and 2, 4-D).

8. **Parthenocarpic fruit:** Grapes, Banana and Orange (IAA).
9. **Flower initiations:** Pineapple uniform flowering and fruit ripening (NAA) and delay flowering (2, 4-D).
10. **Weed eradication:** 2, 4-D.

B. Gibberellins

- It is the active principle isolated from the soil borne fungus *Gibberella fujikuroi*.
- The concentration of GA_3 is usually the highest in immature seeds, reaching up to 18 mg/kg fresh weight in *Phaseolus* species, but it decreases rapidly as the seeds mature.
- In general, roots contain higher amounts of GA_3 than shoots. Gibberellins have also been found effective in overcoming both kinds of dormancy in buds as well as seeds.

Role of gibberellins

1. **GA:** Synthesis in leaf and induce shoot elongation (IAA + GA_3), by effecting cell elongation or cell division or both.
2. **Enhance metabolic activity:** Mobilization of reserved food material, promote growth and height, increase root activity and kinetin production in root- translocation to growing bud.
3. **Shoot elongation:** GA_3 spray increases height of seedlings.
4. **Delay senescence:** Increase photosynthetic and protein synthesis so decrease abscission.
5. **Increase cambial growth and differentiation:** Induce flower and fruit set (IAA+GA_3).
6. **Dwarf plant (genetically) to normal height:** GA_3
7. **Promote flowering in long day plants**: Substitute for long day condition and cold treatment (vernalization).
8. **Induction of parthenocarpy in grapes**: Three physiological events: Rachis cell elongation, flower thinning and berry enlargement.
9. Breaking dormancy and leaf expansion.

C. Cytokinins

- First endogenous cytokinin was isolated from maize kernels named as zeatin.
- Germinating seeds, roots, sap streams, developing fruits and tumor tissues are rich in cytokinins.

- Cytokinins imbibed seeds germinate better in dark than unimbibed lettuce seeds.
- Similarly cytokinin together with gibberellins effectively breaks the photodormancy of celery (*Apium graveolens*) seeds.

Synthetic cytokinins are: Kinetin, Benzyladenine and Ethoxy ethyladenine.

Role of cytokinin

1. Cell division, elongation and enlargement.
2. Tissue culture morphogenesis.
3. Induction of flowering and fruit development.
4. Parthenocarpy.
5. Apical dominance overcoming.
6. Breaking dormancy.
7. Delay senescence.
8. Improves N_2 metabolism.

D. Ethylene

- Neljubow (1901) is credited with having identified the active growth regulating component of the illuminating gas as ethylene.
- Ethylene is formed naturally in plants in amounts sufficient to bring about regulatory effect and it might be considered as plant hormones.
- Recently a synthetic chemical known as ethrel, ethephon, chloroethyl phosphonic acid (CEPA) has been reported to release ethylene when applied to plants.

Role of ethylene

1. Breaking dormancy.
2. Induce ripening of fruits.
3. Induce abscission of leaves.
4. Inhibit elongation and lateral bud growth.

Growth retardant: The term growth retarding chemical or growth retardant is that chemical slows cell division and cell elongation of shoot tissues and regulate plant height physiologically without formative effects e.g: AMO 1618, Phosphon-D, CCC, Chloromequat and Alar.

These do not occur naturally in plants and acts in retardation of stem elongation, preventing cell division. Plant growth retardants are defined as synthetic organic chemicals that cause a retardation of cell division steps in pathways of hormone biosynthesis without evoking substantial growth distortions.

Inhibitors: These suppress the growth of plants. There are phenolic inhibitors and synthetic inhibitors and abscisic acid (ABA).

Phenolic inhibitors: E.g. Benzoic acid, Salicylic acid, Coumaric acid and Chlorogenic acid.

Synthetic inhibitors: E.g. Maleic hydrazide (MH), Tri-Iodobenzoic acid (TIBA), SADH etc. an inhibitor from young leaves of *Betula sps.* prevent the growth of apical buds eg. ABA and Dormin.

Role of abscissic acid (ABA): It should appear as 5th growth regulator in the group; add introduction to ABA; take this before growth retardant.

- To stop elongation.
- Induce dormancy.
- Delay germination.
- Inhibit growth process.

Add method of preparation of growth regulator formulations.

Methods of application

Growth regulators can be applied in different ways like:

- Spraying method.
- Injection of solution into internal tissues.
- Root feeding method.
- Powder form.
- Dipping of cuttings in solution.
- Soaking in dilute aqueous solution.

Various Uses of Plant Growth Regulators

1. **Propagation of plants:** A number of plants are propagated by stem, leaf cutting and by layering. For promotion of rooting, the most commonly utilized hormone is IBA followed by NAA.

   Gibberellic acid causes inhibition of root formation in cutting. Cytokinins also help in quick and profuse root formation in cuttings and layers. By use of auxins, profuse root formation is observed in cuttings of guava, fig, pomegranate, crotons, rose, hibiscus, etc.

2. **Seed germination:** Many seeds have natural dormancy which can be got over by dipping the seeds in auxins. Soaking seeds of french beans and peas in 10-20 ppm solution of GA for 12 hours before sowing, significantly improves the yield and quality. Dipping sweet potatoes in 5ppm GA solution for 5minutes before sowing increases sprouting and yield of potatoes.

3. **Control of plant size:** In fruits and vegetables, application of higher doses of nitrogenous fertilizers spraying cycocel (growth retardant), the superfluous growth of leaves is checked. By spraying 10ppm solution of morphactin in potato, the growth of plant is reduced and thereby the size of tubers is increased. The growth retardants are useful in checking the growth of hedges in ornamental gardens there by reducing the cost of trimming the hedges.
4. **Regulation of flowering:** In Pineapple, due to later flowering the fruit get ready in rainy season. This deteriorates the quality of the fruit. This difficulty can be overcome by spraying 5-10 ppm solution of NAA before flowering. Application of 100-200 ppm GA in Dahlia plants induces early flowering. Sometimes, it is necessary to delay flowering eg. Crossing of varieties which do not flower simultaneously. Hence, the crossing becomes difficult.
5. **Control of sex expression:** In number of cucurbits, such as ridge gourd, bitter gourd, watermelon, cucumber and pumpkins which have proportion of male flowers is more than female flowers. For better yield, it is necessary to increase the number of female flowers. This can be achieved by application of auxins which increases the number of female flowers and decreases the number of male flower. The commonly used auxins are NAA and ethrel.
6. **Control of fruit set and growth of fruit:** Spraying NAA, TIBA, and PCPA on flowers increases the fruit set. Dipping of grape bunches (young fruits) in GA solution increases the berry size in Thompson Seedless grape.
7. **Control of fruit drop:** In Nagpur Santra, the fruit drop can be controlled by spraying 10-20 ppm NAA or 10 ppm 2,4-D after fruit set. The fruit drop in mango can be controlled by these two auxins.
8. **Thinning of fruits:** Sometimes it is necessary to thin the fruits so as to bring a balance between the supply of nutrients and development of fruit. In such cases spraying with mild solution of ethrel or morphactin reduces the fruit load by 25-30 per cent.
9. **Early ripening and development of fruit colour:** If the fruits could be brought in the market in early part of the season, they fetch good price. Spraying with 2,4,5-T and B-9 hastens maturity of apples by 1-4weeks.
10. **Prevention of sprouting:** In potatoes and onions, after harvest, in storage, the buds start sprouting which makes them unfit for cooking. Spraying of malic hydrazide (MH) solution before storing prevents sprouting and these can be stored safely for 6 months.
11. **Control of weeds:** The conventional method of controlling the weeds is to remove them by uprooting manually. Successful control of weeds is obtained by spraying 2, 4-D in many crops.

Chapter 17

Breeding Approaches in Horticultural Plants

The current status of advances in fruit breeding is through the development of different scientific approaches augmented by ever-increasing knowledge and application of genetics, statistics and biotechnology. These innovative approaches very specific for a species in most of the cases, are the major tools of the fruit breeders to tackle the different objectives of fruit improvement programme at present Fruit improvement is a very slow process due to the long generation cycle varying from species to species, thereby reducing the chances of exploiting genetic recombination. Besides this factor, most of the fruit species are either highly heterozygous or polyploidy in nature. Due to this reason the asexual propagation of fruit plants is a conventional means while wide segregation occurs upon sexual reproduction. Such expectation is not unlikely because the types selected as commercial varieties are definitely to be vigorous ones, and a positive correlation exists between vigour and heterozygosity.

This discussion on breeding of fruit plants involves different aspect of the species concerned is so essential as well as fundamental that discussion of them must procede any consideration of breeding methods themselves. The plant species are grouped into two-self-pollinated and cross-pollinated. These two groups have emerged on the basis of pollination mechanism which plays significant role in the method of breeding application. To emphasize the difference in the reproductive systems of these two groups one should know the details about floral biology, mechanism of pollination control, reproduction by asexual and sexual means and self and cross-pollinated plants.

A. Reproductive System of Horticultural Plants

For achieving success in plant breeding the knowledge of reproductive system of the plant is very essential. The plant species are grouped in to two self pollinated and cross pollinated. The mechanism of pollination play and important role in the method of breeding application. For a succesfull breeding programme breeder should know the mechanism of pollination, floral biology, mode of reproduction in asexual and sexual plants and self pollinated and cross pollinated crops.

Floral Biology

In fruit breeding the characteristic features of flowers-morphological and behavioural, play an important role. The studies on floral biology of any plant species involving the following aspects are most important.

i. Type and morphological features
ii. Sex
iii. Time and length of flowering
iv. Pollen fertility
v. Female fertility
vi. Receptivity of stigma
vii. Time of pollinations
viii. Storage life of pollen

Floral Morphology

The type and morphological features of flower are very important from the breeding point of view. Unlike field crops, fruit plants show a degree of variation in type and morphology, even among different varieties within the species. Regardless of difference in size, shape and colour of petals, the number as well as arrangement of petals differs among genotypes. As for example, in peach two types viz rosaceae and compannulate types of flowers are found. Most of the varieties bear single whorl of petals, while tripple whorl (cv. Honey Sweet) and double whorl (cv. Matchless) genotypes are also there. The importance of petal length is also important in peach cultivar like Ranjit Bagh Early that bears very small petals which are not enough to cover reproductive organ which when protruding may receive injuries from early spring frost, if occurs. Similarly, the position of the flower on the inflorescence is a criterion determining fruit set in many species.

Types of Sex Form

There are three sex types of flowers hermaphrodite, pistillate and staminate. Hermaphroditic flowers are called perfect or complete in which both the stamens and pistils are functional. Pistillate flowers are devoid of anthers. Reverse of pistillate flowers are staminate ones with non-functional pistils. All the three sex types of flower are found in grapes, strawberries, papaya etc.

Depending on the presence of unisexual flower i.e. staminate or pistillate, plant species are categorised as monoecious when staminate and pistillate flowers are borne separately on the same plant and as dioecious in which the staminate and pistillate flowers occur on different individuals. Walnuts, chestnuts, pecans, filberts are typical examples of monoecious type.

Similarly date palm, jojoba (*Simmondsia chinensis*) are typical dioecious fruit species. Further specification generates designations as gynomonoecious and gynodioccious. Ficus carica is a gynodioecious fruit species, having two distinct forms of tree; the caprifig which is monoecious, and the fig which is pistillate. The syconia of caprifig contain short-styled pistillate flowers and staminate flowers while the syconia of fig tree contains only long styled pistillate flowers.

Time, Length and Behaviour of Flowering

The time of flower opening and its length of duration, time of maturity of pollen and the receptivity of the stigma, pollen viability in situ and in storage condition, female fertility are significant characteristics for the mode of reproduction in plant species. A prior knowledge about these aspects of flowers helps the breeder in making desired crosses.

In many horticultural plants, the time of flower opening depends on the environmental conditions. The length of flowering period is also depended upon the temperature and humidity. The avocado flower is perfect. In this fruit species, a given tree (or cultivar) is classified as 'A' type if each flower is functionally female (pistil-receptive in the morning and functionally male (pollen-shedding) the following afternoon; or 'B' type if each flower is 'female' in the afternoon and then 'male' in the following morning. An A type flower opens for the first time in early to mid-morning, remains open and pistil-receptive till noon, then closes and remains closed till the afternoon of the second day. When it reopens and starts shedding pollen the pistil no longer remains functionally receptive, finally closing permanently that night. Flowers on B trees behave analogously but with transposed timing. This important flower behaviour, of course, is regular only under certain weather parameters, with diurnal temperatures raising about 26^{0}C and nocturnal temperatures remaining above about 15^{0}C. This dichogamy of avocado flower is described as protogynous dichogamy with synchronous daily complementarity.This phenomenon of differential maturity of staminate and pistillate flowers, commonly known as dichogamy, is evidently complete mainly in monoecious fruit species viz. pecan, walnuts, filberts etc. In protandry, maturation of anthers takes place before pistils and protogyny is the reverse of protandry. Homogamy i.e. synchronised flowering of both type of flowers, becomes important for persuming inbreeding, if necessary, but of least importance in fruit plants which possess self-sterility viz. filberts in few plants like fig, this dichogamy is pronounced. The flowers of the caprifig tree are protogynous, the pistillate flower mature three or more months ahead of the staminate ones. In chestnuts, the phenomenon is called as duodichogamy. Two types of inflorescence occur, the unisexual staminate catkin at the lower parts of the shoots and the bisexual catkins towards the terminal end of the shoots. The lower staminate unisexuals bloom first, then pistillates of the bisexual catkins and lastly the staminates of these catkins at least after ten days of anthesis of the staminate flowers of unisexual catkins. This sequence of O, Q and then O, Q maturation in chestnut is known as duodiehogamy. However, variation in degree of dichogamy prevails among cultivars, location, weather and season as a result of genetic and environmental effects.

Female Receptivity

Receptivity of stigma, its onset, duration and peak period, is very much important in terms of controlled/artificial crossing to achieve success in a significant way. Depending on the cultivar and climatic conditions, the duration of receptivity either extends or shortens. The fluctuations in temperature affect considerably the stigma receptivity viz. peach.

Pollen Characteristics

Pollen viability particularly when immediate pollination is not possible, in storage for short time or long duration, is also an important consideration in fruit breeding. Besides this, pollen viability varies during the period of anthesis. In peach, viability attains maximum (55%) between 9 a.m. and 2 p.m. on the day of anthesis, while in some fruit plants viz. commercial lemon and orange cultivars fertility percentage is as low as 25%. Hence, the prior knowledge on pollen viability, of optimum time for pollen collection helps a lot in making successful crossing in fruit plants.

Control of Pollination and its Mechanism

The plants are broadly categorized into two, self-pollinated and cross-pollinated as mentioned earlier. In the systems involving monoecy, protandry and protogyny cross-pollination is not enforced but encouraged leaving, thereby, the scope of self-pollination to a limited extent. The scope can be utilized to develop inbred lines of these plants species through artificial selfing. These systems encouraging cross-pollination only, do not involve genetic differences among individuals. No genetic problem arises, therefore, during artificial control of pollination in the species. On the other hand, the systems that enforce complete or nearly complete cross-pollution are, however, genetically controlled. This can be ignored while pollination is done artificially. Dioecy and incompatibility are the two main types/ systems which involve individuals genetically differentiated. The other controlling system is male sterility, having similar characteristics in the artificial control of pollination.

Dioecy

The term dioecy means male and female flowers are found separately in the same species. Dioecy is found in papaya, date palm etc. The other important but not edible, fruit plant jojoba (*Simmondsia chinensis*) is also dioecious. For these dioceious plants, male-parents are essential to develop fruits which are the commercial products. Interestingly, the inheritance of male and female characters in these plants in not fully understood. Though male plants produce no fruit but essential to produce pollen. Conventional practice of propagating date palm is the removal of side-shoots from the desired plant followed by its establishment in field. Similarly with jojoba, male plants except a few ones are rouged out at the time of first flowering. The recent development of in-vitro technique or micro-propagation has opened the scope of improvement in these fruit plants. The results await commercial success in *Phoenix dactylifera*, *Carica papaya* and *Simondsia chinensis,* although commercial micro-propagation is now practiced in papaya and banana.

Incompatibility

Incompatibility means plants where male and female both parts are functional but due to certain reason they cannot pollinate to each other. The important reasons are heterostyle, maturity of male and female part, polygamous nature of the plants etc. The system which is genetically controlled and prevents self-pollination for enforcing cross-pollination in hermaphroditic plant. This is due to the arrest of post-pollination events as different levels. Incompatibility occurring between species referred as inter-specific incompatibility, and self-incompatibility while within species. Inter-specific incompatibility prevents fertilization between gametes of distantly related species, the causes of which are many, in intra-specific self-incompatibility, the failure of fertilization between gametes of the same or other individuals of the same species is caused by genetic factors. Incompatibility may be of two types-heteromorphic and homomorphic. In heteromorphic system, individuals of the species produce either two or three types of flower differing in length of stamens and styles, and fertilization occurs only when pollens fall on sigma bearing similar length of style as that of stamens. This system is not found among common fruit plants. Homomorphic incompatibility is governed by multiple genes termed s alleles. Pollen tube having a particular S allele is inhibited in the style carrying the same S allele. Determination of genetics of self-incompatibility is a laborious process involving extensive breeding programme for many generations. It may be of two types-gametophytic and sporophytic.

Among fruit plants, the self-incompatibility is widespread in apple, pear sweet cherries, almond and plum. In ease of apple, practically all cultivars are self-incompatible to some extent. Unlike apple, all the pears are diploid but out-breeding in them is ensured by gametophytic incompatibility. The self-incompatibility system in pears breaks down on doubling of chromosomes. Self-incompatibility in 11 out of 23 *Rubus* species is caused by stylar inhibition and keeps observed two alleles S_1 and S_2 responsible for it. In cultivated almond, gametophytic incompatibility is found. The almond cultivars set fruit when cross pollinated with the pollen of a different genotype. The self-fertility can be transferred to almond from self-fertile species viz. peach. The first generation hybrids of almond with self-fertile species are also self-fertile. The self-fertility system (sf) is dominant over self-incompatibility system (si) in almond. Similarly self-incompatibility in plums is a genetic character and multiple allelomorphs are believed responsible for it. In mango, the occurrence of self incompatibility (sporophytic) has been reported in Dashahari, Langra, Chausa and Bombay Green.

Apomixis

Apomixis means development of seed without pollination and fertilization. This form of reproduction occurs in many plants of hybrid origin viz. *Malus sp.* Generally the apomictic fruit plants are polyploid and perpetuate themselves easily by apomictic seeds, though they are capable to produce sexual hybrids when crossed with other diploids. The main effect of apomixis is an increase in the proportion of maternal individuals through prohibition or modification of genetic segregation and recombination.

Parthenocarpy

Parthenocarpy means development of fruit without pollination and fertilization. Its importance lies mainly with seedless fruit production. However, it is not common in fruit plants though desired in some cases. Parthenocarpy is a characteristic feature of all common type and of persistent caprifigs. Trees lacking this trait develop blank syconia in caprifigs and seedless fruits in figs. On the other hand, seedlessness in grape is not a case of parthenocarpy. It is stenospermocarpy where abortion of embryo takes place at an early age of development. In pears also many cultivars produce fruit parthenocarpically but it is undesirable for poor quality, lack of flavor etc.

Mode of pollination

Pollination means transfer of pollen from male part (anther) to female part (stigma). The transfer of pollen either by air (aenemophyllus) or by insect (entegmophyllus) or by water (hydrophyllus). When the pollen grain from an anther falls on the stigma of the same flower on the same plant (variety) is termed as self pollination or autogamy, whereas the pollen grain from the flower of the plant is transfer to the stigma of the flower of another plant (variety) is termed as cross pollination or allogamy. Third situation is known as geitonogamy when pollen from flower of a plant falls on the stigma of other flower of the same plant (variety).

Cleistogamy

Cleistogamy means dehiscence of pollen grain take place before opening of the flower i.e. grape and sapota.

Homogamy

Homogamy means where male and female parts of the flower mature at the same time which favours to self pollination i.e. citrus, peach and apricot.

Dichogamy

Dichogamy means where male and female part in hermaphrodite flower mature in different time which favours the cross pollination. Dichogamy is of two types 1. Protandry means maturation of androecium first then gynoecium e.g. walnut and coconut, 2. Protogyny means where gynoecium mature first then androecium e.g. annona, banana, plum, pomegranate, avocado and fig.

Male sterility

Male sterility means impotency of pollen grains which favours to cross pollination e.g. triploid banana, triploid apple, etc.

B. Breeding Techniques in Horticulture Plants

The plant breeding strategy to be used in improving specific character of a fruit plant species involves a number of important considerations which decide the approach that may be most efficient and fruitful for the characters in question. The same technique as well as the same strategy may not be useful for all types of fruits. It may vary depending on the type of character, its inheritance if known, and mating systems of the fruit plant concerned. The presence of incompatibility and sterility barriers to crossing, inbreeding depression and the occurrence and frequency of spontaneous mutations also influence the selection of an appropriate breeding strategy.

In fruit plant species, most commonly used breeding techniques are hybridisation, mutation and polyploid inductions, introduction and clonal selection. In recent times biotechnological approaches i.e. in vitro technique of tissue and organ culture, and also gene cloning are gaining importance in fruit improvement programme.

Hybridization

Controlled hybridizations are usually made between parents that have the best phenotypes for the characters desired. If the character to be improved is highly heritable and genetic variance is additive, genetic advance can be achieved smoothly. On the contrary, if dominance or epistasis is present, selection of parents should be done on the basis of progeny performance, otherwise, genetic advance would be low. The progeny test is useful if the characters can be assessed in early stage. However, often a number of undesired characters accompany the desired characters transferred through hybridization. The method of backcrossing is used to overcome it. Many cultivars developed through hybridization are in good existence at present in each type fruit species.

Mutation

Mutation occurs spontaneously in nature. It can also be induced artificially with the help of mutagenic agents either physically or chemically. The mutated bud or shoot is maintained by asexual propagation. Alter proper evaluation it is released as varieties. So many examples of bud mutant or 'sports' have been reported in different fruit plants.

Polyploidisation

Like mutation, polyploidy has a significant role in fruit improvement. In grapes polyploidy has been successfully used to obtain self fertile inter-specific hybrids with muscadins or large berry yielding forms of desirable genotypes. Similarly the cultivated form of strawberries is octaploid. In general, polyploidy offers greater vigour, larger fruit size and higher self-compatibility viz. tetraploids of pear.

Inbreeding, Outbreeding and Backcross Breeding

Inbreeding is done by either selfing or mating between closely related parents. In contrast outbreeding means mating between individuals not closely related. Whereas, in backcross, breeding recurrent backcrosses are made to one of the parents of a hybrid, accompanied by selection for a particular trait.

Inbreeding results an increase in homozygosity in all loci. The intensive inbreeding for a long time fixes genetic characters, thus separating the population into genetically distinct groups. The self-fertilisation is a clear system of inbreeding. For this reason self-pollinated species are more homogeneous than outbreeding species. Most of the fruit species are outbreeding and they maintain a wide heterozygosity. Hence, while inbreeding occurs in these cross-pollinated species, deterioration is maximum in comparison to that of a self-pollinated type. The most important methods applicable to outbreeding fruit species are backcross breeding, hybridisation of inbred lines, recurrent selection etc. The backcross breeding in case of fruit plants is used to introduce one specific character into another in the background of single gene resistance to disease.

Intergeneric and Interspecific Hybridisation

In fruit plants though not common but not rare. In strawberries there are reports on crossing of *Fragaria* with *Potentilla*, though the objective was not fulfilled. Like intergeneric crosses, there are several reports on successful interspecifie crosses in *Prunus sp., Fragaria sp.* The cultivated almond crosses readily with peach and plum: similarly apricot with plum and so on. The main objective of interspecific crossing is to transfer the characters from one species to other. As for example, self-fertility in almond is absent. It has been transferred through hybridisation with peach.

C. Non-Conventional Techniques

The need to insist on non-conventional methods i.e. biotechnological tool, in fruit breeding was felt necessary while the conventional methods of plant breeding were proved to be of limited value. The following methods included in non conventional techniques.

Somatic Embryogenesis and Clonal Selection

In somatic embryogenesis embryos arise from single cells and small volumes of the culture can give rise to thousands of seedling plants. The technology of somatic embryogenesis is highly potential to enlarge the scope of clonal selection in fruit breeding. The realisation of the full potential of somatic embryogenesis depends on the efficient technique of plantlet regeneration which awaits considerable progress in major fruit plants. Exceptionally a significant progress has been achieved in case of Grapes, Strawberries, *Rubus sp.*, Pineapple etc.

The potential of clonal selection in vitro is dependent on the somatic heterogenity as well as the probable chimeras among the clones, providing sources of variation. Among many difficulties, the greatest one in clonal selection is low yield of somatic embryos and poor germination' rates in fruit plants. The second one is a suitable screening method.

Polyembryony

The occurrence of polyembryonic seeds have been reported occasionally from temperate fruit species. Polyembryony occurs by budding or cleavage of the zygotic embryonal mass. Such budding or cleavage is much more common in proembryonic stage than embryos of advanced stage. The nucleus or integument tissues can be used to regenerate adventitious embryos which on complete plantlet development are true to type plants and virus free. In contrast, plantlets developed from other tissues generally show variation. Thus production of polyembryos in vitro could be a useful tool in breeding of fruit plants. Success has been achieved in *Citrus sp.*

Protoplast Fusion or Somatic Hybridisation

Protoplast fusion or somatic hybridisation is used (i) To produce novel plants and combine characteristics of otherwise sexually incompatible species, (ii) To produce cybrids and to exploit the cytoplasmic variability. (iii) To develop cytoplasmic male sterile lines, and (iv) For the uptake of organells. Relatively little research has been done in this area on fruit crops, though it is the promising area from which several benefits should accrue.

Gene Cloning and Development of Transgenic Plants

Genetic engineering is the latest developed technique by which successful insertion of desired genes into the genome in target for modification takes place. Three types of techniques which are applied to transfer the genetic material to the host are achieved by (i) Biological vectors (e.g. Agrobacteum), (ii) Direct introduction (e.g. particle bombardment), and (iii) Cell fusion (e.g. protoplast fusion). The numbers of plant species which have been changed through genetic engineering are increasing rapidly. At present about 50 different species are in the list, mostly of horticultural importance including two fruit species and walnuts. Identification of biodiverse spices for breeding or conservation through DNA barcoding has been suggested. This method also cheeks extincion of species, innovation of organism's fragmentary material for testing and conservation.

Chapter 18

Physiological Disorders of Horticultural Plants

Physiological disorders are abnormalities in plants which are associated to non-pathogenic factors. A plant or its parts may show unusual growth, function or deformity. Such abnormalities are widely referred to as disorders. These may be incited by nutrients deficiency or excess, hormonal imbalance, abnormal growing conditions etc. Some commonly observed disorders have been dealt in here suitably.

FRUITS

MANGO

Malformation- It is of two types, vegetative and reproductive.

The vegetative malformation is observed at seedling stage in nursery. On the affected plants following symptoms is noticed:

- Bunching of leaf at terminal portion of leaf.
- Shortening of internodal length.
- Shortening of the size of leaf lamina of the plants.
- Reduced length of petiole.

The reproductive malformation manifests following symptoms:

- Compactness of panicle.
- Shortness of rachis.
- Greeniness of panicle.
- Crowded and enlarged flowers with thicker pedicels, calices, and petals.
- Attachment of panicle even during off-season.

Causes

- Lower level of RNA, DNA, soluble protein and total nitrogen.
- Lack of auxin. Malformed panicle had lower level of all the four fractions of auxin (free neutral, free acidic, bound neutral and bound acidic).

- Higher level of carbohydrates (reducing, non-reducing, polysaccharides and carbohydrates) in vegetatively malformed shoots.
- Higher content of zeatin, abscisic acid and ethylene.
- Involvement of malformin like substances.
- Cultural practices, nutritional practices, mites and fungi.

Control

- Deblossoming during January.
- Spray of NAA 200 ppm during October.

Varieties like Bhadauran, Alib and Illaichi are free from malformation.

Black tip

Symptom

- Development of small, etiolated area at the distal end of fruit.
- Mesocarp and seed remain unaffected.
- Softening, pre-mature ripening and early drop of fruit.

Causes

- Gases emanating from brick kilns-CO, CO_2, SO_2 and ethylene are important in this regard.
- Dashehari is highly susceptible and Lucknow Safeda the least, to black tip.

Control

- Brick kilns should be located 1.8-2.0 km away from orchard.
- Height of the chimney should be 18- 20 m from ground level.
- Spray of 0.6 % Borax during flowering initiation, full bloom and after fruit set.

Spongy tissue

Symptom

- Development of non-edible, sour, yellowish and sponge like patch in pulp of the fruit.
- Non-ripening of the fruit due to un-hydrolyzed starch.
- High acidity, low ascorbic acid, carotene and sugar contents than normal fruits.

Causes

- Convective heat arising from the soil.
- Alphonso variety is highly susceptible.

Control

- Sod culture in orchard using green vegetation or leguminous crop.
- Mulching at pre-harvest stage.
- Harvesting fruits at ¾ th maturity.

Jhumka (Clustering)

Symptom

- Formation of a bunch of fruitlets at the tip of panicles.
- Turning of fruits to yellow.
- Adherence of fruits to panicle for longer period.
- Dark green much more curved fruitlets.

Causes

- Lack of adequate pollination and fertilization due to unfavourable weather conditions.
- Spray of insecticide like Monocrotophos during flowering hampering insect visit for pollination.
- Simultaneous vegetative and fruit growth leading to diversion of photosynthate to the vegetative part depriving fruits.

Control

- Spray of NAA 200-300 ppm during November.
- Minimized use of pesticides during full bloom.

Soft nose

Symptom

- Breakdown of the pulp on the ventral side and towards the apex.
- Overripe appearance of pulp on the ventral side towards the apex while the pulp around the shoulders and on the dorsal side is unripe.
- Tissues in affected fruits are greyish black and spongy.

Causes

- Allowing the fruits on the trees for longer time and ripening on tree. Fruits harvested at semi-ripe stage manifested lesser incidence of soft nose.
- High nitrogen level (especially in Kent mango).
- Improper level of calcium in plant

Control

- Care of causes constitutes control of the malady.

Taper tip

Symptom

- Intensification of normal green colour.
- Abrupt tapering and often curved appearance of fits.
- Smaller size fruits

It is very common in Dashehari

Control

- No control measure has been developed as yet.

Fruit pitting

Symptom

- Development of pits on fruit peel when fruit is of half grown size.
- The pits appear in almost equal portion on all sides of fruits.

Causes

- Deficiency of boron in soil.
- Dashehari variety is more susceptible

Control

- Spray 400-500 g borax/tree to the bearing trees

Jelly seed

Symptom

- Disintegration of pulp surrounding the stone into jelly like mass.
- Disintegration of entire pulp leading to development of internal cavity.
- Softening of the beak.

Control

- Highly susceptible variety Tomy Atkins

Girdle necrosis

Symptom

- Disfiguring of lower halves of the fruits and appearance of brown dotted etiolated area on the other half.

- Development of large necrotic lesion.
- Development of necrotic girdle of tissues around sinus region of the fruit leaving green lip healthy in the initial stage. In advance stage, tip also turns necrotic and it can't be easily differentiated from black tip.

Causes

- Fumes of brick kilns.

Control

- Similar to black tip.

BANANA

Kotta Vazhai (Seed banana)

Symptom

- The word 'kottai' means seed. There is conspicous development of enlarged ovules.
- Affected fruits remain dark green.

It is very serious disorder in Poovan variety.

Causes

- It is suspected to be associated with the incidence of banana streak virus.

Control

- Spraying of 2, 4-D @ 120 ppm.

Neer Vazhai (Water banana)

Symptom

- Neer means water and vazhai means banana. As the name indicates, the affected fruits exude watery fluid.
- Delayed shooting.
- Lanky bunches with few hands.
- Immature unfilled fingers.
- Poor growth.

This is very severe problem in Nendran and Poovan cultivars.

Causes

- Infected suckers transmits the malady.
- Virus or mycoplasma like organisms (MLOs) may be associated in causation.

Control

- Spray NAA.

Degrain

Symptom

- Drooping of ripe fruit from the bunch due to rotting of pedicel.

Control

- Avoid excessive application of nitrogenous fertilizers.

Yellow pulp

Symptom

- Abnormal and premature development of banana fruits.

Causes

- Excess potassium in relation to nitrogen and sulphur deficiency.

Control

- Application of sulphur.

Gooseflesh

Symptom

- Ripe fruits show wilted and shrivelled appearance.
- Peel turns brown.

This is very common during dry winter when atmospheric humidity falls to low level.

White leaf

Symptom

- Younger leaf show white discolouration.

Causes

- Unbalanced nitrogen content in soil and plant.

CITRUS

Frenching/Mottle leaf/Little leaf/Foliocellosis

Symptom

- Chlorosis between the veins.
- Greeniness of the area adjoining the mid-rib and lateral veins.

- Small pointed and narrow leaves in acute case.
- Bushy appearance of the plant.
- Rapid die-back.
- Death of the plant.

Causes

- It is due to zinc deficiency.

Control

- Spray 0.5 % zinc sulphate.

Granulation

It was reported by Bartholomew is 1934 from California. It is also known as corkiness crystallization, dry end, kaosarn, selerocystosis.

Symptom

- Juice sacs of fruit become tough, enlarged and turn greyish in colour.
- Thicker wall of juice sac.
- High pectin content in fruits.
- Excess Ca, Mg. Na and K is juice sacs.
- Decreased soluble carbohydrates and organic acid in juice sacs.
- Lignifications of juice sacs.
- Increase in rag and peel proportion.
- Higher proportion of rind with thick albedo.
- Less number of viable secd

Causes

- High relative humidity.
- High temperature during fruit development.
- Frequent irrigation.
- High vigour (luxuriant) of the plant.
- Large fruit size.
- Heavy crop load.
- High nitrogen supply.
- Use of vigorous rootstocks like Rough lemon, Karna Khatta, Trifoliate orange, Sour orange.
- Older tree which are pruned heavily and produce luxuriant growth.

- Heavy pruning.
- Any other treatment which favours luxuriant growth.

Sweet orange cultivar Hamlin and Musambi and mandarin cultivar Dancy tangerine are highly susceptible.

Control

- Less frequent irrigation.
- Controlled nitrogen fertilization.
- Spray of micronutrients Zn, Cu, K each at 0.25 % commencing from August till September during fruit development.
- Avoid use of vigorous rootstock.
- Early harvesting.

Blastomaenia

Symptom

- Sprouting of multiple buds in the axil of leaves in terminal portion of the plant.
- Witches broom like appearance of sprouts.
- Reduced leaf size forming a cluster like bouquet with chlorotic appearance and dropping of the malformed leaves eventually.

Causes

- New bud transmissible disorder.

Control

- Spraying oxytetracycline hypochloride (250 ppm) five times at weekly interval gives good success.

Creeping stem

Symptom

- Creeping habit of plants.
- Leaves and twigs remain tender green for a long time.
- Sterile branches.

It is a problem in acid lime and Sathgudi sweet orange.

Fruit cracking

Symptom

- Long, narrow, deep crack at the styler end of the fruits.
- Sometimes cracks originate between the ends.
- Growth of harmful fungi, bacteria and insect on affected fruits.

Causes

- Sudden rain or irrigation following prolonged drought.
- Fluctuating soil moisture level.
- Variation in temperature and relative humidity.
- High N content.
- Deficiency of Boron and Calcium.

Control

- Regular irrigation especially during summer months.
- Avoid excessive application of N.
- Spray NAA 100 ppm or GA_3, 100 ppm or Borax 0.8% during fruit growth.

Exanthema/Ammoniation/Dieback

- It is the major problem of citrus fruit.
- It is found the irregular fruit.

Causes

- Due to Cu deficiency.

GUAVA

Bronzing

Symptom

- Interveinal tissues of old leaves turn red to purplish red.
- Terminal one or two pair of leaves remain green.

Causes

- Deficiency of P. K. and Zn.

The incidence is severe during rainy season and mild during winter.

Control

- Follow good orchard management practices adopting balanced nutrition.
- Avoid condition of extreme water stress.
- Acidic condition of soil helps minimize the incidence.

Allahabad Safeda is comparatively free from disorder.

GRAPE

Barrenness of vine

Symptom

- Development of unproductive wood.
- Failure to bear normal crop.
- Reduced productive life of vine.

Causes

- Faulty training and pruning.
- Heading back to have developed healthy limbs.

Water berries

Symptom

- Lack of firmness in berry.
- Soft to feel when touched
- Dull colour, watery berry which shrivel and dry by the time of harvest

Causes

- Over cropping and inadequate nourishment.
- Frequent application of nitrogenous fertilizer and frequent watering leading to excessive shoot vigour and continued shoot growth.

Control

- Bunch and berry thinning.
- Cluster clipping.
- Limited watering and nitrogen application.
- Use of potash and oil cakes.
- Application of boric acid 0.2 %

Shot berry/Millerandage/Coulure

Symptom

- Development of some smaller berries in otherwise normal bunch.

Causes

- Poor pollination or fertilization.
- Poor carbohydrate nutrition.

- Boron deficiency.
- Improper application of GA

It is a major problem in varieties which bear compact bunches, such as Beauty Seedless and Perlette.

Control

- Pre-bloom application of GA_3.
- Avoidance of boron and zinc deficiencies.
- Berry thinning by the use of auxins.
- Dipping of bunches at berry set stage in the solution of ethephon 25 ppm.

Hen and chicken disorder

Symptom

- Presence of many small berries around a bold berry in a cluster. The bold berry is taken as indicative of hen and the small berry of chicken and hence the name.

Causes

- Impaired fertilization.
- Growth of many berries without embryo formation following the use of growth promoters.
- Deficiency of zinc and boron. In case of zinc deficiency berry size is reduced but the shape is as usual. Whereas, in case of boron deficiency the berry is spherical/oblate.

Control

- Spray zinc (0.5 %) and boron (0.3 %) following proper schedule before flowering.

Bud and Flower drop

- It is also known as Coulure or Shelling.

Symptom

- Excessive shedding of flower buds about 8-10 days before full bloom.
- Loose and straggly bunches.

Causes

- Moisture stress.
- Imbalanced C/N ratio in plant.

- High ABA and low auxins.

This is very severe in Beauty Seedless, Thompson Seedless, Early Muscat, Kishmish Beli, Cardinch, Gold and Himrod.

Control

- Prevent moisture stress.
- Spray NAA before anthesis.
- Timely spray of Zn and B.
- Proper canopy management.

Pink berry

Symptom

- Development of red streaks on the peel of the few berry.
- Development of pink berry in bunches during ripening before harvest.
- Turning of pink colour to dull red rendering the bunch unattractive.
- Watery berry.

Causes

- Large diurnal variation in temperature during berry ripening.
- Moisture stress.

This is very serious in Thompson Seedless and Tas-A-Ganesh varieties.

Control

- Avoid moisture stress.
- Application of adequate dose of potash.
- Cluster dipping in 10 ppm Benzyl adenine.

Uneven ripening

Symptom

- Green coloured unripened berry in otherwise ripened bunches.

Causes

- Inadequate leaf area.
- Non-availability of food reserve.

This is a problem is Bangalore Blue, Bangalore Purple, Beauty Seedless and Gulabi.

Control

- Cluster thinning.
- Stem girdling.
- Application of ethephon 250 ppm at colour break (veraison) stage.

LITCHI

Fruit cracking

Symptom

- Cracking of epicarp.
- Splitting of fruits

Causes

- Rains after prolonged drought.
- Sudden heavy irrigation.
- Fluctuation in soil temperature.
- Temperature above 38°C.
- Humidity lower than 60%.
- High N.
- Deficiency of B and Ca

Cultivars with thin skin, few tubercles/unit area and rounded to flat in shape are less prone to crack.

Control

- Regular irrigation.
- Spraying with either 200 ppm NAA, or 40 ppm GA, or 10 ppm 2, 4-D or 2,4, 5-T or Ethephon during fruit growth.
- Spray of 0.8 % borax or $ZnSO_4$ 1.5 % is equally effective.

AONLA

Fruit necrosis

Symptom

- Browning of innermost part of mesocarp at the time of endocarp hardening.
- It follows browning of epicarp.
- Development of black area on the fruit surface.
- Turning of mesocarp completely black, corky and development of gummy pockets on the fruit surface.

Causes

- Boron deficiency.

Francis variety is highly susceptible to the malady.

Control

- Spray 0.6 % Borax during September- October at 15 days interval.

PAPAYA

Freckles

Symptom

- Spotted appearance of ripe fruits.
- Young fruits of less than 40 days are free from this malady.

Causes

- Unknown.

Control

- Wrapping young fruits with white paper bag.

POMEGRANATE

Fruit cracking

Symptom

- Splitting of fruit at styler end. Sometimes, splitting originates between ends.

Causes

- Sudden rains.
- Heavy irrigation.
- Fluctuating soil moisture.
- Low humidity.
- High N.
- Deficiency of Boron and Calcium

Control

- Regular irrigation.
- Mulching during summer.
- Spray of NAA/GA_3 100 ppm/Borax 0.8 %

Internal Breakdown

Symptom

- Softness of aril.
- Turning of aril to light creamy brown to dark blackish brown.

Control

- Harvesting 130-135 days old fruit.

ANNONACEOUS FRUITS

Stone fruits

Symptom

- Fruits turn brown and become hard.
- Ceased further growth.
- Retainment of hard fruits on trees.

Causes

- Entering of tree into dormancy during winter well in advance before harvesting all fruits.
- Moisture and nutrient stress.

Control

- Proper application of manures and fertilizers.
- Timely irrigation.
- Proper upkeep of plants favouring flowering well in time and consequently proper ripening.

Woodiness

Symptom

- Presence of woody seed pockets.
- Presence of gritty lumps in pulp.
- Brown discoloration of pulp.

Control

- Use of dwarfing inter stock of *Annona squamosa* or dwarfing rootstock of *A. Cherimola.*
- Maintaining proper level of calcium in plants.

Sun-burn

Symptom

- It is observed in young trees.
- The affected parts crack and the bark peels off.

Causes

- Heavy pruning and exposure of branches to sunlight.

Control

- White washing of exposed part.
- Management of canopy.

LOQUAT

Shihan-sho/Purple spot

Symptom

- Fruits turn reddish brown.
- Mizuho Oobusa, Satomi and Nojimawase have high incidence.

Control

- Use of gray paper bag, black inside with a low light transmittance reduces incidence.

Macadamia decline

Symptom

- Leaves are bronzed necrotic and abscise.
- Terminal clump of young, small and deformed leaves on branches which fall later on.

Causes

- High demand of carbohydrate by developing fruitlet.
- Imbalanced allocation of nutrients.
- Starved root for carbohydrate and consequently starvation of leaves for water and nutrients required to maintain photosynthesis.

Control

- Restoration of adequate supply of carbohydrate to root system. In this regard, maintaining orchard in healthy growing condition is useful.

MANGOSTEEN

Gamboge

Symptom

- Exudation of yellow gum from the fruits and branches.
- Fruits turns white.
- Pulp turns yellow.
- Emission of unpleasant flavour from fruits.

Causes

- Fruits exposed to direct sunlight.
- Summer maturity of fruits.
- Heavy and continuous rains at the time of fruit ripening.

Control

- Covering of fruits to avoid direct contact of sunlight.

PINEAPPLE

Fasciation/Multiple crown

Symptom

- Appearance of multiple crowns as against usual single crown.
- Flat and broad top of fruits.
- Corky and insipid fruit.

Causes

- Higher vigour of the plant.
- High fertility of the soil and warm weather favourng vigorous vegetative growth.
- Advance ratoon crop.

It is more pronounced in Cayenne group of cultivars.

Control

- Restriction of growth by selecting proper soil type.
- Avoidance of ratoon crop

Sunscald

Symptom

- Damaged peel of the exposed surface of the fruit.

Causes

- Leaning or falling of peduncle bearing the fruit one side exposing the fruit to direct sunlight.
- Wide space planting.

Control

- Fruit covering with straw or banana leaves or its own leaves during April-May.
- High density planting.

Black heart

- It is also known as internal browning.

Symptom

- Development of brown translucent spots at the base of fruit close to the core.
- Black discoloration of entire centre of fruits.

Causes

- Low temperature and exogenous application of GA.

Translucent flesh

Symptom

- Senescence of fruit pulp thereby turning the fruit transparent.
- High pH, TSS: acid ratio and weight of fruits.
- Lower acids.

Causes

- Preceding three months before harvest lower maximum temperature (23°C) and lower minimum temperature (15°C).
- Fruits with small crown.

COCONUT

Barren nuts

Symptom

- Nut without developed kernel.
- Oblong shape nut.
- Less husk.

- Embryo absent, if present, embryo is in stage of decay.
- Cracking of shell.

Causes

- Poor pollination.
- Poor fertilization.
- Deficiency of K and B

Control

- Proper application of K and B nutrients.

Crown choking

Symptom

- Shorter and crinkled leaves.
- Tip necrosis of leaflets.
- Leaves fail to unfurl.
- Choking of frond.

Causes

- Boron (B) deficiency

Control

- Soil application of Borax@50 g/plant during February-March and September-October.

APPLE

Bitter pit

Symptom

- Development of small, brown, dry pockets usually spherical in shape below peel and also in cortex.
- The spots are confined more towards the calyx end.
- The peel becomes corky.

Causes

- Deficiency of calcium (Ca).
- Heavy dose of nitrogen.
- Irregular water supply.
- Excessive fruit shedding.
- Heavy pruning.

Control

- Spray of 0.5 % calcium chloride after flowering until harvesting.

Water core

Symptom

- Water soaked area in the pulp.
- Dull peel of fruit.
- Spongy appearance of fruit.

Causes

- Excessive level of Boron.
- Delayed harvesting.

Cultivars like Delicious, Jonathan, Cox's Orange Pippin, Bramley's Seedling. Worcestor etc. are susceptible to water core.

Control

- Maintain proper level of boron.

Brown core

It is also known as core browning or core fresh.

Symptom

- Turning of fruit pulp near the core brown.
- Slight discoloration of pulp between the seed cavities.

Causes

- Storage of fruits at -1^0 to 2^{0}C.
- Increase in level of fruit potassium.

Control

- Storage of fruits at proper temperature.

Jonathan spot

Symptom

- Appearance of dark brown, black depression on the fruit.

Causes

- High level of boron forcing early maturation and consequently increased incidence of Jonathan spot.

It is common in Jonathan cultivar of apple.

Control

- Spraying of calcium chloride 0.5-0.7 % 2-6 weeks before harvest.

Cork spot

- Development of small blushed area on the fruit peel above the brown spot anywhere in the cortex between peel and core.
- Higher proportion of spots in pulp.
- Appearance of spots earlier than biter pit in growing season.

Control

- Spraying of calcium chloride 0.05%.

Scald

Symptom

- Browning of epidermal and hypodermal cells of the fruit.

Causes

- Oxidation of α-farnesene formed in the waxy coating of the fruit.
- Early picking of fruits which contain higher level of α-farnesene.

Control

- Application of anti-oxidant products like ethoxyquin and disphenylamine, use of diphenylamine 2000 ppm and $CaCl_2$ (2-3 %) two weeks before harvest is very effective.

Endoxerosis/June drop

- It is also found in apple fruit.
- It is found in drought areas.

Causes

- Due to water difficiency

Control

- Application of irrigation as per requirement.

PEAR

Hard end

Symptom

- Hardening and blackening of fruits approaching maturity over the blossom end

Causes

- Use of oriental rootstock (*Pyrus serotina*) for raising plant.
- Unfavourable water relationship between the fruits and other plant parts.

Control

- Use of European pear as rootstock.

Pink calyx

Symptom

- Development of pink coloration near the blossom end of the fruit.
- Occurrence of core breakdown and softening.
- Failure of fruits to ripe.

Causes

- Abnormal growing season before harvest.
- Night temperature lower than 7.1°C and day temperature lower than 21°C for few days are inductive to disorder.

PEACH

Sun scald

Symptom

- Scaling and peeling off the bark.

Causes

- Exposed trunk and scaffold branches.

Control

- Shading of the branches by wrapping straw or hay.
- Painting of exposed surface with lime paste.

Split pit

Symptom

- Splitting at the joint of dorsal and ventral sides of the fruit.

Causes

- Condition favouring development of larger fruits.
- Heavy rain after a long dry period.

Control

- Normal growing and maintenance of garden.

Gumming

Symptom

- Exudation of gum from fruits.
- Filling of entire pit cavity surrounding the kernel with gum.

Causes

- Seed abortion.
- Heavy rain after a long dry period.

CHERRY

Fruit cracking

Symptom

- Cracks on the surface of fruits.

Causes

- Sudden rain or heavy irrigation followed by drought.
- Fluctuating soil moisture level.
- High temperature.
- Less humidity.
- High N level.
- Deficiency of Boron (B) and Calcium (Ca).

Control

- Follow regular irrigation.
- Use proper dose of N.
- Spray 100-120 ppm GA_3.
- Spray 0.8% Borax

STRAWBERRY

Albinism

Symptom

- Development of white or pink area on the surface of fruits.
- Pale colour of pulp.

- Lack of uniform ripening of fruits.
- Poor flavour and more acidic fruits,
- Waxy appearance of fruits.
- Susceptibility of fruits to fruit rot during storage.

Causes

- Dense planting.
- Excessive fertilizer application.
- Growing of crop in sandy, low pH soils and soils with high N, P and K.
- Growing of crops in tunnels with hampered ventilation.
- Use of black film mulch as against white film. The black film mulch raises the incidence probably due to high N mineralization which generates higher temperature.

Elsanta is worst affected variety by albinism.

Control

- Avoid dense planting and also excessive application of fertilizers especially N, K.
- Avoid use of hay or paddy straw as mulch material.

Malformation

Symptom

- Undeveloped achenes at the distal end of receptacle.
- Malformed fruits.
- Changed shape of berries.

Causes

- High N level.
- Insufficient pollination.
- Lack of growth promoting substance.
- Planting of more vigorous plants.

Control

- Arranging bee hives for proper pollination.
- Planting of young and less vigorous plants.
- Avoidance of excessive use of nitrogenous fertilizer.

Fasciation

Symptom

- Abnormal flattening of fruit bearing stem and fruit.
- Witch's broom appearance of the plants.
- Failure of plants to produce runners.
- Broadening of flower buds.
- Barrenness of the plants.

Causes

- Unfavourable growth condition especially to short day unfavourable for normal development of fruit.

Control

- Proper management of plantation.
- Provision of suitable pollinator.

RASPBERRY

White drupelets

Symptom

- White coloured fruits.

Causes

- Exposure of fruits to higher temperature. Temperature higher than 42^{0}C for 4 or more hours of ultraviolet radiation.

Control

- Covering of fruit with suitable covering either of white polyester or black fabric at least one to three week before harvesting.

KIWI FRUIT

Sun scorch

Symptom

- Development of sunken, brown, leathery scar on surface of fruit exposed to sun.
- Insipid fruits.

Causes

- High solar radiation.

Control

- Thatching of the branches with hay, paddy straw or dry grasses.

Flats

Symptom

- Development of flattened fruit.

Causes

- Improper pollination.

Control

- Hand pollination.
- Arrangement of bee hive in garden to effectivate pollination.

Water strain

Symptom

- Occurrence of dark strains down the side on the fruits.

Causes

- Deposition of tannin which leach out from the dead tissue of the fruit by rainfall.

Control

- Removal of dead tissue from the plant.
- Removal of blemishes from fruits using mild solution of citric acid.

PERSIMMON

Calyx cavity

Symptom

- Development of cavity beneath the calyx of the fruits.
- Growth of bugs and fungus in the cavity.

Causes

- Trees producing heavy crop load.
- Resorting cross pollination in orchard.
- Heavy rainfall during autumn.
- Deep, fertile and poorly drained soil.

Control

- Avoid excessive application of N and K.
- Fruit thinning to avoid heavy crop load.
- Ensuring proper pollination.

Sujika

Symptom

- Appearance of white lines on rind.

Causes

- The malady is common in low yielding tree.

PECAN NUT

Mouse ear

Symptom

- Shortening of the mid-vein of the leaflets.
- Round and wrinkled leaflet turning alike cap.
- Smaller leaflet.

Causes

- Deficiency of manganese.

Control

- Avoid manganese deficiency in the soil.

Rosette

Symptom

- Bronzing and crinkling of leaflets.
- Bunching of leaflets.
- Die-back of twigs.

Causes

- Zinc deficiency.

Control

- Spray 0.5 % zinc sulphate.

OTHER FRUITS

AVOCADO

Grey pulp

- Moisture content of pulp down to 75 %.
- It is prevalent in fruits grown in warmer areas.

Pulp spot

- Black discoloration of vascular bundles at cut ends of the fruit stalk.

Tip burn

- Necrosis of the tips and margin of leaves.
- Falling off of leaves.
- Chloride toxicity is responsible for the malady.
- Deep ploughing, incorporation of organic matter to the soil and irrigating the orchard is helpful in controlling the malady.

Post Harvest Disorders

Such disorders are encountered due to adverse pre-harvest or post-harvest environment especially temperature or to a nutritional deficiency during growth and development. Some important post harvest disorders accounted to low temperature has been discussed.

Apple

- Superficial scald-Sunken skin discoloration.
- Sunburn scald-Brown to black colour on area facing sun side.
- Senescent breakdown-Brown mealy flesh accounted to over-mature and overstored fruits.
- Low temperature breakdown-Browning of cortex.
- Soft scald- Soft, Sunken, Brown to black, sharply defined areas on the surface and extending a short distance into flesh.
- Jonathan spot-Superficial spotting of lenticelles. It occurs at higher temperature.
- Brown core-Browning along core line.
- Water core-Translucent areas in flesh.
- Brown heart-Brown area in flesh, cavity in flesh.

Pear

- Core breakdown-Brown, mushy core in overstored fruit.
- Neck breakdown, vascular break down-Brown to black discoloration of vascular tissue connecting stem to core.
- Superficial scald-Grey to brown epicarp speckles. It occurs early in storage.

Grape

Storage scald-Brown skin discoloration of white grape variety

Citrus

- Storage spot-Brown sunken spot on surface.
- Cold scald-Superficial grey to brown pitches.
- Flavocellosis- Bleaching of rind.
- Stem end browning- Browning of shrivelled areas around stem end,

Peach

- Wooliness- Red to brown, Dry areas in flesh.

Plum

- Cold storage- Brown, Gelatinous areas on epicarp and flesh breakdown.

VEGETABLES

TOMATO

Blossom end rot

- Discoloration on the blossom end of fruit.
- Development of black spot over one-half to two-third portion of the fruit.
- Dark grey to black discoloration of epidermis of fruits.

Causes

- Use of ammonium sulphate as a source of nitrogen supply.
- Imbalance of magnesium and potassium.
- Deficiency of calcium in the blossom end portion.

Control

- Spray of 0.5% calcium chloride at fruit development.

Cracking

- Fruit cracks.
- Furrows like appearance on fruits.
- It is radial or concentric in nature.

Causes

- Rain following a long dry spell.
- Reduced transpiration increasing cell turgidity.
- Boron deficiency in soil.

Control

- Growing of resistant variety like Sioux, Manalucie, Punjab Chhuhara.
- Soil application of borax 10 18 kg/ha or spray @023 per cent at the fruiting stage.
- Maintenance of proper moisture.

Puffiness

- Unfilled locular jelly of fruit.
- Light weight fruits.
- Lack of fruit firmness.

Causes

- Non-fertilization of ovules.
- Necrosis of vascular and placental tissues.
- High or low temperature.

Control

- Care of factors of causation.

Catface

- Distortion of the blossom end of fruit.
- Appearance of ridges, furrows and indentation on the fruit.

Causes

- Improper pollination.

Blotchy ripening

- Greenish yellow and whitish patches on the ripe fruits in stem end portion

Causes

- Imbalance of nitrogen and potash in soil.

Control

- Balanced application of nitrogen and potash containing fertilizers.

CARROT

Carrot splitting

- Splitting of roots.

Causes

- Heavy rainfall after a period of drought.
- High nitrogen.

Control

- Application of balanced quantity of nitrogen.
- Proper irrigation.

Cavity spot

- Formation of hollow root.

Causes

- Deficiency of calcium.
- Excess of potassium.

Control

- Control of factor of causation.

Forking

- See under radish.

RADISH

Forking

- Appearance of branched roots.
- Reduced length of roots.

Causes

- Cloddy field.

Control

- Proper soil preparation.
- Fine tilth of soil.

Akashin

- It is found in radish.

Causes

- Due to Boron diffieciency.

Control

- Use of borax

CAULIFLOWER

Buttoning

- Development of small curds.
- Inadequate foliage.
- Small leaves enable to cover curd.

Causes

- Transplanting more than six weeks old seedlings leading to poor development of roots.

Control

- Timely transplanting of seedlings.
- Avoidance of overcrowding in the field.

Blindness

- Plant without terminal buds.
- Collapse of growing point.
- No curd formation.
- Development of thick, leathery, large and dark green leaves.

Causes

- Low temperature.
- Damage to growing point.
- Injury by insect-pests.

Browning

- Dark green and brittle young leaves.
- Puckered and chlorotic old leaves.
- Development of water soaked, light to dark brown spots on the stem.
- Formation of cavity and hollowness of the stem.
- Irregular water soaked spots on the curd.
- Small curd with bitter taste.

Causes

- Deficiency of boron.
- Decreased availability of boron at neutral soil pH.

Control

- Application of borax/sodium borate/sodium tetraborate @ 20 kg/ha.
- Spray of 0.25 to 0.50 per cent solution of borax.

Riceyness

- Appearance of loose, granular curd.
- Elongation of peduncle-stalk bearing flowers.

Causes

- Heavy dose of nitrogen.
- High relative humidity.
- Temperature above or below optimum.

Control

- Follow up of recommended package of practices.
- Cultivation of genetically pure seeds.

Leafiness

- Development of small, thin green leaves in between curd segments

Causes

- Prevalence of high temperature.

Control

- Selection of proper variety

Whiptail

- Un-developed leaf blade.
- Large bare midrib of leaves.
- Ruffled and distorted leaves.

Causes

- Deficiency of molybdenum.
- Acidic pH of soil having high manganese concentration hindering uptake of molybdenum.

Control

- Application of lime to correct acidic pH of soil.
- Use of sodium or ammonium molybdate @ 1-2 kg./ha as soil application.

Calcium deficiency is responsible for many disorders in many fruits and vegetables. These a summarized as under:

- Apple-Bitter pit, cork spot, cracking, low temperature breakdown, internal breakdown, water core, jonathan spot
- Avocado-End spot
- Bean-Hypocotyl necrosis
- Cabbage-Internal tipburn
- Carrot-Cavity spot, cracking
- Celery-Black heart, cracking
- Chickory-Black heart, tip burn
- Lettuce-Tipburn
- Mango-Soft nose
- Pear-Conespot
- Pepper-Blossom-end rot
- Potato-Tipburn, sprout failure
- Strawberry-Leaf tipburn
- Tomato-Blossom-end rot, blackseed, cracking
- Watermelon-Blossom-end rot

FLOWERS

Bent neck

Symptom

- Bending of floral stalk below bud is reffered to as bent neck. It is observed when flowers are placed in vase after cutting from mother stalk.

Control

- Addition of two much sugar in vase solution.

Control

- Use of proper concentration of sugar in rose solution. Usually sucrose 0.5-3.0% concentration is used in vase solution.

CARNATION

Calyx splitting

Symptom

- Stretching of calyx exposing corolla.
- Improper opening of flower.
- Disproportionate shape and ruined appeal.

Control

- Use of rubber band at the point of maximum diameter of the flower. The band should be placed when flowers have started opening. It shouldn't be applied when the buds are too small, otherwise, it results in misshaped buds.

TULIP

Stem topple

Symptom

- Development of water soaked spots on the upper half of the flower stalk or on the lower part of the stalk near the neck of the bulb.
- Shrivelling and collapsing of flower stalk.

Causes

- Calcium deficiency.
- Insufficient ripening of bulb after wet and cool summer weather.
- Excessive high temperature during forcing.
- Improper air circulation.

Control

- Avoid forcing under high temperature and moisture condition.
- Application of 0.05 % calcium nitrate with irrigation water.
- Lowering of greenhouse temperature.

Lily

Leaf burn

symptom

- Burning of leaf or leaf tip.

Causes

- Collapse of palisade cells under the epidermis of leaf.
- High relative humidity.

Control

- Spray of 0.05 % calcium nitrate.

FREESIA

Thumbing

Symptom

- Separation of the lowest two or three florets of the inflorescence.

Causes

- Wide gap in florets.
- Flower inducing temperature exceeding 15°C.

Control

- Maintain proper flower induction temperature.

SPICES

FENNEL

Gummosis

Symptom

- Oozing of gum from inflorescence.
- Shrinking and drying of inflorescence.

Causes

- Not yet known.

Control

- Use of disease free healthy seeds.
- Adoption of long duration crop rotation.

Chapter 19

Vegetable Nursery Management

Seedlings of several vegetables are first raised in well prepared nursery beds, followed by transplanting in the field. Raising of seedling in the nursery beds is economical as well as easier to take care of young, tender seedlings against pest and diseases. Further, raising of seedlings in nursery allow more time for land preparation.

Site and soil for nursery

In selecting a site for nursery beds, following points should be considered viz sunny situation, good drainage and irrigation facilities. Sandy loam soil with plenty of organic matter are ideal for starting nursery beds. In case of heavy soils it is desirable to add coarse sand to modify the soil condition. Before sowing seed it is essential to sterlize the beds by steam or formaldehyde or any other chemical to do away with problem of damping-off disease. Burning of leaves or straw in the beds is quite helpful in controlling certain soil borne diseases and pests.

Preparation of beds

Beds of 100-120 cm wide and 3-4 metre in length and 8-10 cm high are ideal. It is desirable to allow 20-30cm space between two beds. Apply 5-6 kg FYM, 200-250 g superphosphate and 200-250 g muriate of potash per square metre of the bed. Manures and fertilizers should be spreaded uniformly in the beds and mixed. If beds are dry, irrigation of the beds helps in proper decomposition of manures and fertilizers. Seed should be sown 5-7 days after the application of manures and fertilizers in the beds. At same time the beds should be treated against soil borne diseases also.

Seed treatment against seed borne diseases

Before sowing the seed in the field or in the nursery it is essential to treat the seed against seed- borne diseases. For seed treatment either hot water treatment or with chemical *viz.,* Thiram or Bavistin or Trichoderma can be tried. Dry-dressing method is easy to adopt. In this method the seed is first moistured (not wet) with clean water, followed by spreading the seed evenly on a news paper or white polythene sheet. The chemical is dusted with a duster evenly on the seed. Ensure that the wet seeds have a coating of chemical on them. If necessary mix the chemical with hand. Keep the treated seed in a cool dry place for 20-30 minute for drying. The thoroughly dried seed should be used for seeding.

Seed treatment for hastening germination

The delayed germination of seed may be due to hard seed coat or due to presence of inhibitors or due to dormancy. Growth regulators have been reported to be very effective to overcome such problems. Auxin IBA, NAA, Kinetin and potassium nitrate are reported effective in promotion of germination. Whereas gibberellin and ethylene (chloroethyl phosponic acid) are quite effective in promotion of germination in dorment kind of seeds. The rate of application depends on the kind of seed and duration of treatment. Gibberellic acid are used at the rate of 200-500 ppm. Where auxin are used 500-1000 ppm.

For hastening earlier and uniform germination the chemical, viz., Naphthalene, acetic acid, Indole butyric acid or potassium nitrate or thiourea are used. The rate of chemical will depend upon kind of seed and duration. The gibberellic acid are used at 5-200 ppm, NAA 100-250 ppm, nitrate 1000-5000 ppm per pot. The treatment duration varies from 20-30 minute.

For hastening germination the seed beds needs be covered with 300-400 gauge polythene which will promote earlier and better germination. On small scale or for fine seeds, the use of planting plug or plastic cup require, better care of seed and germinating seedlings.

Treatment of seed beds (soil treatment)

Before sowing seed in the prepared beds, it is essential to sterilize the beds to do away with problem of seed-borne diseases. For sterilization the simplest method, is to spread a 2-4 cm. thick layer of dry leaves on the beds, followed by burning of the leaves. The other method is to cover the nursery area with black polythene of 250-300 gauges. The edges of the polythene sheet should be pressed into the soil to minimize the air-circulation. Keep the beds in this condition for a period of 10-15 days. Ensure that beds remain covered and moist. The nursery beds should be sprayed with 0.1-0.2% solution of bavistin or with 1.0-1.5% of *trichoderma viridi.* The treated beds can be used after 3-4 days after the treatment.

Seed sowing

In the prepared beds the seed should be sown by opening a 2.0-4.0 cm deep miniature furrows. It is desirable to allow 8-12 cm space between two rows. After sowing seed the furrow should be covered with leaf-mould or coarse sand or with a mixture of leaf-mould and sand (2:1). Beds be irrigated by using sprinkler. Avoid over irrigation. It is desirable to cover the seed bed with polythene or straw. As soon as the seedling starts germinating the covering material should be removed. In order to protect the tender seedlings against strong sun rays or rains the bed to be covered with a thatch prepared with straw leaves and placed about a metre above from the bed surface.

After care

If young seedligns be irrigated with 0.5% urea or 1.0% CAN solution at an interval of 20-25 days during the early stage of seedlings will accelerates their growth. Bavistin or Calxin at 0.1% alone or mixed with CAN or urea spray will, helps in overcoming the problem of damping-off disease. One or two application of Rogor or Malathion at 0.01% is effective to prevent attack of pests. The weeds should be removed as and when they appear.

Hardening

Prior to lifting the seedlings from nursery for transplanting, it is desirable to "harden" the seedlings. "Hardened" seedlings accumulate carbohydrate and thus are able to withstand transplanting shock and adverse environmental conditions. Hardening can be accomplished by withholding irrigation for couple of days.

Transplanting

Too old or too young seedlings both are unsuitable for transplanting in the field. Seedlings having 4-6 true leaves or 10-15cm tall are ideal for transplanting. Seedling can be transplanted bare-rooted or with a soil ball containing roots. Bare rooted seedlings undergo root-damage and transplanting shock, both check the growth. Seedling, with soil around the roots need be pressed after transplating. Use of "starter solutions" containing nitrogen, phosphorus, potassium or growth-regulators after transplanting will proves beneficial in establishment of the seedling in the field. Early establishment of seedlings in the field results in healtheir growth and higher production.

Chapter 20

Seed and Dormancy

Seed

A seed is a mature ovule consisting of an embryo together with stored food, all enclosed by a protective coat. It is product of the ripened ovule of gymnosperm and angiosperm plants which results as a consequence of fertilization and some growth within the mother plant [illegible] reproduction. The embryo develops from [illegible] integument of ovule. A seed has three parts [illegible] and embryo. Embryo includes [illegible] Seed is located [illegible] plant part which is used for [illegible] Thus in case of potato stem and tuber are [illegible] results in (1) Better germination (2) Vigorous [illegible] stand (4) Better quality of produce (5) [illegible]

Development of seed: Successful [illegible] prerequisites to produce a viable seed [illegible] transferred from anther to the stigma [illegible] secreted by the stigma. The fluid [illegible] pollen grains. The pollen tube grows downwards [illegible] until it reaches the embryo sac and discharges [illegible] with a female gamete and forms the zygote [illegible] polar nuclei to produce endosperm (3n) [illegible] embryo embedded in nutritive tissue develop [illegible] tissues surrounding these structures provide [illegible] development. Like fruit, the seed also exhibits [illegible] sigmoid pattern of growth. Various changes [illegible] development and the sequences of development [illegible] keeping the basic theme unaltered.

Seed production: Seed production [illegible] and should be taken up only in a [illegible] breeder's seed is used to produce foundation [illegible] to produce certified seed. The seeds [illegible]

Chapter 20

Seed and Dormancy

Seed

A seed is a mature ovule consisting of an embryo together with stored food, all enclosed by a protective coat. It is product of the ripened ovule of gymnosperm and angiosperm plants which results as a consequence of fertilization and some growth within the mother plant formation of seed completes the cycle of reproduction. The embryo develops from zygote and the seed coat from the integument of ovule. A seed has three main parts these are seed coat, endosperm and embryo. Embryo includes the root, the cotyledon and embryonic leaves. Seed is located inside fruit and a fruit is a mature ovary. In broad sense any plant part which is used for commercial multiplication of crop is called seed. Thus in case of potato stem and tuber are also known as seed. Improved seed results in (1) Better germination (2) Vigorous seedling growth (3) Higher crop stand (4) Better quality of produce (5) Ultimately in higher crop yield.

Development of seeds: Successful pollination and fertilization are the prerequisites to produce a viable seed. During pollination the pollen grains are transferred from anther to the stigma and get stuck there in the sticky fluid secreted by the stigma. The fluid contains sugar which induces germination of pollen grains. The pollen tube grows downward through the style in the ovary until it reaches the embryo sac and discharges two male gametes-one is fused with a female gamete and forms the zygote (2n) and the other is united with two pollar nuclei to produce endosperm (3n). The zygote develops and gives rise to embryo embedded in nutritive tissue developed from endosperm. The nucellus tissues surrounding these structures provide necessary energy for their proper development. Like fruit, the seed also exhibits sigmoid and sometimes double sigmoid pattern of growth. Various changes occur during the course of seed development and the sequences of development may vary from species to species keeping the basic theme unaltered.

Seed production: Seed production of any variety is a highly specialized technique and should be taken up only in a propitious agro-climatic condition. In general, breeder's seed is used to produce foundation seed and foundation seed is used to produce certified seed. The seeds man should have working knowledge of the nature of growth of the plant, its genetically makeup, mode of pollination an susceptibility to various pests and diseases. The seed plot should be located in a place with abundant sunshine. The recommended agronomic package and practices in respect of seed treatment, seed rate, fertilizer dose, irrigation, weeding and plant protection measures must be followed to obtain a healthy crop. The proper isolation distance from plot to plot should be maintained depending on the mode of pollination to avoid natural cross pollination. This distance depends on the direction of insect flight, if the varieties are insect pollinated, or the direction of the prevailing wind, if the varieties are wind pollinated. The seeds are harvested from the mother plant when they are mature and contain moisture ranging from 15 to 17 per cent. Delay is harvesting may reduce the quality of seed which is of prime importance. Proper care should be taken during mechanical manipulation (i.e., processing and drying) of seeds to prevent from damage and varietal admixture. Storage of seed is an important aspects, which needs proper attention, to maintain viability.

Dormancy

Seeds of some species and varieties do not germinate immediately after maturation and extraction from the fruit. The mechanism controlling germination process is known as dormancy. The control of onset of growth of seeds is governed by external factors (temperature, moisture etc.) as well as internal factors associated with seed (physical, mechanical and chemical barriers). A seed is called dormant when it consists of an alive embryo but fails to germinate even under congenial environment.

Rest period: Sometimes the internal physiological conditions of a seed inhibit the process of germination even if it is placed in most conducive atmosphere. Seeds of this category require some biochemical and physiological changes after harvesting leading to the initiation of new growth. This phenomenon is known as rest period

Germination of seed: Seed germination refers to the resumption of metabolic activity and growth of an embryo, resulting in the rupture of seed coat and emergence of plantlets. The prerequisites for germination process are (i) seed must be viable, (ii) it must be nondormant and the embryo is quiscent, and (iii) the seed must be placed in conducive atmospheric conditions (light, temperature, moisture, oxygen) which vary from species to species. A series of changes pertaining to morphological, biochemical and physiological conditions, take place within the seed during the process of germination, including (i) Seed hydration, (ii) Increased respiration, (iii) Enzyme turnover, (iv) Increase in adenosine phosphate, (v) Increase in nucleic acid, (vi) Digestion of stored foods and transport of the soluble products to the embryo where cellular components are synthesized,

(vii) Increase in cell division and enlargement, and (viii) Differentiation of cells into tissue an organs. The growth of embryo is the resultant effect of rapid increase in cell division and cell elongation which occur simultaneously. The sustained demand of the embryo for energy is met from the reserved food materials until the leaves are fully expanded and become active for photosynthesis and roots are developed to absorb moisture and nutrients from the soil. As the embryo resumes growth, the radicle and plumule emerge out respectively from the base and apex of the embryo axis. This constitutes the over ground framework of the plant.

Factors Affecting Germination of Seed

1. External Factors

i. **Water:** Seed becomes physiologically active and resumes germination only after hydration. The initial phase of water absorption is colloidal, while the osmotic forces are predominant in the later phase of hydration. The germination percentage and germination rate vary with the amount of water absorbed by the seeds. The water requirement of seed for resumption of growth was relatively small, amounting to not more than 2 to 3 times the weight of the seed. Seeds absorb moisture from the seedbed, therefore, decrease in level of moisture supply or presence of excess soluble salts may drastically reduce the germination rate, Temperature plays a major role in inhibition of moisture by the seeds. In general, higher the temperature, upto certain limit, greater is the moisture absorption.

ii. **Temperature:** Temperature requirement for germination of seeds vary from species to species. In general, the optimum temperature for seed germination of temperate crops is lower than that of tropical crops. The optimum temperature for seeds of non-dormant plants ranges between 25°C to 30°C. High temperature accelerates the germination rate, upto certain limit, while it declines with the fall in temperature. However, seeds of many species exhibit same degrees of germination over a wide range of temperature. Temperature not only affects the germination process but regulates the subsequent growth of seedling.

iii. **Oxygen:** Seed is a living body and for sustaining its life, proper respiration has to be ensured. The oxygen demand increases rapidly during the early phase of seed germination. To obtain rapid and uniform germination of seed, supply of adequate oxygen is a must, failing which the seed, may decay. Rate of oxygen intake is an indicator of germination process and proportional to the amount of metabolic activity. The requirement of oxygen for germination varies among seeds of different species.

iv. **Light**: Seed germination of some species is affected by light while many are insensitive to light. Depending on the responsiveness to light, seeds can be grouped into two: (i) Positively photoblastic i.e. the germination process is accelerated in presence of light e.g. strawberry, blueberry etc. (ii) Negatively photoblastic i.e. the germination is retarded or prevented by light (eg. Nigelia, Allium, Amaranthus, Phlox). However, some workers identify some seeds which are neutral to light reaction.

The germination responses to light is controlled by a photo-chemically reactive pigment called phytochrome present in plants. Which is a light receptive protein pigment complex. Germination of seed is augmented by red light (660 n/u to 730 n/u), whereas, the far-red (720 to 800 n/u) light inhibits it. It is a reversible photoreaction and can be repeated indefinitely. If the inhibited seeds are exposed to red and far-red light alternatively, the ultimate effect depends on the last exposure. The stimulating influence of red light to germination is nullified if it is followed by far red light. On the contrary, if far-red is followed by red light, germination process is accelerated. The exposure of photoblastic seeds to red light causes perceptible increase in metabolic activity and mitosis in embryos, while they are inhibited by far-red light. Temperature and period of water absorption play major role in regulating the red-light requirement for germination.

The red light, gibberellic acid, cytokinin, ethylene, moderate low temperature (less than 20°C) are denoted as germination promoting agents, and far-red light, abscisic acid, moisture stress and high temperature as germination inhibiting agents.

2. Internal Factors

The germination process of seed is also influenced greatly by a number of factors resident to seed itself which are described below:

i. **Seed coat:** The seed coats of some species (mainly leguminous plants) are impermeable to water due to presence of a layer of palisade like macrosclereid cells and coating with a cuticle layer. The non-dormant embryo is incapable of developing and emerging out from the seed because of moisture stress condition even though sufficient moisture may be present in the soil.

   Seed coats of some species (walnut, stone fruit etc.) are so hard that the tender embryos fail to rupture them and develop subsequently.

ii. **Rest period**: Post extraction rest period, as stated earlier, is seen to be prerequisite for seed germination of some fruit plants (i.e. Fig).

   In some cases, the high concentration of phenolic compounds and abscisic acid strongly inhibit the quick germination of seeds leading to a reasonable duration of rest period.

Means to improve germination

The ability of seeds to germinate and to produce acceptable seedlings, which is commonly known as viability depends on a number of factors such as pre-harvesting ambient environmental condition, proper handling during post extraction period, environmental condition of the storage etc. Even if all the conditions are satisfactory, some seeds require special treatments for quicker and better germination. The treatments which are commonly used are described below.

1. **Soaking in water**: Soaking of seeds in water promotes germination by softening the hard seed coat, activating the enzymes and diluting the effects of inhibitors. Duration of soaking varies from overnight to 3 or 4 days depending on the nature of seed coat. Hot water treatment has been found to be very useful in breaking the seed dormancy. In this method seeds are placed in hot water. The seed are then allowed to soak the water for 12 to 24 hours and sown immediately after the treatment. Care has to be taken so that the embryos are not damaged.
2. **Scarification**: Scarification is the process of injuring the hard seed coat by any means to accelerate the water absorption and to improve the gaseous exchange for hastening the process of germination. This can be achieved by (a) Mechanical scarification or (b) Acid scarification. In mechanical scarification the surface of the seed is scratched or injured by rubbing against rough surface or sand paper. The extent of scarification depends on the species. In acid scarification the seeds are dipped in concentrated sulphuric acid for varying duration from 10 minutes to 3 hours depending the hardness of the seed coat. Seeds are then washed thoroughly in water to remove the traces of acid.
3. **Stratification:** Exposing the seeds to low temperature (0 to 5°C) for a considerable period helps in accelerating the process after ripening and breaking of dormancy resulting into stimulation of the germination. This cold treatment is known as stratification. Seeds are placed in wooden box containing moist sand and kept in low temperature a little above the freezing point. The duration varies with species from one month to six months.
4. **Chemical treatment**: Various chemicals viz, gibberellic acid (200 to 4000 ppm), thiourea (0.25 to 0.5 %) and potassium nitrate (0.2 %) have been found to hasten the germination of seeds. Seeds are soaked in the aqueous solution of these chemicals for 12 to 24 hours before sowing. These chemicals are also reported to have strong influence on the seedling growth after germination.

Apomictic Seedling

In some species an embryo is formed from the diploid cell in the embryo sac or nucleus tissues and not due to the fusion of male and female gametes. The genetic makeup of this embryo is identical to the mother plant and hence regeneration of plant by this seed is equivalent to asexual propagation. This phenomenon is known as apomixis and the seedling produced in this manner is called apomictic.

a. **Recurrent apomixis:** In this type of apomixis, an embryo develops from the diploid egg cell or from some adjoining cell, without occurrence of meiosis, having the normal diploid number of chromosomes, akin to the mother plant e.g. malus etc.

b. **Non-recurrent:** In non-recurrent apomixis an embryo develops directly from the haploid egg and so the resultant embryo is also haploid. Having been haploid in nature these plants are always sterile and do not exist more than one generation.

c. **Adventitious or nucellar embryony:** In this type of apomixis an embryo forms the nucellus tissues or integuments outside the embryosac e.g. citrus.

d. **Vegetative apomixis:** In some species vegetative buds are produced in place of flowers in inflorescence which subsequently develops into new plants.

Chapter 21

Vegetable Gardening

The purpose and the mode of marketing of vegetables determine the type of vegetable gardening. The various types of vegetable gardening are as follows.

1. Home or Kitchen gardening
2. Market gardening
3. Truck gardening
4. Processing gardening
5. Vegetable forcing
6. Seed production gardening
7. Floating vegetable gardening

1. Home or Kitchen Gardening

Growing of vegetable within the residential area for the purpose of family need is termed as kitchen or home gardening. The basic considerations in kitchen garden are

1. Choice of family members
2. To meet daily requirement of vegetables.
3. Growing of nutritive and leafy vegetables.
4. Growing of vegetables free from pesticides and insecticides
5. Growing of rare or special kind of vegetables.

Layout of kitchen gardens: In order to meet the daily requirement of vegetable is 300g per head per day in which 75g tuber and root vegetables, 125g leafy vegetables and 100g of fruits vegetables are required in a balance diet.

In order to meet daily need of vegetables it is essential to grow the vegetables by adopting the following considerations.

1. Location and site of field
2. Layout of field
3. Kind of vegetables and their varieties

4. Arrangement of crops in the field
5. Perennial vegetables
6. Adoption of crop rotation.
7. Compost pit and path

1. **Size and location of kitchen garden-** For family of five members (adult and young both) 250-300 square meter of land is adequate to grow vegetable. The length and breadth of the beds should in ratio of 3:2. The ideal shape of each bed should be rectangular. Each bed should be connected with irrigation channel. It is desirable to prepare a layout map on the paper, which will help in working out the cropping scheme.
2. **Location of the kitchen garden-** The location of the kitchen garden will depend on the location, size of the residence and open space for vegetables. As far as possible the location should be very close or attached with the residence. The selected site should be free from large trees or building so that crop could receive sun light for 6-8 hours every day.
3. **Selection of vegetables-** Maximum area should be given to leafy vegetables, followed by tubers and bulbs crops. In selection of vegetables following points should be kept in mind :
    1. It is desirable to grown early season and late varieties of each kind of vegetable. This will enable to get vegetable of one kind for large family.
    3. Selected vegetable varieties which are known for high yield and free from pest & diseases.
    4. Select short duration varieties & early maturing vegetable and late varieties for further requirement.
    5. Select varieties which are nutritive and pest or disease resistance.
4. **Manures and fertilizers-** Use organic manures viz. FYM, compost, cake and green manures should be used. The chemical fertilizer and inorganic pesticidies should be avoided as far as possible. Never apply any pesticide three to four days before harvesting of the crops.

2. Market Gardening

Market gardening refers to the type of vegetable gardening when the vegetables are grown for the nearby market. In other words growing of vegetables within 15-20 km radius of the town or city. Farmer should prefer to grow early and late varieties of vegetable as these fetch higher price in the market. In the market gardening land is occupied with crop all the year round. Thus success of market gardening largely depends upon the ability of assured irrigation and manures of organic and inorganic fertilizers as far as possible resistant varieties should be grown. In case of attack of pest & disease as far as possible organic pesticide should be used.

3. Truck Gardening

Truck gardening refers to growing of vegetables on large scale and marketing has the produce far away from the place of production. The selection of lands depends upon labour and irrigation supply. The cost of production should be relatively cheaper due to land and labour cost. Two-three crops in each season are grown on large scale. The land, labour and irrigation facilities are also less expensive as well as easily avilable.

4. Processing Gardening

When vegetables are raised for supply to the processing factory then it is termed as processing gardening. The choice of vegetable and their varieties to be grown depends on the processing unit. The entire crop of a farmer is consumed by the processing industry. This helps the farmer in getting good income of his produce. Usually processing unit are always located in area where certain kinds of vegetables are grown in large scale. Farmers have to grow varieties of vegetable which are ideal for processing. The vegetable which are used on large scale for processing industries are tomato, onion, garlic and cauliflower. For processing industries vegetables are supplied in bulk at a lower rate.

5. Vegetable Forcing

Growing vegetable other than their normal season is termed as vegetable forcing. Vegetable grown in other than normal season as they fetch higher price due to less avalabilities of vegetable. Vegetable forcing is possible by adopting protective cultivation technique, which means growing of vegetable in polyhouse or green house or poly tunnel is fully air temperature control. The temperature, light and irrigation fully control. The temperature is adjusted to the need of the vegetable. Green houses are prepared of poly carbonate or fibre glass for certain kind of vegetables. In polyhouse crops such as cucumber (Kheera) capsicum, tomato, and european vegetables are grown as these crops fetch high price in normal season.

6. Seed Production Gardening

Refers to the type of gardening, which deals the seed production of vegetables crops. This type of farming requires skill and protection measure. For seed production vegetables crops are in two groups viz.

i. Self pollinated crops.
ii. Cross pollinated crops.

For cross pollinated crops such as cauliflowers & cabbage should be kept in isolation distance from 1500 to 2000 meters.

For seed production the crop may be grown in situ are full grown plants are shifted to some other suitable location.

In order to obtain high yield from the seed crop the crop should be raised in well fertilized field & the area is also protected from wild animals.

7. Floating Vegetable Gardening

In Dal Lake of Srinagar, J&K the farmer grow vegetables on boat, due to lack of agriculture land near the town. On the boat 8-10 cm thick layer of straw or grass is spread followed by a layer good garden soil or compost layer of 10-12 cm thick is spread. On this layer either seed is sown or vegetable seedlings are transplanted. Usually leafy and short duration crop are preferred as the leafy and green vegetables are in great demand.

Organic Farming of Vegetables

Organic farming refers to growing of vegetables without using any synthetic fertilizers, pesticides, fungicide or herbicide for control of weeds.

The inorganic farming produce are polluted and they have adverse effect on plants, animal and human body, several diseases are caused by chemical pollution.

Further the inorganic fertilizer increases the soil pH. Increased pH effect the population of soil micro-organism i.e. water holding potential is poor. The use of fertilizers always increases the emission of carbon dioxide (CO_2) gas in the atmosphere which results in increasing the change in the climate.

The produce of organic farming are of high grade and fetch higher price in the market. There is great demand of organic fruit and vegetable within country and as well as for export. The dietic value is always high in organic produce because they are more tasty, nutritious and free from harmful chemicals.

There is feeling that in organic farming the crops production is low, which does not hold true. It is possible that in first two years of organic manures yield may not be high, afterword the yield is higher than that of inorganic farming.

Merits of organic farming

1. Increased consumer demand due to improvement in quality with lesser cost of production.
2. Higher yield.
3. With lesser cost of production.

4. Less expense on plant protection.
5. Improvement in soil fertility.
6. Control of soil and water pollution and increase in soil micro-organism population.

Chapter 22

Seed Production of Vegetables

Vegetable crops: A seed is borne on fruit and fruit is a mature ovary and ovary is a typical part of flower. Flower in angiosperm, consists of four parts these are calyx/sepal, corolla/petals, androecium/stamens and gynocium/pistil, outer whorl of flower is collectively referred to as calyx. The individual components of calyx are called as sepal. Petals are collectively referred to as corolla. Petal is a unit of second inner whorl after sepals. Stamen is part of flower bearing the male reproductive parts composed of anther and filaments. Pistil is part of flower bearing the female reproductive parts composed of stigma style and ovary.

Seed Production Techniques in Vegetable Crops

Share (%) of F_1 hybrids- Cabbage 85%, Watermelon 70%, Okra 23%, Tomato 80%, Chilli 80%, Cauliflower 50%. Among the Asian countries, India is the 2nd largest production of hand pollinated hybrid seed in vegetables.

Hybrid seed production male: female ratio- Okra-1:4, Muskmelon-1:3, Cucumber-1:5, Watermelon-1:6, Summer squash-1:5 etc.

Placentation- The manner of arrangement of seed within the ovary is called placentation.

There are three basic types.

i. **Parietal**- Seed are attached to the ovary wall.

ii. **Axil**- The ovary is divided by partition called septa and seeds are attached to central axis.

iii. **Free central (basal)**- Seed are attached to the central axis but there are no partitions or septa.

Basic structure of seed- Development of four megaspores through meiosis is known as mega-sporogensis. Three haploid megaspores normally degenerate. Development of female gametophyte or embryosac from the functional megaspore through three successive mitotic divisions leads to one large cell enclosing eight haploid nuclei. This process is known as mega-gametogenesis soon these nuclei arrange themselves within the enlarging embryosac and cell wall form. Out of eight nuclei, three nuclei with cell wall at one end/pole are called antipodal cells. Two poler nuclei without cell wall occupy central place inside the embryosac. There is egg apparatus consisting of one egg cell between two synergid cells. Two polar nuclei fuse subsequently to form one diploid (2n) nucleus. This arrangement leads to formation of seven celled structure known as mature gametophyte or embryosac or megagametophyte.

During flowering pollen (haploid) is transferred from anther to stigma is called pollination. The mature pollen grain germinates on the stigma. A pollen tube with two male gametes grows down the style into the ovary until it reaches the embryosac having 8 haploid nuclei within the ovule. Two male gametes from the pollen tube are discharged in to the embryosac. One male gametes unites with the female gametes surrounded by two synergids to produce zygote. This process known as fertilization the second male gamete fuses with two polar nuclei to produce endosperm which triploid (3n).

The relationship between floral parts and fruit or seed can be illustrated as follows.

Ovary (pericarp) – Develops into fruit.

Ovule – Develops into seed

Integuments – Develops into seed coat (testa)

Nucellus – Develops into perisperm

Two polor nuclei + sperm nucleus – Develops into endosperm

Egg nucleus + sperm nucleus (zygote) – Develop into embryo.

Global seed markets- According to estimates provided by International Seed Federation (ISF), global players in world seed production and marketing could be listed as follows :

- Monsanto – USA
- BASF – Plant Science – Germany
- Dow Agro Science – USA
- Dupont –USA
- Limagrain – France
- Rijk Zwaan – Netherlands
- Syngenta – Switzerland
- Bayer Crop Science – Germany

Indian Seed market- The major players (Indian/joint venture/foreign seed companies) in Indian vegetable seed industry are represented by about 200 seed companies in India.

- Advanta Seed- **Bangalore**
- Tropical Seed – **Bangalore**

- Bayer Crop Science - **Gujarat**
- Bioseeds – **Hyderabad**
- Ganga Kaveri Seeds – **Hyderabad**
- Pioneer – **Hyderabad**
- Ankur Seed – **Nagpur**
- Bejo Sheetal – **Jalna**
- East-West Seed – **Aurangabad**
- Indo-American Hybrid Seeds – **Bangalore**
- Kaveri Seeds – **Sikandarabad**
- Mahyco – **Jalna Maharastra**
- Sygenta – **Mumbai**

General principles of vegetable seed production: Majority of vegetable crops are propagated by true seed while few like pointed gourd, coccinia, garlic, drumstick etc. are propagated vegetatively. The production of vegetatively propagated crop is easy as compared to seed production of botanical (tree) seeds. The maintenance preservation and multiplication of pure seed have greater significance as the variety is generated by the breeders after investing of very precious time, labour and money for that purpose. Therefore seed production of crop is done following definite procedures, which vary depending on the nature of the crop i.e. self or cross pollinated or asexually propagated and the type of variety (pureline, hybrid, synthetic or composite).

In general seed production involves the following steps-

1. **Selection of crop and variety:** Only those crop and varieties should be taken for the seed production which are high in demand, having potential or established market and performing well in the area.

2. **Selection of seed:** Unless initially the pure seed is procured from a reliable source, no effort can help to maintain its purity. The pure the seed, the lesser will be the effort involved in maintaining the varietal purity. It is therefore must to verify the source of seed.

3. **Reporting to monitoring/certification agency:** Improved seed production is subject to legal umbrella and it must undergo monitoring under the supervision of the authority defined in Seed Act. Therefore proper reporting by the seed grower or institution to the monitoring agency should be ensured.

4. **Selection and preparation of field:** Selection of the field is the key to success of a seed production programme. The field should be uniform in topography, fertility, texture etc. which enables the seed crop to express all

the passport traits uniformly. Soils are well fertile well drained, free from soil borne disease and weeds. The proper tillage and herbicides should be used and a favourable seed bed should be prepared.

5. **Cultural practices:** This is vary with crop and geographic location. These practices also play a key role in obtaining good seed harvest likes adjusting the sowing time for seed crops, maintaining proper inter and intra row distance in such a way that plants express full vigour and their maturity may fall in the drier part of the season. Necessary steps should be taken for timely control of insect and disease. In case of severe disease, prophylactic spray is applied.
6. **Appropriate male: female ratio:** Male: female ratio is relevant particularly in case of hybrid seed production where the F_1 seed is the result of cross pollination between two parents. In such cases only the female parent bears the hybrid seed. In order to minimize seed cost, male: female ratio is generally kept in favour of the female parent. The male: female ratio is decided on the basis of experimental investigations and may be 1:1, 1:2, 1:3, 1:4 etc.
7. **Maintenance of recommended isolation distance:** Isolation means keeping the seed plots away from other fields of the same crops and crossable species. Ensuring the proper isolation distance from the nearby field of the same crop and crossable species is the most important prerequisite for multiplication of seed vis-a-vis maintaining its purity.
8. **Field inspection:** Field inspection refers to the scrutiny of seed production plots by a team of qualified persons. The primary objective of field inspection is to ensure that seed production is being carried out of the designated variety and there is no contamination (physical or genetically) beyond the specific maximum limits. It also ensure that the step necessary to minimize genetic and physical contaminations have been taken properly and in time field inspection is done by a team of qualified persons to verify the source of seed, prescribed land requirement male: female ratio and prescribed isolation or border row in case of hybrids, presence of off type and objectionable weeds, disease incidence of specified disease and similar other requirements. That may be specified for the crop concerned.

   In general field inspection may be done at the following five stages.

   1. Pre flowering
   2. Flowering
   3. Post flowering
   4. Pre harvest
   5. Harvest stage.

In asexually propagated crop such as potato, sweet potato, pointed gourd etc growth stage like pre flowering and post flowering may not be relevant.

9. **Roguing:** Roguing is the removal of off type plants from a field. Off types are those plants that are phenotypically different from plant of the variety grown as seed crop. It is an essential component of seed production programme as it helps to attain desirable level of genetic purity. A rogue plant may cause genetic impurity due to mechanical mixture and by out crossing with the true to type plants of seed crops. Roguing is however continued till crop maturity in order to remove off type plants based on fruits that become distinguishable only at the later stages of development e.g. tomato fruit colour. In case of nucleus or breeder seed production roguing is performed under the direct supervision of the breeder or his associates.
10. **Harvesting:** Harvesting of seed crop at appropriate maturity is essential to avoid the wastage like dropping of over ripe fruits and seeds in the field. In some cases such as okra and brinjal first picking for consumption or sale does not affect the ultimate seed yield but adds to the farmer's income in addition to other beneficial effects like reducing the disease inoculums build up. The seed produced on plant under moisture deficit are usually light and shriveled with poor vigour and are more prone to hardseededness. It is assumed that when soil fertility becomes limiting plant responds by producing less seed.
11. **Seed processing:** It is carried out to improve the quality of harvested seed through a series of operation *viz.,* Drying, cleaning, grading, testing, seed treatments, bagging and labeling.

Basic objective of seed processing

a. Improving the seed quality by removing adulterants and unfit seed.
b. Taking preventive measures that maintain seed viability.
c. Provide information about seed quality standards to the perspective buyers.
d. Making seed handling easier.

1. **Seed drying:** Seed should be dried to reduce the seed moisture to safer levels. Its basic purpose is to sustain the seed viability and longevity by minimizing attacks of storage pests and pathogens and avoiding heat damage due to higher respiration rates in moist seeds. Seed can be dried under natural condition (under sun) or in artificial condition using various types of dries. Artificial drive by bag driers, box driers, bin driers, flat storage drier, continuous flow tower drier etc. can be used for drying seed to the desired level eg- Moisture content (%) for drying crops tomato, brinjal, chilli 8% ordinary and 6% vapour proof pack, okra 10% ordinary and 8% vapour proof pack.

2. **Cleaning and grading:** Cleaning is the separation of physical impurities like trash, dirt, weed seeds etc. from the seed lots, whereas the grading refers to removal of under sized or underweight seed from the seed lot. Before cleaning and grading pre conditioning of seeds may also be done. Pre conditioning also includes pre cleaning, which refers to removal of large sized particles light weight chaffy material and seed of small size from the lot. All cleaning operations basically involve separation of adulteration based on size, density or shape. Hand sieves can also be used for grading on small scales.
3. **Seed treatment:** It refers to exposing the seed to certain agents, physical or chemical which are able to protect them from pests and ensure good health of seeds and emerging plants. Its main aim is to protect the seeds from pests and pathogen such as bacteria, fungi, nematodes and insects. The most commonly used fungicides for seed treatment are captan, thiram and carbendazim. Equipment used for seed treatment is drum dry seed treater, slurry seed treater or mist osmatic seed treater.
4. **Seed packaging:** Seed should be packed in smaller unit to avoid risks of physical gradients, particularly vapours pressures which arise in large bulks. Packaging in smaller units makes identification, transportation, handling and marketing easier. Packaging material and amount of seeds to be packed depends on several factors such as kinds of seeds, duration of storage, storage environment, moisture content etc. Packaging materials can be classified into three types -
   i. **Moisture vapours permeable** - Jute bag, cloth bag, paper bag
   ii. **Moisture vapours resistant-** Jute bag laminated with thin polythene film
   iii. **Moisture vapours proof-** Tin cans, polythene bag (700 gauges), aluminum foil pouch etc.
5. **Seed storage:** The storage of seed by the growers is mainly for short term (3-9 months) but occasionally growers needs to store up to 18 months. The purpose of seed storage is to maintain the seed in good physical and physiological conditions from the time of harvest to the sowing.

Factor affecting seed longevity in storages

1. Kind of seed.
2. Initial seed quality.
3. Moisture content.
4. Temperature and relative humidity during storage.

Point to be considered for seed storage

1. Storage in a cool and dry place.
2. Effective storage pest control.
3. Proper sanitation in seed store.
4. Drying seeds to safe moisture limits before storage.
5. Controlling storage conditions depending upon length of storage period and prevailing climatic conditions.

Chapter 23

Principles of Gardening

The planning of a garden is an art. It is said that a poet is born, and in that sense a garden architect is also born. But that does not mean that a garden architect has nothing to learn. On the contrary he should learn enough of geology, geography, garden history, styles of gardening, and above all should have a profound knowledge about plants. It is imperative to know [illegible] landscape gardening. A landscape may be def[illegible] small, on which it is possible or desirable to [illegible] landscape gardening may be described as the [illegible] methods and materials with a view to impr[illegible] designing is known as "landscape architecture" [illegible] gardening" is also popular.

Before discussing the principles of gardening [illegible] make some useful suggestions. The first and th[illegible] another garden which has secured a prize in a [illegible] one's own design giving due consideration [illegible] mistake which is commonly made is to plan [illegible] garden can accommodate causing overcrowdin[illegible] difference in levels has to be taken advantage of [illegible] will be costly to create artificial undulations. [illegible] at least one feature or there be a second these [illegible] other. Before planning a design one must be sure [illegible] utility or beauty or both.

Landscaping is an art of beautifying a piece of land [illegible] material non-living material in order to create a [illegible] natural. Landscaping makes a place more [illegible] pleasing, where people can rest and enjoy [illegible] Landscape gardening is landscaping of a garden [illegible] gardening and painting on a canvas or paper [illegible] colours are used to form a picture, only difference [illegible] 2D image and garden is collection of living plants [illegible]

Chapter 23

Principles of Gardening

The planning of a garden is an art. It is said that a poet is born, and in that sense a garden architect is also born. But that does not mean that a garden architect has nothing to learn. On the contrary he should learn enough of geology, geography, garden history, styles of gardening, and above all should have a profound knowledge about plants. It is imperative to know at the outset what is meant by landscape gardening. A landscape may be defined as any area, either big or small, on which it is possible or desirable to mould view or a design, whereas landscape gardening may be described as the application of garden forms, methods, and materials with a view to improving the landscape. The art of designing is known as "landscape architecture," although the older term landscape gardening" is also popular.

Before discussing the principles of gardening in detail, it will be worthwhile to make some useful suggestions. The first and the foremost thing are not to imitate another garden which has secured a prize in a competition. One has to develop one's own design giving due consideration to the local conditions. One more mistake which is commonly made is to plant many more specimens than a garden can accommodate causing overcrowding. In a landscape garden any difference in levels has to be taken advantage of, but in a perfectly flat land it will be costly to create artificial undulations. In each garden the care should be at least one feature or there be a second these two should harmonize with each other. Before planning a design are must be sure for what purpose the garden is utility or beauty or both.

Landscaping is an art of beautifying a piece of land or a landscape with planting material non-living material in order to create a picturesque effect or to imitate natural. Landscaping makes a place more peaceful, beautiful, appealing of pleasing, where people can rest and enjoy with their family and friends etc. Landscape gardening is landscaping of a garden, more or less landscape gardening and painting on a canvas or paper sheet is similar. In both cases colours are used to form a picture, only difference is that painting is non-living 2D image and garden is collection of living plants with non living things in 3D form. It is not necessary and also possible to follow all the principles at a time in a landscape plan but there are 8 basic principles one should follow during landscape planning, which are discussed below.

Simplicity: The plan must be simple. It should not contain too many themes or overcrowding of plants or other garden ornaments, as this creates confusion and hinders in getting the theme and also distract the viewers.

Unity: It increases aesthetic beauty of the garden. It can be expressed by harmonious placement of garden features in proper way. It can be created by repetition of single component or by blending different component in harmony in such a way that every feature expresses the total effect independently.

Harmony: It is an overall effect of various features, style and colour schemes of the total scene. It is arranging different things in garden in such a way that it creates relation between all and makes them all look one.

Balance: Balance in a design is an essential part for unity, harmony and proportion of design. Therefore, correct balance in different planting materials like annuals, shrubs and tree should be maintained. Balance in size, shape, colour and form of building and different plant should be maintained.

Proportion: In this every feature should be in relation with total space available for the garden. The space provided for lawn, paths, herbaceous borders, shrubbery, tree, building and other garden object should be in a right proportion. It should be seen in mughal garden like size of building, tree, lawn and paths etc.

Scale: Scaling of components, size, shape and form unites the different component of design, create harmony and incorporate balance and proportion in design. In general in a design, area can be divided in following manner which may vary with personal choice and type utility. Where on the lawn (25-30%), paths (15-20%), herbaceous border (8-10%), shrubbery (12-15%), trees (15%) and building (25-30%).

Accent/focal point: Accent is a center of attraction which is generally an architectural feature focused as a point of interest. The focal point attracts viewers to a point from where a single view can be seen and from where the whole plan could be understood and all components looks one which avoids monotonous view. The hidden focal point is called as vista. Mostly objects like fountains, tree and statues etc. are used. In English gardens statues are used as focal point. It may be anything, a flowering tree, shrubbery, focal clock, fountains and lakes etc.

Rhythm: Repetition of same object or objects at equidistance is called rhythm. It can be created through the shapes, progression of sizes or continuous line movement. Rhythm creates movement of eye. For example in Mughal gardens trees of single species of equal height and shape, fountain and water canals are planted to create this effect. In present day situation, light are used for this purpose.

Initial Approach: In theory, everyone would like to have a perfect plot of land, but in actual practice the plot available for gardening, in three out of five cases, either will not be in a good or the shape and size will not be ideal. Whatever may be the case, one should not throw hands up in despair even if the site appears to be hopeless. A good designer is one who will make best use of such a site. As has already been stated, land with natural undulations should never be levelled, but rather the differences in levels should be utilized with advancing, though may not look artistic is essential in any garden. But the fencing should be such that it looks naturals far as practicable and it should not obstruct any natural view. For example, if there is natural forest scenery or a hillock just outside the boundary it should be incorporated in the garden design in a thoughtful manner so that it appears to be part of the garden.

A building or machinery, once it is complete, takes a final shape. But with living plants it is impossible to visualize how a garden design will look like in the long run when the plants attain full size, even though the design may have been completed. For example, a tree which is normally expected to grow to a height of 10 m, remains dwarf for some reason or other thus jeopardizing all calculations. One more difference with inanimate objects and living plants is that while the final design for a building or machinery can be completed on paper this cannot be so with living plants, and as such each design should be adaptable. The man on the spot who will actually implement the design should be given enough scope to change it to adapt to the local needs and personal taste of the owner and/or designer. It is only the formal gardens, not having any trees that can be drawn on paper and implemented without any appreciable change.

The other terms and principles used in landscape designs are briefly discussed below.

Axis: This is an imaginary line in any garden around which the garden is created striking and balance. In a formal garden, the central line is the axis. At the end of an axis, generally there will be a focal point, although another architectural feature such as bird-bath or sundialn can also be erected

Mass Effect: The use of one general form of plant material in large numbers in one place is done to have mass effect. To see that such mass arrangements do not become monotonous, the sizes of masses should be varied.

Unity: Unity in a garden is very important as when this is achieved it will improve the artistic look of the garden. Unity has to be achieved from various angles. First, the unity of style, feeling, and function between the house and the garden has to be achieved. Secondly, the different components of the gardens should merge harmoniously with each other. The aim is to give the visitor an overall impression of the garden rather than blowing up some special features. The last point, which is also very important, is to achieve some harmony between the landscape outside and the garden. A garden laid out in complete defiance of the local conditions may look exotic, but is not a successful garden. As for example, cacti planted in a seashore garden is completely out of place as these are inhabitants of dry localities.

Space: The aim of every garden design should be such that the garden should appear larger than its actual size. One way of achieving this is to keep vast open spaces, preferably under lawn and restrict the plantings in the periphery, normally avoiding any planting in the centre. But if any planting has to be done in the centre the branches at a higher level on the trunk (or the lower branches are removed) and not a bushy shrub. Such planting will not obstruct the view or make the garden appear smaller than its size. Another way of creating an illusion of distance, which was in vogue in older a yes but not practised much in recent times, is to make lines converge slightly at a distance. For example, paths in a garden are gradually narrowed or the sizes of the farthest trees diminish in size. But such tricks will give a reverse impression from the other end. Another suggestion to create the illusion of more space in a large public garden is to alternate large. A large open space planted haphazardly all over with trees looks smaller than its size. The tecnique of creating an illusion of more space is also referred to as forced perspective

Divisional Lines: In a landscape garden, there should not be any hard and fast divisional lines. But there is the necessity of dividing or rather screening a compost pit or a malis quarter or a vegetable garden from the rest of the garden. In fact areas under lawn, gravel, stone or cement path, and shrubbery border have their natural divisional lines from its immediate neighbour though these are not discreet. This is what is exactly needed. The divisional lines should be artistic with gentle curves and these should also be useful. Above all these lines should harmonize with one another.

Proportion and Scale: Proportion in a garden may be defined as a definite relationship between masses. For example, a rectangle having a ratio of 5:8 is considered to be of pleasing proportion. As this ratio comes down the form looks neither a square nor rectangle, and the design becomes undesirable. There is no set rule as regards scale or proportion in a garden. But a simple rule is that a design should look pleasant. It is better to have an ad hoc design first and then try it out on the actual spot. If the design looks appealing as well as pleasing, it is implemented. When a shrubbery border has to be planted the outer design is marked by arranging a rubber hose or thick wet rope in different designs on the spot and the one which looks best is adopted. Then sticks of different heights, representing the various shrubs, are planted in various positions and by the method of permutation and combination the most proportionate looking arrangement is adopted.

It will be worthwhile to give a few more examples to illustrate the importance of scale in a garden. A narrow step leading from a wide terrace is completely out of scale. The steps in a garden, should not only be broader than those inside the house but should, have deep treads (the stepping) and low risers also. This means the steps are spaced wider, making climbing easier and pleasant. Moreover, a very wide flight of steps dividing two lawn areas, at different levels, make the transition easy and inconspicuous. The common practice of laying out a small rockery at the base of a large tree with small thorny specimens looks not only ugly but is also out of scale and proportion under the large canopy of the tree. A tiny pool in the midst of a large lawn also looks disproportionate.

Texture: The surface character of a garden unit is referred to as texture. The texture of the ground, the leaves of a tree or shrub will all determine the overall effect of the garden. The texture of rugged looking ground can be improved to an appreciable extent by laying meticulously chosen small pebbles from the riverbeds, if establishing a lawn is out of the question. A gulmohar is a fine textured tree when in full leaf, whereas *Spathodea companulata* is a coarse textured tree. The placement of all these various textures with harmony and contrast has to be achieved to get the ultimate desirable effect.

Time and Light: In a category of time in a garden. First comes the daily time, which provides different quantities and qualities of light during the course of the day. As the morning sun is vital for all flowers, the designer has to take this into account while planning. In most parts of India the garden design should be planned in such a way that in the afternoon it is possible to sit in a shaded place from where the best part of the garden should be visible. The second type of time is the seasonal changes in the year. A good planner must roughly take into account.

Mobility: In a temperate country, the garden changes colour very sharply and contrastingly from one season to the other thus symbolizing mobility or movement. As for example, many trees in the temperate regions attire themselves with wonderful huss due to the changes in their leaf colour in the autumn. Then suddenly in the winter leaves fall and everything goes to rest bringing an atmosphere of melancholy and dulinsss all around. Again in the spring the plants spring back to life with the appearance of the new leaves, In most parts of Tropical India, though these contrasting changes cannot be achieved, it is possible to bring in some subtle changes, such as Bengal or Indian Almond (*Terminalia catappa*) which changse its leaf colour into striking red twice annually before falling or *Lagerstroemia fosreginae* which also changes the colour of the leaves to coppery shade in the autumn befors shedding, or *Madhuca indica* and *Ficus retigiosa*, the new foliage of these appearing as coppery red in the spring, should be planted in some parts of the garden.

Style: Lastly, one has to decide about the style to be adopted for one's garden, broadly speaking, every garden lover has to invent his own style of gardening commensurate with his budget, taste, and the nature of the site. But a man can develop his own design only when he studies carefully all the great garden styles of the world and grasps the underlying principles in them, There is no doubt that persons not having enough specialized knowledge will commit mistakes; nevertheless, one should not get deterred by this fact, One word of caution to a novice gardener is that he should not get used to his mistakes, but critically assess every feature and try to correct the mistakes and improve upon the design with the acquiring of new knowledge through experience and learning from others.

Elements of landscape design

1. **Line:** In landscape design, lines differentiate two or more elements or components or parts of design. In landscape, line can be drawn by repetition of same objects like planting Ashok tree, shrubs, etc. along the roads; hedges along the paths; annuals along the path or side of a tree to give a sense of tree canopy, edges, etc. In formal garden, lines are straight and it is important in creating mirror image in other half of garden. In informal design, lines are curvy and of irregular size and shape which has the same functions as in formal garden. Line gives a sense of border to a particular object in landscape and avoids mixing of two or more components.

2. **Colour:** Colours are the most essential element in a landscape design. This imparts beauty and cut boredom, monopoly of green colour. Colours are divided into three groups.

   Primary colour: Red, Yellow, Blue.

   Secondary colour: Green, Violet (purple), Orange.

   Tertiary colour: Mixture of primary and secondary colours. White, grey, black and silver colours are considered neutral.

   Colours include three terms namely hue or chroma, value and intensity. Hue or chroma refers to the relative purity or strength of the colour. Value determines how light or dark the colour is, whereas, intensity refers to how bright or dull it is

3. **Texture:** In landscape design, appearance of objects and their surface is referred as texture. Texture can be physical or visual. It must be seen as

comparison and can be analysed by comparison between objects. Coarse texture (large leaf tree), medium texture (medium size leaf plant) and fine texture (small leaf tree) are the three categories of texture. The texture of garden decides its overall view. Coarse texture is mostly used for focal point. Planting coarse and fine textured plants together attracts viewer's eye movement.

4. **Habit:** Habit of planting material (straight, globular, columnar, bushy shape of crown) attracts viewer's eye movement in different directions. Straight growing plants move viewer's eyes towards up where sky and tall plants jointly give a scenery view, adding sky in landscape design. Globular plants move eyes in horizontal direction which relates earth and other small components. Habit of plants play an important role in viewer's eye movement and help the viewers by guiding what landscaper wants to show or the beauty of his design. Habit can be compared with silent direction signs, indicator or guide.

5. **Form:** In landscape design, form refers to shape of objects. Shape given to trees and hedges adds beauty, harmony, rhythm, unity and help to establish focal point.

6. **Light:** It has become an important element in landscape design. Light helps to create shade effect which can be utilized in imparting beauty to landscape. Light are used in fountains, water bodies to give visual effects. Light adds colour in landscape if used smartly

7. **Space/Volume:** Design must be planned according to space available. The design should not be crowdy. It is possible to make a garden appear larger, longer, wider, shorter by manipulating the apparent perspective and proportion. The garden design should be such that it gives illusion of being larger than its actual size. If space is less then design should be planned in such a manner that less space also look more in volume than actual.

8. **Mobility:** In landscape design, mobility refers to change in garden or landscape with time in space and volume. Use of annuals according to season changes colour in garden which give sense of change in garden. Likewise, running water, deciduous trees, evergreen trees, flowering trees, shrubs and climbers etc. give mobility to design. It can also be understood by example of temperate countries where garden changes colour very sharply and contrasting from one season to the other symbolizing mobility or movement. In tropical countries trees like Pride of India (*Lagerstroemia speciasa*), Pipal (*Ficus religiosa, Ficus infectoria*), Mahua (*Madhuca longifolia*) and Indian almond (*Terminalia catappa*) can be planted to create mobility in the garden.

9. **Style:** It may be formal, informal, free or wild style of gardening. In formal style, space, form, paths, line, etc. are geometrical. In this, land is selected according to design or converted according to designs requirement. Here, paths cross at 90° angle and balance is symmetrical e.g. Mughal, Persian, Italian, French, Japanese gardens etc.

Chapter 24

Lawn

Lawn

Lawn is a natural green carpet, and it is important feature of a landscape and a garden without a lawn is not considerd complete. Lawn is an area of land closed mowed grasses it is primarily developed for aesthetic and recreational purpose. A lawn is an integral part of a garden and landscape besides aesthetic and recreational purpose and several other purposes. Lawn provides a place for taking rest after tiring of the day, holding parties, social functions, passive and active recreation. Distinguishing characteristic of turf grasses is the ability to with stand close mowing and still providing a functional dense healthy ground cover. Lawn is also called as heart of garden. Lawn can be called as turf pitch a field, sod, yard, are green depending upon the plantation usage continent. Lawn is a ground cover of perennial grass, ditch, persists enclose mowing and require proper management practice.

J.B. Olcoth designed first experiment in lawn grass at Monchester in USA in the 19th century. Festuca and Agrostis species were used to make turf (Lawn) during 1880 in U.K. In the early 19th century lawn become wild spread out side of parks golf course. Now a day in many metro cities of India lawn has become a cultural of the passion of many homes.

Selection of Grass

There are mainly two types of grasses are used for planting lawn.

a. **Bermuda grass** (*Cynodon dactylon*)- It is commonly called as doob or hariali. This is very commonly used for planting lawn due to its fast, growth, hardiness, less water requirement and response to frequent mowing. This makes an excellent turf. It is highly suitable for large area and a playground on account of it's tolerant to water and has good recuperation habit.

   Variety of bermuda grasses- Kalkatiya, Hariyali, Selection 1, 5, 8, Palna, Panam etc.

b. **Korean grass (*Zoysia japonica*)-** It is native of Japan, Korean and Philippine island. This kind of grass is recently introduced in India and has become very popular in short span of time due to its velvety growth and more cold tolerance. It makes cushion like turf. This is highly suitable for smaller areas and home lawns.

Type of Lawn Grasses

Warm season- Warm season grasses grow luxuriantly in warm climate they starts growth at the temperature above 10°C and grow fastest when temperature are between 25-35⁰C and they are comparatively harder than cool season grasses. Warm season grasses are more popular for making lawns, they require less care and maintenance eg. Doob grass/bermuda grass (*Cynodon dactylon*), Korean grass (*Zyosia japonica*), Buffalo grass (*Buchloe dactyloides*), Carpet grass (*Axonopus affinis*) and Bahia grass (*Paspalum notatum*) etc.

Cool season- Cool season grasses start growth at 5°C and grow at their fastest rate when temperature prefer between 10-15⁰C. Some important cool season lawn grasses are Tall fescue (*Festuca arundinacea*), Chewing fescue (*Festuca rubra*), Annual rye grass (*Lolium multiflorum*), Creeping bent grass (*Agrostis palustris*), and Kentucky blue grass (*Poa pratensis*) etc.

Purpose of a Lawn

- It is an important element in garden.
- It leads to unity in garden design.
- It is natural green carpet and is the carpet floor of outdoor room.
- It is a heart of garden and the center for social life.
- It gives restful appearance to the eyes through its green outlook all the time.
- Prevent soil erosion.
- Enhance ground water recharge.

Characteristic of Lawn Grass

- Look fresh and green throughout the year.
- Cold and drought resistance.
- It should not be patchy.
- Free from attach of disease and insect.
- Quick growing.
- Should not give fowl or bed order.

Preparation of Soil

1. Dig soil up to 45cm depth and expose sun May and June.
2. Turn soil 2-3 times remove stone rocks and break big clouds

3. Spread 10-15 cm thick layer of well rotten weed free FYM and thoroughly mixed in soil.
4. Sandy loam soil is best for lawn grasses growing which are pH ranges between 5-6.
5. Irrigation the field thoroughly and allow all weeds to germinate.
6. Remove the entire weed along with roots manually or spread non selective type of herbicide, like Paraquat or Gramaxone at the rate 1-1.5 liter in about 800-1000 liter.

Planting Methods of Lawn

Following are different methods of planting lawns:

1. Seeding Method

- This method is common to grow cool season lawn grasses.
- About 25-30 kg seed/ha is mixed in 200-500 kg sand and saw dust and broadcast evenly in prepared field.
- Do light rolling.
- Sprinkle water regularly until seedling emergence.
- Less labour is required but lawn is not even.

2. Dibbling Method

- A small bunch of grass alone with roots and little stem is taken.
- Planting is done a spacing of 10 cm apart both row to row and plant to plant.
- Do regular watering until establishment.
- It is done in June to September.
- Lawn develop by this method is quick uniform and with more labour and cost.

3. Sodding Method

- Sodding is expensive than others vegetative propagation method.
- This method is recommended where quick cover is required.
- The sod should not be laid when the day time temperature excess 32^{0}C for an extended period.

4. Sprigging Method

- Grass root along with little stem are chopper into small pieces.
- Spread this over prepared field during rainy season.

- Do small raking to mix grass in soil.
- Do light rolling.
- Do light watering with sprayer.
- Do moving after 70-80 days.

5. Turfing Method

- Small pieces of well prepared lawn or turf are cut into square or rectangular shape. Preferable plants are planted in polythene sheet.
- Fix these in thoroughly prepared field.
- Do heavy rolling.
- Lawn prepared in clean and weeds free.
- Quickest method of lawn raising.

6. Plugging Method

- The planting of 5-10 cm diameter square, circular or plucked shape piece of sod at regular interval is called plugging.
- Care should be taken that plugs or well watered but must not be soggy (muddy).
- There is 10 times more planting than sprinkling.
- Quick establishment of lawn, it is advised to plant plugs closely.

7. Stolonizing Method

- Stolonizing is the broad casting of stolons on the soil surface.
- Covering by top dressing or pressing into the soil.

8. Aritificial Lawn Making

- When the seeding are about 10 cm heights, do light mowing.
- Greenery for short duration can be achieved by sprinkling pine need less in any area.

Managment of Lawn

Mowing and rolling : The newly planted lawn is not mowed till has established well. In the beginning the grass should be trimmed with the help of grass cutter (Mower). It is the cutting of lawn grass for maintaining it's the activeness and for maximum utility. Mower discover by "Edwing Budding" in 1830 in England. Light rolling should be done on dry ground to suppress the upright growth to anchor the grass firmly in the soil and to keep the level of ground. Interval of mowing of an established lawn depending upon season. In rainy and winter season mowing is required at an interval of 7-10 days. During spring season mowing is required at the interval of 15 days whereas during summer it is done at monthly interval.

Manures and fertilizers : The regular application of fertilizers keeps the grass to grow luxuriantly and maintains the lush green colour of the lawn. Sun hemp is very good green manure before lawn planting. In 30 m^2 lawn 3-5q. FYM, 10-20 kg lime and 10-20 kg SSP. Broadcast a mixture of 50-60 gm/m^2 or 1.5 kg/30 m^2 (2 CN: 1 SSP: 1 K_2SO_4) twice in Feb-March and Aug-Sept. and spray of urea at 0.3%

Irrigation : Water requirement of lawn depend upon season, type of soil, grass used weather and planet. Grasses are surface fedder and hence adequate watering should be done frequently. It should be done before wilting is internal water stress. Increased watering inters well result in deeper root development, then by decreasing water requirement. Irrigation required up to 5-15cm on depth at 8-10 days interval is ideal as frequent light watering is harmful. Korean grass needs more frequent watering than Calcutta grass.

Weeding : Regular mowing checks weed growth by removing upper portion of the weeds and starvation of root. But still there may be large population of weeds which grows fast and needs removal. For controlling broad leaved weed spread 2-4-D at 0.005% and for narrow leaved weed spray Atrazine @ 1.5 kg/ha in 1000 litter. In lawn of Korean grass spray Benefine or Sylvex at 0.1%.

Scraping of lawn : It is done to renovate the old lawn when it becomes old and grass become compact. After 3-4 years during summer month i.e. during June, lawn should be scraped completely with the help of khurpa and raking should be done both ways. Before the starts of rains top dressing of mixture consisting of garden soil, sand and sieved leaf mould (1:2:1) should be applied to cover the upper 3-5 cm.

Disease

- Damping off, root rot, gray leaf, mould, leaf spot, powdery mildew, fairy ring are most important disease of lawn.
- Bordeaux mixture 4: 4: 50 at fortnightly interval.
- Dithane-M-45 (0.1 %) + Bavistin (0.1%) at fortnightly interval.

Insect

- Termite (0.03% Chloropyrophase), cut worm (Spinopad at 0.05%) and root grub (Phorate 10-12 kg).

season mowing is continued at interval of 7-10 days. During spring season mowing is required at the interval of 15 days whereas during summer it is done at monthly intervals.

Manuring and fertilizers: The regular application of fertilizers keeps the grass to grow luxuriantly and compliments the lush green colour of the lawn. Sun hemp is very good green manure before lawn planting. In a new lawn 5-10 t FYM, 10-20 kg lime and 10-20 kg SSP. Broadcast at a time of 50-60 g per m² of (2 CN : 1 SSP : 1 K [illegible]) in between [illegible] March and Aug-Sept and spread it on the lawn.

Irrigation: [illegible] where [illegible] and ornamental plants are grown and [illegible]. Watering should be done frequently. It should be done before wilting as internal water stress. Increased watering interval will result in deeper root development thereby decreasing water requirement. Irrigation [illegible] up to 5-7 cm on depth at 5-10 days interval is ideal as frequent light watering is harmful. Korean grass needs more frequent watering than Cynodon grass.

Weeding: Regular mowing checks weed growth by removing upper portion of the weeds and starvation of root but still there may be large population of weeds which grows fast and needs removal. For controlling broad-leaved weed spread 2,4-D at 0.05% and for narrow leaved weed spray Atrazine @ 1.5 kg a.i. in 1000 litres. In lawn of Korean grass spray [illegible] or Sythan at 0.1%.

Scraping of lawn: It is done to renovate the old lawn when it becomes old and grass become compact, once in 3-4 years during summer months. During June lawn should be scraped completely with the help of khurpa and raking should be done both ways. Before the rains organic top dressing of mixture consisting of garden soil, sand and well decomposed farm yard manure (1:2:1) should be applied to cover the exposed surface.

Diseases [illegible]

- Damping off, root rot, brown patch, mould, leaf spot, powdery mildew, rust [illegible] are most important diseases of lawn.
- Bordeaux mixture 4:4:50 at fortnightly interval.
- Dithane M-45 (0.2%) + Bavistin (0.1%) at fortnightly interval.

Insect [illegible]

- Termite (0.2% Chlorpyriphos), cut worm (Sumicidin at 0.05%) and white grub (Phorate 10 G [illegible]).

Chapter 25

Types and Styles of Garden

Garden

Garden is a place where vegetables, fruits and ornamental plants are grown mainly for recreation. The garden incorporates both natural and man-made materials.

Types of garden

The major garden types which shall be discussed are: English garden, Mughal garden, Persian garden, Italian garden, French garden, Japanese garden etc. Out of these the Mughal, Persian, Italian and French styles fall in the category of formal gardens, whereas the English and Japanese gardens are classified in the informal style of gardening.

The famous features of the major types of garden are given bellow:

1. **Feature of English garden-** With the mind famous British garden architects repton and capability brown advocated the concept that the British gardens should look like the countryside. In which lawn mixed border especially of herbaceous annuals as well as herbaceous perennials, shrubbery and rock garden. The English climate suits admirably well for the growth of herbaceous annuals. Typical grassland climate in England and gardening is hobby of rich people. English men were very fond of flower essential feature.

2. **Feature of Mughal garden-** Site near hill, slope with perennial rivulet. A garden enclosed with walls and fitted with tall gate and has at least 7, 8 or 12 terraces symbolizing 7 planets, 8 paradises, 12 zodiac with interest at the lowest terraces. The running water in canals and terminal building. Baradari with 12 doors, 3 in every direction (Safed baradari in Lucknow) symbolism and plant material.

3. **Feature of Persian garden-** Based on idea of heaven. Strictly formal and symmetrical. Beautiful architectural work and laid out after cutting terraces. Plants cypress a symbol of eternity.

4. **Feature of French garden-** Formal garden in perfection. The moral of French garden style of Le Notre seems to teach the lesson 'how to think big'. Unexampled scale of mass and sweep of design. His style dominated the gardens of civilized Europe for a longe time.
5. **Feature of Italian garden-** Came into existent at the time Renaissance and resemble Mughal or Persian garden. Fountains, sculptures, water canal, box on yellow, hedge, topiary arbaur, trellis and architecturally beautiful garden e.g. Plant of rose.
6. **Feature of Japanese garden-** It is the both the Persian and Japanese garden design were based on their respective ideas of heaven. The Japanese continued the same style for centuries but still remain popular. Ornamental water ponds, streams waterfall, fountains, wall, water basin. It should be a place where the mind finds rest and relaxation.

Plants in Japanese garden

- **Evergreen-** Abies, Chytomeria, Juneperus, Mangolia, Podocarpus etc.
- **Decidous-** Acer sp, Populus, Morus, Salix, Prunus etc.
- **Shrubs-** Azaleas, Gardenia, Camellia, Lagerstroemia, Rhododendron etc.
- **Climber-** Clematis, Wisteria, Loocera etc.
- **Annuals-** Aster, Chrysathemum, Carnation etc.
- **Bulbous-** Canna, Gladiolus and Lilly etc.

Types of Japaneese garden

A Japanese garden may either be in the form of a large public park or a small family garden designed for living which is seen usually by members of the family or he family guests. The Japanese gardens are further classified based on positions, shape, and purpose. The important types are: i) Hill garden, ii) Flat garden, iii) Tea garden, iv) Passage garden and v) Sand gardens.

1. **Hill garden:** Out of the various styles, this one is considered to be the ideal by many garden enthusiasts. This style is known in Japanese as Tsukiyama-niwa or Tsukiyama sansui, meaning hills and water. Though this garden can be laid out in a space of any size by making use of perspective to maintain a reduced scale, it is obvious that a fairly large area is much suitable as laying out a mountain scenery needs considerable space, The hill garden is made up of one or more hills designed with earth mounds and exposed weathered stones, The other features of this garden are water in the form of a stream or a pond or a waterfalls or all the three with or without islands and also bridges, lantern, stones, and trees, If it is not possible to introduce

water in the garden, its presence is effected by a dried bed of stream or a dry shoreline. The important points in the garden are decorated with stones and selected trees. But pine trees may be planted to give the effect of being swept by wind, untrimmed stepping stones are placed over the walks.

An island is general an usual feature in a hill garden. When the island is present it should be decorated with a "Worshipping stone", called raithai-seki in Japanese, a "Snow-viewing" lantern and a pine tree.

2. **Flat garden :** As the name implies, Hira-niwa or flat gardens are laid out in flat ground without hills or ponds. Flat gardens are supposed to represent a mountain valley or a meadowland. These gardens were popular during the era of Muromachi (1392-1573).

   A flat garden is not necessarily as flat as a pan-cake. Since it stimulates a mountain valley, low rounded hills designed with the help of stones or earth mounds or both will look quite appropriate in a flat garden. But some others opine that there should not b any ups and downs in a flat garden. The usual features to break the monotony of a flat garden are a well, a water-basin made of stone in the shape of an urn, stones lying close to the ground, stepping stones, and trees. The trees are trained to lie close to the ground. In a flat garden, the principle is to avoid strong vertical lines represented by tall pines. In olden days the flat gardens were simple in design consisting of a few low-growing trees and flat rocks but in modern times many features of the tea garden, like water-basin, have been incorporated in this type of garden also.

3. **Tea garden :** The tea garden is laid out based on certain principles and customs of the Japanese tea ceremony and hence needs a considerable space of at least about 200 square metres, for its designing. Since the performance of the tea ceremony needs an atmosphere of intimacy it is essential that the garden be enclosed by a fence. But the fence should be rustic in nature, with a gale made of very light material such as bamboo. To protect the tea house from the noise of the outer world, the tea gardens are divided into an outer garden (soto-roji) and inner garden (uchi-roji).

   The outer garden is comparatively a narrow area, with a waiting place where the guests are supposed to wait until the master of the house appears to welcome them. This waiting place has a water-basin for the convenience of the guests who can wash their hands and a stone lantern for illumination, but n present days this serves more as a decoration piece. A stone path, usually of stepping-stones, leads to the inner garden. The inner garden is also separated from the outer garden by a rustic fence and a gate made of light material.

4. **Passage garden :** The passage gardens, the Roji-niwa, are those which are laid in narrow passage, as for example a narrow space between two houses or approaches to buildings. As such areas are generally narrow the garden lay-out should be simple and not overcrowded.

   In such gardens there should be hardly any ornaments such as lanterns, basins or other man-made features. The common features of a passage garden are a few key rocks, slabs of stones, and only a couple of types of plant. Bushy shrubs and trees are unsuitable in a passage garden; instead, plants with open form and slender shapes are selected.

5. **Sand garden :** It is the simplest style of gardening, though not liked by many as it is totally devoid of plants. The most famous sand garden exists in Kyoto and is known as Ryoanji garden. The garden consists of a rectangular area of about 350 m^2 adjoining a Zen Buddhist temple. The main feature of this style of gardening is to arrange a few vertical and prostrate stones in groups of 2 or 3 and to fill in the gap between the stones with fine white gravel. The gravel is raked in most simple patterns simulating the ripples flowing water. The raking has to be repeated often to keep the garden in its best shape. This style of garden looks pleasant and effective only when confined to a limited area.

Styles of garden

Styles of garden is a good appearance typically determine by the principle according to which gardening can be worked out. Besides the term landscape gardening the other two of familiar terms in gardening are the formal and informal gardens. The following terms are given below.

1. **Formal:** In this garden the design is still as everything is done in a straight and narrow way. In such garden everything is planted in strait lines e.g. Mughal, Persian, French and Italian.

2. **Informal:** In an informal garden, the whole design looks informal, as the plants and the features are arranged in a natural way without following any hard and fast rules e.g. English, Japanese and Chinese.

3. **Free style:** In which also study the both formal and informal garden. Which in the found middle of the systematic and non systematic in nature e.g. Rose garden (Chandigarh).

4. **Wild:** The concept of wild garden is not only against all formalism but it also breaks the rule of landscape styles and naturalize plants in shrubbemes. Wild style garden are found unsystematic planting of tree, shrubs and bulbous plants etc.

5. **Ornamental garden:** In planning a garden several factor like size of the house and the space available for garden, availability of border, cost of laying the garden its maintenances have to be taken into consideration eg. Park (Private and public).

Though in India from history and ancient literature we find that gardening was quite in vogue in olden times, but unfortunately there is no garden style called 'Indian Garden' which can claim a place in the major gardening styles of the world. The famous garnden style of India the "Mughal Gardens" are nothing but a replica of the ancient Persian Gardens.

The features of the major garden styles are given bellow:

A. Features of formal garden

- First plan is made on paper and then land is selected accordingly.
- Land is leveled.
- Symmetrical design.
- Geometrical (Square, Rectangular, Circular beds border).
- Roads and path cut a right angle.
- Balance is symmetrical as a same feature replicated on both side of center axis.
- Hedge, edge, topiary trimmed.
- Tree can be selected as individual feature.
- They are usually small to medium in size.
- It has east and west orientation Mughal garden, Persian, Italian and French American.

B. Features of informal garden

- Plan is forced to fit the land.
- Main aim is to capture natural scenery.
- Land is not labeled.
- A symmetrical design.
- Non geometrical beds and border, untrimmed hedge, edge, and topiary.
- Individual plant as not selected as feature.
- Much more variety of elements is use.
- Animal like, Umbrella, Seats, Cassettes, Rockery, Water pull etc. Such as Japanese, Chinese, English etc.

C. Features of free style garden

- A new approach to gardening that allows developing a garden with what on land.
- This style combine the good point of both formal and informal as well as naturalistic feature and aesthetic mixed to create a picturesqure effect.
- This style is suited to almost all situations.

D. Features of wild style garden

- Wild styles garden no rules are followed but aim is to make the garden is beauty and natural "William Robinsons".
- Aim is to make garden more beautiful and natural.
- Such gardens are laid out for more agreeable communication in nature.
- Wild variety of trees, shrubs and creepers are used in natural lays.
- No formal rules are followed and allowed to give in their natural shapes.

Chapter 26

Hedge, Edge and Topiary

Hedge

When shrub is planted on boundary for fencing, it is also called as hedge. In other word shrubs or trees planted at regular intervals to form a continuous screen is called a hedge. It may be ornamental or protective or both. Hedge also become an important feature of formal layout to serve various function as screening of the area out building, tennis court, vegetable garden, hardening of unwanted place etc. All the shrubs cannot be planted for making an ideal hedge due to different nature of growth.

For selecting an ideal shrub for a hedge, it should have fallowing characteristics.

- It should have thick texture and quick growth.
- It should stand trimming to shape.
- It should be easily propagated through seeds or cutting.
- It should with stand drought condition.
- It should not attract reptile's animals.

Classificatin of Hedge

Hedge are planted to protect the area to avoid the trespassing to man or animals or to beautify the boundary of different therefore according to purpose hedge can be classified as-

- Tall protective hedge.
- Dwarf protective hedge.
- Tall ornamental hedge.
- Dwarf ornamental hedge.

1. **Tall protective hedge :** The height is about 1-3m and growth is very dense along with thorns eg. *Inga dulcis*, *Carissa carandus* and *Bougainvillea species* etc.
2. **Dwarf protective hedge :** Dwarf shrubs grow about 1m and have thorns and protective in natures eg. Euphorbia (*Euphorbia bojori)*, Nagphani

(*Opuntia species)*, Agave (*Agave species)* and Davils tree (*Pendilanthus species)* etc.

3. **Tall ornamental hedge-** Shrubs grow 1-3m tall and have attractive foliage plant produce colour full flower are also eg. Heena (*Lawsonia alba)*, Duranta (*Duranta plumieri)*, Rukmani (*Murraya panniculata)*, China rose (*Hibiscus rosasinensis)* and Fire bush (*Hamelia patens*) etc.

4. **Dwarf ornamental hedge-** Height of dwarf hedge is about 1m and plants are very attractive eg. Acalypha (*Acalypha pecies)*, Wild jasmine (*Clerodendrum inerme*), Lantanas (*Lantana species)* and *Thunbergia errecta* etc.

Growing of Hedge

Purpose- A garden hedge can serve the purpose of a compound wall, give shelter from strong gails, ensure privacy i.e. serve the purpose of a screen from a background for a floral display such as herbaceous border, as a part of the garden on its own merit, separate one component of a garden from the other (vegetable garden from the flower garden) and screen the ugly and unwanted spots such as manure pits, lavatory, servants quarters etc. in the garden.

Critaria for selection a hedge plant- In a garden a headge is planted with two motives: a) protective, which means protection against theft, trespass, wind etc. and b) for ornamental purposes or screening. For the first category a hedge plant should have the following characteristics- quick growing, hardy, including drought resistant characters, thorny, dense, should responced to frequent pruning and clipping and can be raised quickly by seeds or cutting.

Preparation of soil- Hedge plants can be grown in various kinds of soil. For better growth of plants soil should be deep, well drained and fertile therefore, planning and preparation of ground should be done carefully. For making a good growth of hedge a trench about 60-75 cm deep and 30-60 cm width should be dug up and left exposed for a fort night or so before planting in order to destroy harmful micro flora and insects by scroching sun.

Planting time- The most suitable time of planting hedge is rainy season in the beginning of monsoon, weather condition are hot and humid. Planting can also be done during Feb.-March depending upon the availability of regular supply of water and planting material.

Planting method- Rooted cutting or seed are planted. Under Indian conditions the planting of hedge is undertaken at the beginning of the monsoon season in June-July. A headge is started by sowing seeds or by putting cutting in situ or by planting rooted cutting, generally in double rows. The distance of planting for tall hedge should be about 60-90cm and for dwarf hedge it should be about 20-30cm. The planting should be done by triangular system, show that it makes a good dense hedge.

Maintenance- Hedge does not like weed growth at the base and these should be uprooted as and when they appear. Keeping reserve plants are essential, otherwise the casualties are to be replaced by seeds or new cutting, again the uniformity in growth will be lost.

Irrigation- Water requirement of hedge depends upon climate and soil types. During rainy season generally not irrigation required for hedge planting and during winter season generally water required once in 10-15 days and at weekly intervals during summer season.

Manuring- Manuring is one aspect which receives least attention by the gardeners. One may be inclined to believe that manuring of hedge is a sheer waste. Once in a year the hedge should receive before the rains well rotten cowdung at the rate of 4 kg per running metre. It should be well incorporated in the soil. Fertilizers can also be added twice a year at the rate of 30g each of superphosphate, bonemeal and ammonium sulphate per metre row of hedge.

Trimming- When the hedge plants attain a height of 15cm height with the topped back to 10cm height with the garden shears topping is done many times till desire height is acheved. Later on hedge can be trimmed to different shape. The top of hedge can be kept flat, wavi, black of square or any shape. In rainy season frequent trimming is required because plant make faster growth than winter or summer season.

Clipping and pruning- It is the hedge are most important to keep the hedge neat and in good shape. They should be done at regular intervals and no stage the top growth should exceed 15-20 cm in length.

Edge

When low growing perennial plants are grown on the border of plots or beds. They are called as edge plant or an edge. These plants hardly grow up to 20-30 cm. In garden edge are also planted around rockery, big tree, alongside walks pathway and to divide the area. Like an edge they also become a part of formal or informal landscape designs. The edge plants are usually propagated through terminal cutting during rainy season and stand against trimming eg. *Eupatorium cannabium*, *Justicia species, Iresin lindenii* and *Alternanthera versicolour* etc.

Edging- The term edging can be defined as any material of any description which is employed in garden for dividing flower bed borders etc. from road wall or path for demarcating spaces allotted for particular purpose.

Kinds of edging

1. **Living edging-** Colourfull flower
   a. **Foliage plants-** *Alternanthera tricolor, Aspidistra sps., Coleus blumei, Iresine sps. and Pilea muscosa* etc.
   b. **Flowering plants-** Sweet allysum (*Allysum mauritinum*), Candytuft (*Eberis amara*) and Marigold (*Tagets sps.*) etc.
2. **Mechanical edging-** Brick in vertical and horizontal.

Topiary

It is an art of training plants into different shape i.e. of birds, animals, domes, umbrellas, etc. Topiary was first introduced in Roman garden in the first century and letter revived in 12th century in the monastic garden. For simple geometric topiary shape frame is not required and the plant can be trained free hand. However, for larger shape, iron, frame is required to trained the plant on it. It is an old art and now a day. It is becoming common in City Park to provide passive, recreation to the visitors specially children. The ideal plant should be quick growing with small foliage and stands against trimming which is done frequently.

Suitable plants like *Clerodendrum inerme*, *Cupressus macrocarpa*, *Duranta plumier*, *Bougainvillea species* and P*utranjiva roxburghii* etc.

Training frames are employed for making topiary. The frames are generally made by soft steel rods or galvanized wire frame. Making frames true to shape is highly technical and artistic for true depiction of figures. The figures of lady with a pitcher, elephant, giraffe, camal, ox, monkey, birds, peacock, farmer and bullocks and umbrella etc. are liked by everybody. For picturesque topiary, there should be a broad base or on plateform of plants. For large animals 2-4 plants are planted at different point. Planting of selected plant at selected place is done at an early stage, stopping of branches is done for dense growth and then frame is placed. Maintenance of topiary plant need special care plant should be liberally watered and fertilized so that plants make a dense and colourful growth.

Chapter 27

Garden Features

Garden Walls : A garden lover will never like to block the view of his garden by putting a wall along its periphery. A garden as it is enjoyed from inside should also be visible from outside.

- Low brick or concrete or stone wall of say 60-90 cm height and to put over it some grills.
- Alternatively walls from 1.8-5.0 m may also be erected depending upon the size of garden.
- One may grow creepers such as *Ficus repens* over the wall.

Flower Beds: The most essential criterion of a flower beds is display the flowers in the best way possible. It may be born in mind that flowers look best when massed in a bed. The flower beds are of special importance under condition of the plains of India since they can be kept planted throughout the year unlike those in England or other parts of Europe where nothing can be grown in the open between November-March. Annuals and herbaceous, perennial flowers, flowering plants are grown in flower beds to provide massing effect of different colours borders is continuous beds of more length than width containing plant of one kind only.

- The flower beds display the flower in their best way.
- More important part of a formal garden.
- These should be simple in design as circular, rectangle, and square.
- It should be simple in design as it is easier to maintain them.
- It is most important part of a formal garden.
- It can be planted during September/October (winter flower), February/ March (summer flower) and April-June (rainy flower).

Path or Garden Drives : A garden must have a carriage drive leading to the house and the garage besides several other paths or walks leading to different parts of the garden. When the planting of low growing perennial plants are grown on the paths it is the also become a part of formal and in formal landscape design. The garden path should never be less than 60 cm wide but should be preferably between 90-120 cm, if sufficient is a available. The ideal plant should be quick growing with small stands against trained which is done frequently. A garden drives leads to the house and the garage while paths walk leads to different part of garden. The principle of construction of garden path are the same as for drives but since these are narrow and not meant for heavy traffic the foundation need not be so deep.

- Paths should not be generally too high or too low from the adjoining ground except in a marsh or a rock garden.
- Garden paths are generally mode of gravel, paving stone crazy paving, bricks, grass etc.
- Garden drives are generally mode of gravel and asphalt or concrete.

Steps : Sometimes it becomes necessary to have steps in a garden as for example when a path goes from one level to the other or one has to climb or get down from the terrace garden. The steps in the garden should be different than those in the building.

- Steps used to move from one level to others.
- To climb or get down from the terrace garden
- Steps can be made of concrete, stones, wood or gravels.
- It should be quite broad and raiser low.

Arches : A garden may need some arches for training climbers or ramblers. A general rule is to have the same width as the height provided space permits.

- Arches are generally erected over walk usually at the entrance and are usually 2 m in height.
- Generally constructed near the gate all over the paths.
- The supporting poles can be made of stone pillar.
- It should be at least 2-2.5 m height.

Pergolas : For growing creepers in a row pergola are ideal structures on which these may be trained. A pergola may be defined as a series of arches joined together.

- It is series of arches joined together generally constructed over pathways.
- It adds beauty to the garden.
- It is useful as resting place.
- In broad pergola it may also be possible to keep a few shade-loving plants to protect them against sun but this may not be desirable all the time.
- Made of wood or stone or brick pillars, angled iron and galvanized pipe.

Terraces- In hilly tract it is not possible to have a large piece of land in one plane for laying a garden and hence gardens are laid in terraces, where it is a natural phenomenon. But, in plains of India the land for gardening may not have any natural undulation for terracing.

- This is common feature in the English or Japanese garden.
- It is the raised flats are gravel section.
- To construct a part or a major portion of the garden.
- It forms a natural links.
- It should give a full view of the garden.

Paved Garden- A paved garden, if properly laid, can be a very attractive feature of a garden. There are some specific plants, which adopt themselves well to a paved garden. These should be dwarf in nature and stand a considerable amount of water and tear from shoes of different weight. But a paved garden should be laid in a path which is not used very often. A special paved garden may also be created if a path suitable for this is not available. Ordinarily a paved garden is meant for walking, although not very frequently and hence the interstices of the paved garden should be planted sparingly.

Carpet Bedding- The art of growing ground cover plants closely and trimming them to a design or alphabetical latter is called carpet beds colour full foliage as edge plants it found to be more suitable for this purpose eg. Alternanthera, Cinararia, Coleus, Irisine, Partulaca etc.

- It is used to cover an area preferably a bed or a series of beds.
- It is arranged in a slope or a slanting position.
- It is the form of a figure or some letters that's cut out.
- Plants having different growth habits or having different colour full leafs are used.

Dry Wall- The term 'Dry Wall' is rather a misnomer, as a wall may be dry but once the plants are planted over it, it no more remains dry but becomes an object of beauty. Whatever may be the name, garden laid on a wall or walls planted with different plants are termed as dry wall in the garden dictionary. Plants growing in the crevices of the stones and hanging down the face of a dry wall look beautiful and are becoming a common feature of the English garden.

Chapter 28

Annuals

Annuals or seasonals are the group of plants which complete their life cycle in one season or in one year. Annuals are commonly known as seasonals as they complete the processes of life (germination, growth, flowering and seed formation)

Chapter 28

Annuals

Annuals

Annuals or seassonals are the group of plants which complete their life cycle in one season or in one year. Annuals are commonly known as seasonal as they complete the process of life like germination, growth flowering and seed formation in one season and finally the plant without. Annuals are widely used for garden decoration, cut flower and pot plants. They are frequently grown as bedding plant and in rock garden on the sides of lily pool and in shrubberies.

Important Feature of Annuals

- These plants can be easily grown.
- A wide variation exists among plants in form, habit of growth, flower colour and flower size.
- Propagation through both sexual and asexual.
- Annuals without aid of other plants keep the garden full and joyful year round.
- Annuals are grown in pots or in ground.

Classification of Annuals

1. According to season

Annuals have different temperature requirement for their growth, development and flowering according.

- Winter
- Summer
- Rainy

a. **Winter season annuals-** The annual that can be easily grown under low temperature with profuse flowering falls under winter annuals. The nursery should be prepared during month of September. Whereas, transplanting should be done in October in hilly area planting during the month of March eg. Calendula, Ice plant, Pansy, Phlox, Partulaca, Sweet sultan etc.

b. **Summer season annuals-** The annuals that thrive well under extremely high temperature during summer fall under summer annuals for this sowing should be done during the end of February and beginning of March and transplanting during the month of March to April eg. Cosmos, Gaillardia, Kochia, Sunflower, Zinnia etc.

c. **Rainy season annuals-** The annuals that can with stand rains and high humidity come under rainy humidity. Sowing time in June and transplanting in July eg. Amaranthus, Balsam, Gaillardia, Cocks comb, Zinnia etc.

2. According to height

In general, medium and dwarf annuals are ideal for growing in pots. Whereas, tall annuals can be used for fence. Depending on their height they can be classified as fallowing.

a. **Dwarf-** Annuals that can grow up to height of 0.45m comes under dwarf category. For edging, these annuals are used eg. Calendula, Pansy, Sweet alyssum, French marigold, Kochia etc.

b. **Medium-** The annuals whose height varies between 0.45-0.75 m is medium use for screening purpose eg. Petunia, Salvia, Candy tuft, Aster, Carnation etc.

c. **Tall-** These annuals are of height more than 0.75m and annuals are commonly used for screening purpose eg. French marigold, Cosmos, Holly hock, Sun flower etc.

3. According to colour

Annuals have got wide range of flower colour in pure form a single or in combination.

a. **Blue and purple colour-** Sweet pea, China aster, Ageratum, Pansy, Corn flower etc.

b. **White colour-** Candy tuft, Petunia, Phlox, Sweet sultan etc.

c. **Pink and Red colour-** Salvia, Phlox, Holly hock, Verbena etc.

d. **Yellow colour-** Calendula, Sun flower, Tithonia, Cosmos, Marigold etc.

4. According to commercial value

a. **Cut flower-** Cut blooms of seasonal are used as vase decoration eg. Aster, Calendula, Carnation, Sweet pea, Zinnia etc.

b. **Loose flower-** Some annuals are used as loose flower for making garland and veni eg. Annual Chrysanthemum, Marigold, Amaranthus, Gaillardia, Balsam etc.

Screening- Using plant to interrupt give can be a way of drawing the eye to word a specific feature or a practical solution for blocking and unsightly view.

5. According to situation

Different annuals are suited to different situations and therefore, right type of annuals should be selected for particular purpose.

a. **For carpet bedding-** Candytuft, Ice plant, Salvia, Sweet alyssum, Sweet william etc.

b. **For climbing-** Sweet pea, *Clitoria terntea*, Nasturtium etc.

c. **For dry flower arrangement-** Nigella, static, Acrolium, Cocks comb etc.

d. **For edging-** French marigold, Pansy, Sweet alyssum, Ageratum, Candy tuft etc.

e. **For fragrance-** Sweet sultan, Sweet william, Sweet alyssum, Stock, Jasmine etc.

f. **For hanging basket-** Petunia, Sweet alyssum, Toroia, Verbena etc.

g. **For ornamental foliage-** Amaranthus, Kochia etc.

h. **For pinching requirement-** Marigold, Ageratum, Zinnia, Petunia, Calendula etc.

i. **For pots-** Balsam, Kochia, Amaranthus, Petunia, Portulaca etc.

j. **For rockery purpose-** Candy tuft, Ice plant, Nasturtium, Phlox, Portulaca, Pansy etc.

k. **For screening purpose-** Nasturtium, Holly hock, Sweet pea, Morning glory etc.

l. **For shady situation-** Phlox, Salvia, Balsam, Torenia, Ageratum, Cineraria etc.

m. **For window purpose-** Aster, Calendula, Petunia, Phlox etc.

6. According to soil requirement

a. **For very poor soil-** Cock's comb, Gaillardia, Balsam, Portulaca, Petunia, Sweet sultan, Sweet alyssum etc.

b. **For alkaline soil-** Balsam, Phlox, Nasturtium, Zinnia, Poppy etc.

c. **For acidic soil-** French marigold, Zinnia, Nasturtium etc.

Cultivation practice

Soil- Annuals grow in well drained fertile sandy loam soil rich in organic matter. Soil should not be acidic are alkaline. The ideal pH 6-7.5 for best cultivation of annuals. In case of clay and sandy soil addition of organic manure will be helpful to improve the soil texture and porosity.

Nursery management- All the annuals are propagated by seed. Seed can be sown in nursery beds, earthen pot, seed pan, seed tray etc.

Management

- Seed bed should be propagated in a place with good drainage system and away from shade.
- Soil should be sandy loam and natural in pH.
- FYM at 10 kg/m^2 should be incorporated in bed.
- Size of seed bed should be 3x1m^2 bed length increase with as per requirement.
- In seed bed are sown in rows 6cm apart.
- After sowing seed must be covered with fine FYM and paddy straw.
- Watering should be done soon after sowing and latter when required.
- In general seedling will be ready to transplant after one month when attend 4-5 true leaf.

Annuals bed and transplanting- Time of transplanting must be during evening hours since the night temperature is beneficial for the successful establishment for seedling. Before transplanting seddling must be harden by check the irrigation for few days.

Planting distance- Distance of annuals will be depend upon the height of the plant. If distance is not properly maintaine the growth of the plant will be adversely affected. The distance for dwarf annual is 30x30cm, medium 45x45cm and tall 60x60cm should be maintained.

Manures and fertilizers- Application of FYM at 5 kg/m^2 should be done during bed preparation and fertilizer NPK (15:10:10gm/m^2) should be applied after 30 day of transplanting. After transplanting of seedling bed must be weed free and irrigate properly.

Intercultural operation- In annuals 3-4 weeding can be done and hoeing and earthing to be followed if necessary.

Plant protection measure

Disease- Damping off, leaf spot, leaf blight, powdery mildew, downy mildew and wilt.

Control- Capton 2 gm/lt, Carbendazim 2 gm/lt, Dithane-M-45, Dithane-Z-78 2 gm/lt.

Insect- Aphids, Bettles, Weevils, and Catter piller.

Control- Imidacloparid 1.5-2.0 ml/lt.

Description of some important annuals

A. Winter season annuals

S. No.	Common name	Botanical name	Family	Flower colour	Plant height (cm)	Remark
1	Paper flower	*Acroclinum roseum*	Compositae	White and pink	45-60	Daisy-like-flower
2	Flors flower	*Ageratum mexicanum*	Compositae	Blue, white pink	20-45	Fliff hads of flowers
3	Hollyhock	*Althaea rosea*	Malvaceae	Pink, scarlet red, maure vilet and yellow	100-120	Majestic plant
4	Sweet alyssum	*Alyssum maritimum*	Cruciferae	White, pink lilac	10-20	Edeging and bedding purpose
5	Snapdragon	*Antirrhinum majus*	Scrophulariaceae	White, pink, yellow foick red and maroom	30-7-	Flowers like dragons jaw on spikes
6	African daisy	*Arctotis grandis*	Compositae	White, orange red	45-60	Bsby, vigorous
7	Daisy	*Bellis perennis*	Compositae	White, pink and crimson	20-30	Dwarf plants
8	Swan river daisy	*Brachycome iberidifolia*	Compositae	White, pink	20-50	Dwarf plant
9	Calendula	*Calendula officinalis*	Compositae	Yellow orange	30-50	Meaning first day of the month
10	Corn flower	*Centaurea cyanus*	Compositae	Blue, pink white	60-80	Weed of the corn field
11	Sweet sultan	*Centaura moschata*	Compositae	White, purple, red, yellow	70-10	Flowers look like power/puff
12	Wall flower	*Cheriranthus cheiri*	Crucifereae	Yellow, burnt orange	30-45	Bedding and pot culture
13	Annual chrysanthemum	*Chrysanthemum coronarium*	Compositae	Yellow white	90-120	Beding purpose
14	Cineraria	*Senecio cruentus*	Compositae	Puple white	30-45	Pot culture, shade loving
15	Clarkia	*Clarkia ebegans*	Onagraceae	White, pink, rose scrlate	60-80	Have long spikes
16	Parrot bill	*Clanthus dampieri*	Leguminosae	Crimson	60-80	Flower are pendulous
17	Coreopsis	*Coreopsis tinctoria*	Compositae	Yellow crimson, brown	45-60	For bedding purposes
18	Cosmos	*Cosmos bipinnatus*	Compositae	Pink, purple, crimson, white	60-100	Good for mass planting
19	Dahlia	*Dahlia variabilis*	Compositae	Yellow, red, blue, white, crismon	60-120	Bedding and pot culture
20	Larkspur	*Delphinium ajacis*	Ranunclaceae	Volat, crimson, pink, blue, white	45-20	Bedding and cut flower
21	Sweet william	*Dianthus barbotus*	Caryophyllaceae	Pink, crimson, mauve, yellow	30-45	Scentd flower

22	Carnation	*Dianthus caryophyllus*	Caryophyllaceae	Pink,white, yellow, mauve, crimson violet	30-60	Cut flower good vaselife
23	African daisy	*Dimorphotheca calendulacea*	Compositae	Yellow, white	30-60	Flowers open during day time
24	California poppy	*Eshscholzia calofomia*	Papaveraceae	Yellow, orange	30-45	Bedding and pot culture
25	Blanket flower	*Gaillardia pulchella*	Compositae	Yellow, orange, lemon, maroom	30-45	Bedding and cutting
26	Freasure flower	*Gazania splendens*	Compositae	Yellow, orange white, red	20-25	Rock garden
27	Boy's breath	*Gypsophila elegans*	Caryophyllaceae	White, pink	30-45	Small lance shaped floor
28	Everlasting flower	*Helichrysum bracteatum*	Compositae	Yellow, pink, red	45-60	Flower long lasting
29	Candytuft	*Iberis amara*	Crucifereae	White lilac	20-30	Flower appear in tufts on spikes
30	Sweep pea	*Lathyrus odoratins*	Leguminosae	White, blue, pink,mauve	90-120	Grown as background,in tufts on spickes
31	Statice	*Limonium sinuatum*	Plumbaginace	White, pink, purple	45-60	Good cut flower
32	Linaria	*Linaria bipartite*	Scrophulariaceae	White, blue, pink, red yellow	0-45	Bed and pot culture
33	Lupin	*Lupines lurens*	Leguminosae	Yellow, blue	40-60	Cutting beds borders
34	Stock	*Mattihola* sps.	Cruciferae	White, red	60-90	Scented cutting
35	Ice plant	*Mesembryanthemum tricolor*	Aizoaceae	Pink, white, yellow	20-30	Rock garden dry wall
36	Nemesia	*Nemesia strumosa*	Scrophuariaceae	White, blue, yellow, orange	45-60	Cut flower
37	Nigella	*Nigella demascena*	Ranunculaceae	White, blue, rose	45-60	Good colour for cut flower
38	Shirley poppy	*Papaver roheas*	Papaveraceae	Scarlet pink white	60-75	Popular flower
39	Phlox	*Rhloxy drummondii*	Polemoniaceae	Pink, crimson, purple, violet	30-45	Bedding plant
40	Nasturtium	*Tropacolum mojus*	Tropacolaceae	Yellow, orange, red	30-40	Bedding
41	Salvia	*Sativa splenders*	Labatae	Red, white, blue, scarlet	30-45	Shade loving
42	Saponaria	*Saponaria calabrica*	Caryophyllaceae	Pink, white, red	60-90	Flowers resembles gypsophilla
43	Pansy	*Viola tricolor*	Violaceae	Purple, blue, yellow	20-30	Pot culture
44	Aster	*Callistephus chinensis*	Compositae	Pink, rose, purple	30-45	Pot and bed culture
45	Sweet sultan	*Centarrea moschata*	Compositae	Purple, pink, blue	30-45	Bed culture
46	African marigold	*Tagetes erecta*	Compositae	Yellow, orange	45-100	Bed culture
47	French marigold	*Tagetes patula*	Compositae	Red, brown, yellow, orange	20-30	Pot and bed culture
48	Verbena	*Verbena hybrid*	Varbinaceae	Pink, red, purple, blue	30-45	Bed culture
49	Lace flower	*Trachymene caerule*	Umbelliferae	White. Pink, blue	45-60	Umbrella like clusters
50	Linum	*Linum grandiflorum*	Linaceae	Red, purple	30-45	Bed culture

B. Summer season annuals

S. No.	Common name	Botanical name	Family	Flower colour	Plant height (cm)	Remark
1	Portulaca	*Portulaca grandiflora*	Portulaceae	Pink, red, yellow, blue, orange	10-15	Pot and bed
2	Blanket flower	*Gaillardia punlchella*	Compositae	Yellow, brown, orange, scarlet	45-60	Easy to grow
3	Kochia	*Kochia scoparia*	Chenopodiaceae		60-75	Green leaves gives
4	Petunia	*Petunia hybrid*	Solanaceae	Pink, blue, purple, white	20-30	Give good effect
5	Zinnia	*Zinnia elegans*	Compositae	Violet, orange, white	70-80	Very hardy, easily grown
6	Sada bahar	*Vinca rosea*		Pink	30-60	Very hardy plant
7	Coreopsis	*Coreopsis tinctoria*	Compositae	Yellow, scarlet	45-60	
8	Sunflower	*Helianthus anuus*	Compositae	Yellow, orange	60-120	Can be grown throughout the year
9	Cosmos	*Cosmos bipinnatus*	Compositae	Pink, orange, yellow	60-70	Bedding purpose

C. Rainy season annuals

S. No.	Common name	Botanical name	Family	Flower colour	Plant height(cm)	Remark
1	Balsam	*Impatiens balsamina*	Balsaminaceae	Pink, red, rose	60-70	Very delicate
2	Cocks comb	*Celosia argentea var. cristata*	Amaranthaceae	Red, yellow orange	30-60	Hardy plant
3	Zinnia	*Zinnia elegans*	Compositae	Violet, orange	70-80	Hardy plant
4	Amaranthus	*Amaranthus caudatus*	Amaranthaceae	Pink, white	45-60	Grown in pots
5	Button flower	*Gomphrena globosa*	Amaranthaceae	White, purple pink	60-70	Bedding, pot culture

Chapter 29

Shrubs

Annuals Border

In this type of border annuals are planted according to their height to beauty of the garden. Annuals border are found two types.

- Single face border.
- Double face border.

Single face border- In this type dwarf plant is kept on front of beds, medium height annuals are planted in the centre while the taller annuals are planted in the back.

Double face border- In this type tall annuals are planted in the center and medium and dwarf annuals are planted in both sides of tall annuals so that full view can be seen from both side.

Herbaceous Border

In this, plant are arranged in irregular group of a kind for harmonious are contrasting colour effect, either all flowering at one time or successfully in such a way that those flowering later should grow up and screen the already flowered. The planting of annuals in the border of a plot is called as herbaceous border. When the border is to be viewed from both sides tall plants are planted in center followed by medium and dwarf planting in both side. Herbaceous border may include all the herbaceous plant including herbaceous perennial (Flowering and non flowering) bulbous and annuals.

Plant Suitable for Herbaceous Border

A. According to height

1. **Tall-** Corn flower, Holly hock, Sun flower, Dahlia etc.
2. **Medium-** Aster, Salvia, Geranium, Gladiolus, Lillium etc.
3. **Dwarf-** Phlox, Iris, Ice plant, Kochia, Gerbera, Anthurium etc.

B. According to colour scheme

1. **Monochromatic colour-** It consists of different tents and shades of one colour and is seldom achieved in its pure from in the landscape. Colour scheme could include white and pink flower with back ground of dark pink and red brick house.

2. **Analogous colour-** It combines colours which are adjacent or side by side on colour wheel. An analogous colour scheme includes green, blue green, green blue, blue and violet blue.
3. **Complementary colour-** Red and green would be complementary colour a complementary colour scheme may be achieved by using plants with green foliage against a red brick house. Transition is gradual change transition in colour can be illustrated by redial sequence on the colour wheel (Monochromatic colour scheme).

Shrubs

Shrubs is a woody plant with several stem and branches arising at the ground level from the main stem. This is perennial in nature and smaller than a tree. Shrubs are very important in the garden as flower, shrubs produce beautiful flower at eye level and fragrant shrubs emit fragrant as nose level. Shrubs produce flower, foliage, fruits and berries and enhance beauty of garden they are hardy in nature and require less care than other ornamental plants.

Importance of Shrubs

- Enhance beauty of surrounding.
- Provide fragrance in garden.
- They take the place of garden boundary wall and provide live lines to the garden.
- Divides different areas are feature in the garden.
- Screen off unwanted sides.
- Reduces wind velocity, soil erosion, weed growth.

Classification of Shrubs

1. According to beauty of plants

a. **For flowers-** There are several shrubs that are grown for their very attractive flowers and enhanced beauty of garden eg. *Barleria cristata*, *Bougainvillea species*, *Crossandra undulaefolia*, *Hibiscus rosa-sinensis*, *Jasminum pubescence* etc.

b. **For foliage-** These shrubs produce beautiful foliage eg. *Codiaem varigatum*, *Euphorbia cotinifolia*, *Manihot species*, Aralia etc.

c. **For variegated foliage-** There are certain shrubs that produce variegated foliage eg. *Duranta plumier*, *D. varigata*. *Manihot utilissima var*, *Tebernaemontana coronaria var* etc.

d. **For flower and foliage-** In these classes are fond as *Acalypha hispida*, Bougainvillea (Archana, Bhabha), Hibiscus (Snow queen and Redhot), *Hamelia patens* etc.

e. **For fruits-** These are a shrub that bears showy fruits eg. *Carissa carandas* (Dark red), *Citrus japonica* (Yellow), *Duranta macrophylla* (Yellow), *Rauwolfia canscens* (Red) etc.

f. **For fragrance-** In which the fragrance flowers are grown for beautification eg. *Cestrum nocturnum* (Rat-Ki-Rani), *Cestrum diurnum* (Din-Ka-Raja), *Jasminum auriculatum, Jasminum grandiflorum, Jasminum sambac* etc.

2. According to requirement of sunlight

a. **For sunny situation-**Bougainvillea, *Hibiscus rosa-sinensis, Jasminum sambac, Jasminum grandiflorum, Lantana camara, Murraya exotica* etc.

b. **For partial or semi shade-** *Jatropha roseia, Mussaenda philippica, Magnolia grandiflora, Nandina domestica* etc.

c. **For both partial and sunny shade-** Acalypha, *Cestrurm nocturnum, Crosandra sps., Hemelia patens, Thunbergia erecta* etc.

3. According to pH

a. **Shrub tolerant to acidic soil-** pH 5.0 below eg. *Juniperus communis, Rhododendron spp., Kalmia latifolia, Aesculus parviflora* etc.

b. **Medium acidic soil-** pH 5.0-6.0 above eg. *Gardenia jasminoides, Hamamelis virginiana, Itea virginica, Hydrangea macrophylla* etc.

c. **Shrub tolerant to alkaline soil-** pH between 6.5-7.5 eg. *Berberis spp., Syringe spp., Hibiscus spp., Viburnum spp.* etc.

4. According to height

a. **Dwarf-** Up to 1 m. *Barleria cristata* (violet blue), *Crossandra undulaefolia* (Yellow), *Ernathemum laxiflorum* (purple-rose), *Jasminum sambac* (white), *Lantana sellowiana* (blue) etc.

b. **Medium-** 1.0 to 2.5m. *Acalypha hispida* (Red), *Allamanda neriifolia* (Yellow), *Cestrum nocturnum*, (White), *Cestrum diurnum* (White), *Jasminum multiflorum* (White), *Lantana camara* (White) etc.

c. **Tall-** 2.5 to 4m. *Buddelia asiatica* (white), *Clerodendrum inerme* (white), *Gardenia jasminoides* (white), *Hamelia patens* (Red), *Hibiscus rosa chinensis* (Red) etc.

Purpose of growing

Specimen- Exceptionally beautiful shrubs can be planted as single specimen in a lawn, area near their special qualities or put on the show eg. *Bougainvillia spp. Camellia japonica, Hibiscus rosa-sinensis, Hamelia patens* etc.

Standard and half standard- Several shrubs may be trained and allowed to develop a single branch at a center height eg. Single stem 1.0 meter for standard, 0.5 meter for half. Standard and half standard plant look more attractive when planted along the path and drives in a formal garden.

Shrubbery

An area of cultivated shrubs in a park or garden is known as shrubbery or any area in the garden fully solely devoted to the shrub plantation is called shrubbery. These shrubs are maintained in formal way therefore, require regular training, pruning and clipping. Maintenance of shrubbery is easy and become less costly if planted properly considering following points.

- Selection of hardy shrubs.
- Shrubs having profuse flowering and beautiful foliage.
- Selection of shrub according to soil.
- Shrub having slow growing habit and required less pruning and management.

Principles and Planning of Shrubbery Border

- Shrubs should be planted in east - south or south-west direction to achieve best result.
- In a large garden shrubbery should be arranged in more area to reduce space and maintenance cost of garden.
- Shrubbery placed in the front of tall tree or along the conifers looks very appealing.
- Flower and foliage colour should be visible from a distant place when tall, medium and dwarf shrub are arranged in the shrubbery.
- Along the path, drives terrace lawn and in front of house small shrub should be planted. Whereas, in front of big tree taller shrubs should be planted for picturesque effect.

Arrangement of shrubbery

Shrubbery is arrange basically in two way i.e.

- According to height
- According to colour

1. **According to height-** In front of an object i.e. Tree, big building. Taller shrubs are planted first, then medium shrub to be planted after that smaller shrubs are place in the shrubbery. Shrubs are arranged in two ways as give below.

a. **Single face shrubbery border-** In this case plantation of shrub is done in front of trees or boundary. Shrubs are arranged according to height then the taller shrub in the last then medium and after that smaller shrubs should be planted.

b. **Double face shrubbery border-** Its observed from both sides in this case taller shrubs are planted between the two medium shrubs besides with smaller shrub are planted in both side.

2. **According to colour-** These shrubs have attractive colour light yellow, white, golden yellow, pink, scarlet, crimson, rose red, violet, blue etc. Three common colour schemes are given below.

a. **Monochromatic colour scheme-** Massing of single or one colour is called monochromatic colour scheme ex. White- *Jasminum sambac* (dwarf), *Cestrum nocturnum* (medium), *Gardenia joaminoids* (tall) and Yellow- *Galphimia gracilis* (dwarf), *Allamanda nerifolia* (medium), *Thevetia peruviana* (tall).

b. **Analogous colour scheme-** It is also called harmonious colour scheme in this scheme shrubs are planted with closely related colour like white, pink, red colour flower or vice versa.

c. **Contrast colour scheme-** It is also called complementary colour scheme. Two opposite colour shrubs are planted in this scheme like blue-orange, red-green and yellow-violet.

Rock Garden

Rock garden is made by the rock or stone, garden look very natural, no symmetrical and unleveled all the garden elements and adornments can successfully used garden with any restriction. It is completely built of industrial and home waste and through away items. Rock garden of Chandigarh is also known as Nek Chandra rock garden after its founder Nek Chandra. Suitable plants are- *Jatropha podagrica*, *Lantana depressa* and *Russellia juncea*

Edging- *Sanchezia nobilis* and *Lantana sellowiana*

Hedges- *Durenta plumieri*, *Murraya exotica* and *Hamelia patens*

Screening- *Jasminum pubescens* and *Duranta repens*

Ground cover- *Lanatana sellowiana* and *Sanchezia nobiliss*

Topiary- *Clerodendrum inerme*, *Cupressus macrocarpa* and *Duranta plumieri*

Pot plants- These shrubs are placed in verandah, terraces, balcony or other place. Size of pot should be of 12-15cm, potting medium consist of soil manure, leaf mould FYM 2:1:1 (S:M:L). eg. *Citrus japonica*, Croton, *Poinsettia* etc.

Planting Care and Management of Shrubs

Propagation

1. **By seed-** Seeds are collected when they are fully ripe they are dried in the shade and stored in air tight bottle in dry places. In rainy season nursery are prepared and seed are sown eg. *Colliandra species*, *Thevetia nerifalia* and *Jatropha species.*
2. **By cutting-** The best season for prorogation by cutting in rainy season although cutting can be mode in Feb.-March if water supply is not limited. The cuttings are made at least 3-5 nodes and about 15-20 cm length eg. *Hibiscus rosa-sinensis*, *Jasminum sambac*, *Bougainvillea species*, *Cestrum nocturnum* and *Cestrum diurnum.*
3. **By layering or air layering-** In rainy season layering done by removing the bark of 0.5-3.5 cm long from stem or branches of shrubs of 20-30 cm long should be selected and wrapped with garden soil and sand mixture eg. *Jasminum sambac*, *Bougainvillia*, Croton and *Ixora species.*

Soil and site preparation-Shrubs are hardy in nature therefore, it can be grown in less fertile and neutral pH soil. Before planting the shrubs soil should be well prepared by addition of organic manure @ 5-6 kg/m^2 area.

Planting- The ideal time for planting is rainy season but if irrigation facility is available it can be planted in February-March as well. In shrubbery border each type of shrubs should be planted at least 2-3 rows at suitable distance. Normally the tall shrub are planted at 1.5-2m distance, medium shrub are planted at 1-1.5m distance and the dwarf shrubs are planted at 0.5-1m distance.

Irrigation- First irrigation should be given just after planting. Frequent irrigation should be given till the establishment. In early age of planting frequent irrigation will be needed. During winter season irrigation should be given at monthly interval whereas, in summer season the plant should be irrigated 15 days interval. In rainy season no irrigation is required.

Gap filling- In gap filling the replanting of the plant will be necessary for filling the gap due to mortality.

Weeding- Wedding in shrubs planting field weeding is essential after two year of establishment.

Pruning- For providing proper shape and enhance flowering pruning is essential. Pruning should be done in the month of December-February in the shrubs like Hibiscus, Jasmine and Hydrangea. Pruning should be done after flowering.

Description of the important flowering shrubs

S.No.	Common name	Botanical name	Family	Flower colour	Flowering time	Method of propagation	Remark
1	Gandharaj	*Gardenia jasminoides syn. G. florida*	Rubiaceae	White	April-June	Air-layering cutting	Popular fragrant 3m tall
2	Gurhal	*Hibiscus rosa sinensis*	Malvaceae	Rose-scarlet		Air-layering cutting	Bushy, 1-2m tall
3	Thalkamal	*Hibiscus mutabilis*	Malvaceae	White in the early morning and canges to pink and deep rose as the day advances	Throughout the year	Seeds cutting	3m tall shrub
4	Rukmini/Raktak	*Ixora coccinea, I. singaporensis*	Rubiaceae	White Scarlet Scarlet	April-June/ July-Sept. Throught the year, Greater parts of the year	Cutting/Layering	2m tall bushy
5	Mussaenda	*Mussaenda frondosa*	Rubiaceae	White	April-Sept.	Layering	Beautiful shrub
		M. luteola		Yellow	April-Sept.	Layering	Beautiful shrub
		M. philippica		Pink	April-Sept.	Layering	Beautiful shrub
6	Kamini	*Murraya exotica*	Rutaceae	White		Seed/ Layering	Used for hedge topiary
7		*Cassia gluca*	Leguminosae	Yellow	Throughout the year	Sed	Beautiful shrub
8	Karonda	*Carissa carandas*	Apocynaceae	White		Seed	Used for hedge, berries
9	Krishnachura	*Caesalpinia pulcherrima*	Leguminosae	Orange-scarlet	Throughout the year	Seed	Beautiful shrub
10	Radhandra	*Caesalpinia pulcherrima var. flava*	Leguminosae	Yellow	Appril-Aug.	Seed	Beautiful shrub
11	Calliandra	*Calliandra inaequilatera*	Leguminosae	Red, pink white		Seed/ layers	Power puff like flower
12	Bougainvillea	*Bougainvillea spp.*	Nyclaginaceae	Various colour	Feb.-June/ Sept.-Dec.	Cutting	Versatile shrub
13	Allamanda	*Allamanda cathartica*	Apocynaceae	Yellow	April-Aug.	Cutting –layering	Can be used as climber
14	Clerodendron	*Clerodendron inerme*	Verbenaceae	White	July-Aug.	Cutting	Used for hedge

contd...

15	Raat-ki-rani	*Cestrum noeturnum*	Solanaceae	Creamy yellow	April-July	Seed/ cutting	Fragrant during night bushy, quick growing
16	Day- Queen	*Cestrum diurnum*	Solanaceae	White	Summer	Seed/ cutting	Bloom during day time
17		*Cestrum auantiacum*	Solanaceae		Feb.-March		
18	Crossandra	*Crossandra spp.*	Acanthaceae	Yellow orange, brick red	Feb.-June	Seed/ cutting	Flower are used for making gujras
19	Golden dew drop balchari	*Duranta plumeri*	Verbenaceae	Blue		Seed/ cutting	Used for making hedge
20	Gandharaj	*Gardenia jasminoides syn. E. florida*	Rubiaceae	White	Feb.-July	Cutting, layering	Have fragrant flower
21	Hamelia	*Hamelia patens*	Rubiaceae	Orange red	April-Aug.	Cutting, layering	Used for making good hedge
22	Barbadose cherry	*Malpighia glabra*	Malpighiaceae	Purple	April-Aug.	Cutting seed	Specimenplant,cherry like fruit
23	Kanel	*Nerium oleander*	Apocynaceae	White, pink, red	April	Cutting layering	Popular shrub
24	Chitra	*Plumbago caoensis syn. P. auriculata*	Plumbaginaceae	Blue	Feb.-Sept.	Cutting layering	Used for edging
25	Poinsettia	*Poinsettia plucherrima*	Euphorbiaceae	Red treats	Dec.-Feb.	Cutting	Rapid growing sun loving
26	Coral pant russelia juncea	*Russelia juncea*	Scrophlariaceae	Coral red	March-Aug.	Cutting	Pendulous branches
27	Chadni, Taggar	*Tabemaemontana coronaria*	Apocynaceae	White	March-Aug.	Cutting	Used for making hedge
28	Pilakaner	*Thevetia nerifolia*	Apocynaceae	Yellow	Throughout the year	Seeds/ cutting	Funnlshaped flower
29	Bela	*Jasminum sambac*	Oleaceae	White	May-June	Cutting	

Description of important foliage shrubs

S.No.	Common name	Botanical name	Family	Method of propagation	Remark
1	Aglaonema	*Aglaonema spp.*	Araceae	Cutting division	Perennial, leaves green with marking of grey or variegated or silver.
2	Alocasia	*Alocasia spp.*	Araceae	Tubers cutting, rhizomes	Beautiful, hardy, indoor plant
3	Aralia	*Aralia spp.*	Araliaceae	Cutting	Hardy lant
4	Satawar	*Asparagus spp.*	Liliaceae	Seed suckers	Beautiful bristle like cladodes
5	Colocasia	*Colocasia spp.*	Araceae		Attractive foliage
6	Cordyline	*Cordyline spp.*	Lilaceae	Node cuttings suckers	Related to bracaena
7	Dracaena	*Dracaena spp.*	Liliaceae	Node cuttings suckers	Long leaves
8	Cycas	*Cycus spp.*	Cycadaceae	Suckers	Good for pod, greenhouse and indoor plant
9	Dieffenbachia	*Dieffenbachia spp.*	Araceae	Cutting	Pot plant, warm, humid conditions plant are poisonours
10	Rubber plant	*Ficus elastica*	Moraceae	Air layering, cutting	Pot plants
11	Maranta (calathea)	*Marant spp.*	Marantaceae	Suckers, cutting	Good pot plant
12	Monster	*Monster acuminate*	Araceae		Root climbers with good foliage
13	Philodendron	*Philodendron spp*	Araceae		Different shapes of foliage
14	Pilea	*Pilea muscosa*	Urticaeae	Stem cutting	Grown in shades place
15	Sansevieria	*Sansevieria cylindrical Sansevieria trifasciate*	Liliaceae	Division for suckers	Perennial, erect, sword like leaves
16	Tradescantia	*Tradescantia albiflora*	Commelinaceae	Stem cutting	Low growing, trailing or creeping

Chapter 30

Trees

Trees

A trees is a woody perennial plant with clear stem or trunk. Trees trend to be long leaved living up to several 100 year.

TREE- logical meaning of each letter

T - Temperature and micro-climate moderation.

R - Removal of air pollutant.

E- Erosion control.

E - Energy conservation.

General importance

1. Trees provide additional necessities such shelter, medicine food, fibre, fuel, timer and tools etc.
2. They create is peaceful, aesthetically pleasing environment.
3. Trees increase quality of life by bringing natural elements and wild life habitats into urban setting.
4. Trees improve air quality, ameliorate climate, conserve water, preserve soil maintain soil fertility and support wild life.
5. Leaves absorb and filter the sun's radiant energy, keeping environment cool in summer.
6. Trees lower the air temperature and reduce the heat in intensity of green house effect by maintain low level of CO_2.
7. They can create the impression of a well established place in new presidential areas and reduce the raw unfinished look.

Classification of Trees

A. According to beauty of plant parts

1. **For flowers-** *Bauhinia purpurea, Butea monosperma, Cassia marginata, Cassia nodosa, Lagerstroemia speciosa* etc.

2. **For foliage-** *Alstonia scholaris, Araucaria cooki, Cupressus funebris, Pinus longifolia, Salix babylonica* etc.
3. **For variegated foliage-** *Rosea morginata, Ficus benjamina, Ficus religiosa, Ornamental orange, Ficus elastica* etc.
4. **For fruits-** *Mangifera indica, Averrhoa carambola, Emblica officinalis, Tamarindus indica* etc.
5. **For fragrance-** *Magnolia grandiflora, Micholia alba, Plumeria rubra, Plueria alba* etc.

B. According to climate condition

1. **For moist areas-** *Alastonia scholaris, Cassia javanica, Lagerstroemia speciosa, Putranjiva roxburghaii* etc.
2. **For marshy area-** *Lagerstoemia speciosa, Salix babylonica* etc.
3. **For dry area-** *Delonix regia, Butea monosperma, Tectona grandis, Cassia fistula, Terminalia arjuna* etc.
4. **For arid area-** *Cassia siamea, Butea monosperma* etc.

Purpose of growing

A. **Specimen trees-** Such trees are planted singly for the attractive shape beautiful foliage, flowers or for drooping branches which reflect humbleness eg. *Cassia fistula, Plumeria alba, Magnolia grandiflora, Salix babylonica, Ficus elastica* etc.

B. **Shade trees-** Such trees have mostly round canopy or umbrella crown leaf so that no or very little sun is allowed underneath them eg. *Azadirachta indica, Alstonica, Ficus religiosa, Ficus benjamina, Mangifera indica* etc.

C. **Ornamental trees-** Ornamental trees are those trees which are planted for enhancing the aesthetic value, fruit, stem, bark, habit and overall frame work are responsible for increasing the aesthetic value eg. *Putranjiva roxburghii, Salix babylonica, Saraca indica, Terminalia arjuna, Ravenala medagascariensis, Plumaria alba, Jacaranda mimosifolia, Grevillea robusta* etc.

D. **Flowering trees** -These trees produce colourful flower and are planted for their beautiful flower eg. *Bauhinia variegata, Casssia fistula, Delonix regia, Butea monosperma, Plumeria alba* etc.

E. **Trees for avenue and road area-** Avenue trees are those trees which are planted along road side. Generally the avenue trees are planted for shade and flowers eg. *Cassia fistula, Jacaranda accutifolia, Ficus infectoria* etc. Avenue trees are planted in different ways.

1. One kind of flowering on both side : *Bauhinia variegata, Gravellia robusta, Cassia fistula, Lagerstromia speciosa* etc.
2. Two kind of flowering tree blooming at one time on both side

   Gravellia robusta (yellow)- *Jacaranda accutifolia* (blue)- *Gravellia robusta* (yellow),

   Cassia fistula (yellow)- *Delonix regia* (red)- *Cassia fistula* (yellow),

   Cassia fistula (yellow)- *Cassia nodosa* (pink)- *Cassia fistula* (yellow).
3. Two kind of flowering tree blooming at different time on both side

   Bauhinia trindra (purple in November)- *Spathodea campanulata* (red in April)- *Bauhinia trindra* (purple in November)

   Cassia fistula (yellow in May)- *Jacaranda accutifolia* (blue in April)- *Cassia fistula* (yellow in May)

   Gravellia robusta (yellow in April)- *Bauhinia variegata* (purple in March) *Gravellia robusta* (yellow in April)

F. **Shady tree on both side-** Tree that are planted as avenue are *Cassia fistula, Cassia siamea, Delonix regia, Butea monosperma, Putranjiva roxburghii, Jacaranda mimosifolia, Terminalia arjuna* etc.

G **Screening purpose-** When tall upright trees are planted very close to give an ultimate look of curtain and screen eg. *Eucaliptus species, Populor species, Polyanathia longifolia* etc.

H. **For fragrance flower-** *Terospermum acerifolium, Plumeria spacies, Magnolia grandiflora* etc.

I. **For checking air pollution-** Industries are major source of pollution and hence in such areas deciduous tree or trees having thick shining leaves will be more successful eg. *Morus species, Ficus infectoria, Ficus religiosa, Poplar hybrida, Anthocephalus cadamba* etc.

Planting care and management of the trees

1. **Climatic factor-** Selection of trees will depends upon prevailing climatic condition of the locality and trees of other climatic conditions may or may not do well or later on decline. This depends upon adoptability of individual types. Trees of tropical climate like *Delonix regia, Neonauclea purpured*, decline later on in subtropical climate similarly tree of temperate climate do not grow well in tropical regions.
2. **Soil factor-** In general trees are adaptable to varying soil condition but specific trees excel in particular condition. In alkaline and saline soil trees

which can be grown successfully are *Cassia fistula, Casuarina equisetifolia* etc.

3. Care and management-

a. **Planting of trees-** Rainy season (June-July) is the best time of planting tree however in North India planting can be done during spring 1-2 year old plants are most suitable for planting because the less chance of plant mortality.

b. **Preparation of ground-** Pit should be dug 60x60x60 cm size and 10-15 kg FYM and 20-25g of 5% insecticide is used in pit filling.

c. **Maintenance and care of trees**

- Staking
- Fencing and tree ground
- Irrigation
- Gape filling
- Training and pruning.

Description of the important flowering trees

S.No.	Common name	Botanical name	Family	Flower colour	Flowering time	Method of propagation	Remark
1	Amaltas the java cassia	*Cassia fistula* *Cassia javanica* *Cassia nodosa* *Cassia siamea*	Leguminosae	Golden Yellow Pink PinkYellow Yellow	April-May May- June May- June May- June	Seeds	Medium sized 10 tall Beautiful flower Medium sized tree Medium sized beautiful Flower avenue tree
2	Gulmohar	*Poinciana regia syn. Delonix regia*	Leguminosae	Orange/Scarlet	April-May	Seed	Flower cover the whole tree
3	Pride of india	*Lagerstroema flsreginae*	Lythraceae	Purple maure	April-May	Seeds	Medium size tree
4	Blue gulmohar	*Jacaranda mimosifolia*	Bigoniacea	Blue mauve	March-May	Seed/semi hard wood cutting	Elegant,deciduous tree
5	Bottle brush	*Callistemon lanceolatus*	Myrtaceae	Scarl	March-Aug., Sept.	Seeds layers	Smalldrooping branches flower born in spikes
6	Flame of forest	*Butea monosperma B. monosrerma var. tutee*	Leguminosae	Scarlet orange yellow	April-May	Seed	Medium size, rough trunkdeciduous
7	Kachnar	*Bauhinia purpurea B. alba*	Leguminosae	Purple deep pink white	November	Seed	Medium size
8	Champa	*Michelia champaka*	Magnoliaceae	White/ cremy yellow	April-May/ Sept.-Oct.	Seed / grafting	Medium size long leaves
9	Pangri	*Erythrina indica*	Leguminosae	Scarlet red	Feb.-April	Cutting	Fast growing, densly branch
10	Madar tree	*Eliricidia maculate*	Leguminosae	Pale Pink flower	Feb.-March	seed	Good looking, medium used for shading cocoa
11	Amherstia	*Amherstia nobilis*	Leguminosae	Vermilion yellow tip	Feb.-May	seed/Leyering	Medium, beautiful tree
12	Indian lilac	*Logerstroemia indica*	Lythraceae		May-Aug.	Seed	Swall tree
13	Himanchampa	*Magnolia grandiflora*	Magnoliaceae	Pink white	April-May	Layering	Evergreen tree
14	Harsingar/seuli	*Nyctanthes arbor-tristis*	Oleaceae	Whit with orange red tube	Sept.-Nov.	Seed/ cutting	Sweet scented flower open at night & fall at day tree
15	Akashneem	*Millingtonia hortensis*	Bignoniaceae	Silvery white		Seed/ root suckers	Quick growing straight 20 mtr

cont...

16	Yellow gulmohar	*Peltophorum inerma*	Leguminosae	Yellow	Feb.-May/ Scpt.-Aug.	Seed/ cutting	Beautiful ornamented tree
17	Temple tree/ pagoda tree	*Plumeria alba*	Apocynaceae	White	March-April/ July-Aug.	Cutting	Evergreen tree
18	Chameli, Gul-e-chin	*Plumeria rubra*	Apocynaceae	White-rose		Cutting	Low growing 6-8m tall tree
19	Sita ashok	*Saraca indica*	Leguminosae	Orange	April-June	Seed	8-10m tall evergreen tree
20	Fountain tree	*Spathodea campanulate*	Bignoniaceae	Scarlet ofange/ crimson	Feb.-March	Seed /root-syckers	20-25m tall ornamental
21	Tecoma	*Tecoma argentea*	Bignoniaccae	Bright yellow	Feb.-March	Seed	5-8m tall tree

Description of the important foliage trees

S.No.	Common name	Botanical name	Family	Flower colour	Flowering time	Method of propagation	Remark
1	Neem	*Azadirachta indica*	Meliaceae	Small white	April	Seed	12-18m tall tree
2	Christmas tree	*Arucaria cookii*	Pinaceae	-	-	Seed	Ornamental tree
3	Siris	*Albizzia lebbek*	Leguminosae	-	-	Seed	Fast growing spreading tree
4	Jhau	*Casuarina equisetifolia*	Casuarinaceae			Seed	10-20m tall tree
5	Shisam	*Dalbergia sisso*	Leguminosae			Seeds cutting	15-20m tall tree
6	Banyan	*Ficus benghalensis*	Moraceae	Crimson berries	Aug.-Sept.	Seeds/ cutting	15-20m tall tree
7	Pakur	*Ficus infectoria*	Moraceae			Seeds/ cutting	15-20m tall evergreen spreading tree
8	Pipal	*Ficus religiosa*	Moraceae			Seed	20-25m tallhuge tree
9	Indian rubber plant	*Ficus elastic*	Moraceae			Air layering	10-12m quick growing tree
10	Silver oak	*Grevillea robusta*	Proteacae	Golden yellow	April-May	Seed	15-20 evergreen tree
11	Mahua	*Madhuca longifolia*	Sapotaceae	Creamish white	March-April	Seed	15-20 tall deciduous tree
12	Mulsari	*Mimusops elengi*	Sapotaceae	White	April-July/ Sept.-Nov.	Seed	10-15m tall dense evergreen tree
13	Ashoka	*Polyalthia longifolia*	Annonaceae			Seed	10-15m tall dense evergreen tree
14	Chir	*Pinus longiflolia*	Pinaceae			Seed	15-20m tall needle like lives
15	Putranjiva	*Putranjiva roxburghii*	Euphorbiaceae			Seed	10-12 m tall dense evergreen tree
16	Poplar	*Populus deltrolides*	Saliceaceae			Cutting	Fast growing, deciduous 5-10m tall
17	Karanj	*Pongamia glabra*	Leguminosae	Lilac	April-May	Seed/cutting	5-10m deciduous tree
18	Arjun	*Terminalia arjuna*	Combretaceae	Yellowish white	March-June	Seed	15-20m tall evergreen avenue tree
19	Morpankhi	*Platycladus occidentalis*	Pinaceae			Seeds	5-8m tall, foliage is fern like
20	Travelers tree	*Ravrenala madagascariensis*	Musaceae			Seed	3-4m tall, banana like leaf
21	Sterculia	*Sterculia alata*	Sterculiaceae			Seed	8-10m tall, leaves are larg, avenue tree
22	Juniperus	*Juniperus chinenss*	Pinaceae			Seed	5-10m tall, hardy, dense, pyramidal decorative tree
23	Chalta	*Dillenia indica*	Dilleniaceae	Large white	July	Seed/ stem cutting	8-20m tall, slow growing evergreen tree
24	Chitwan	*Alstonia scholaris*	Apocynaceae	White- greenish	April-May	Seed	Strong small during night, 6-10m tall tree

Chapter 31

Climbers

Climbers

Climbers are group of plants which have weak stems and ability to climb up the support with the help of modified organs for sunlight and air, twiners differ from climber in the way that they do not posses such modified organs but twine around the support cover it and reach the top. Climber are woody or herbaceous plant which climb up the trees and other tall objects with the help of support of their special modified organ, such as tendrils, root, thorns, rootlets, hooks etc.

Tendrils- *Bigonia gracilis*, *Clematis paniculata* etc.

Thorns- *Bougainvillea species*, *Climbing roses* etc.

Rootlets- *Ficus repens* etc.

Hooks- *Gallium aperine*, *Rubus australis* etc.

Climbers and twiners are important group of plants. Climbers and twiners add the beuty, colour or fragrance in the garden and artificial structure like garden wall, topiary, arches, pergola etc. are made with the help of climbers.

Different Modified Organs in Climbers

Tendrils- A specialized stem leaf or petioles with a thread like shape that is used by climbering plants.

Leaf tendrils- In weak stemmed plant, leaf or a part of leaf gets modified into green thread like structure is called leaf tendrils.

Stem tendrils- Stem when gets modified into green thread like leaf less structure is called stem tendrils.

Thorns- A stiff shape pointed woody projection on the stem which helps plant to climb up.

Climbing root- These are areal adventitious roots that help weak stem to climb on a support.

Clinging roots- These root fix epiphyte on the bark on the supporting tree or pillar.

Rootlet- A small or fine branch of root by which weak stem plant climbed up the support.

Twiners- These are plants which climbed by coiling round the support a phenomenon known as circumnutating they use there on young shoot to twine around there climbing aid as they do not develop their climbing organs.

Ramblers and stragglers- They are still other plants which fail in there attempted to climb but somehow manage to support themselves over the trunk, stems or branches of other plants these are termed as ramblers and stragglers.

Latex- A milky fluid found in many plants which help them to climb up the support on exudates eg. *Ficus pumila.*

Importance of Climbers

- Beautify the surrounding.
- Covering the patio slope as ground cover ugly object and site.
- Create privacy.
- Provide feature in garden.
- Gives attractive view on trend over tree.
- Making topiary.
- Provide background for annuals and herbaceous border.
- Provide shade when trend over pergola.
- Provide fragrance to the surrounding.
- Supplementary.

Properties of Climbers

- Growth of shoots is often extremely rapid.
- Long internodes are produced for very rapid elongation these are often sensitive contact with any support or solid object.
- Commonly there is a long delay in large of leafs until the stem are cylindrical axis becomes wrapped around a support.
- Woody stems are very feasible to permit bending twisting and coiling them are fairly stronger if pulling on two ends but have very little stems when compressed.
- If the supporting tree fails then the entire plants cum-down however these climbers often have a great ability to survive and re-sprout.

Classification of Climbers

A. According to beauty of plant part

1. **Flowering climbers-** *Allamanda cathartica*, *Lonicera japonica*, *Antigonon leptopus*.

2. **For foliage-** *Asparagus plumosus, Ficus pumila, Piper ornatum.*
3. **Flowering and foliage-** *Artabotrys uncinatus, Ipomea quamoclit.*

B. According to nature of climber

1. **Annuals-** Sweet pea, Purple bells, Morning glory, Passion flower.
2. **Perennials-** English evy, Virginia creeper.

C. According to situation

1. **Situation for partial shade condition-** *Clerodendrum splendens, Lonicera japonica.*
2. **Situation for sunny condition-** *Antigonon leptopus, Campasis grandiflora, Quisqualis indica.*
3. **Situation for shade and indoor condition-** *Aparagus plumosus, Monstera deliciosa, Philodendron species.*
4. **Situation for screening wall-** *Ficus pumila, Bignonia unguis-cati.*

D. According to rate of growth

1. **Heavy climbers-** The climber that have fast and good growth and also produce profuse flowers. These climbers are preferred to grow in large area eg. *Bauhinia vahlii, Beaumontia grandiflora, Thunberia grandiflora* etc.
2. **Light climbers-** These climbers have less growth and spreading habit these are well suited for small area eg. *Bignonia unguis-cati, Ipomoea species, Tecoma jasminoides* etc.

E. According to fragrance flowers

1. **Fragrance climbers-** *Jasminum grandiflorum, Lonicera japonica, Solandra grandiflora* etc.

Criteria for selection of climbers

- Amount of sunlight require.
- Habit.
- Spread.
- Texture (fine, medium and course).
- Leaf retention duration.
- Foliage colour (emergence, mature and fall).
- Flower colour (shape, size and fragrance).
- Flowering season and peak flowering duration.
- Fruit (colour, shape, size, season and duration).

Purpose of Growing Climbers

- **For screening purpose-** These climbers are evergreen, easy to grow and provide privacy in garden eg. *Bignonia unguiscati, Ficus pumila.*
- **For arches and pergola-** Climber covering arches and pergola will provide vertical interest outside eg. *Salondra grandiflora, Pyrostegia venusta.*
- **For wall or trellis-** Climbers covering walls or trellis not only screen unsightly areas of the garden, but also brighten up bare walls eg. *Passiflora laurifolia, Ficus pumila, Bignonia unguiscati.*
- **For pot culture-** Light climbers are those having bushy growth are suitable for planting under pot culture eg. *Bignonia purpurea, Climatis flammula, Hoya carnosa.*
- **For porches-** For creating privacy and beautify the porches climber are used eg. *Clematis panniculata, Clerodendron splendents, Wisteria sinensis.*
- **For covering slopes-** Such climbers are used for covering bere patches of soil around tree or shrub eg. *Thunbergia grandiflora, Lonicera japonica.*
- **For making topiary-** Climbers which tolerate frequent pruning and have flexible vegetative growth are suitable for making the topiary eg. *Bignonia species, Clerodendrum inerme.*
- **For hanging baskets-** Plants are suitable for planting in container eg. *Bougainvillea, Clematis, Hedera helix.*
- **For ornamental fruits-** These are the climbers that are properly grown for there beautiful fruits eg. *Dioscoria deltoidea, Hedera nepalensis.*

Planting of climbers- Climbers can thrive well on any soil. The basic requirement is the soil should be fertile, deep, well drained, with good water holding capacity. Planting should be done in a pit of 60x60x60cm size. Before planting it must be refilled with 10-15 kg of well rotten FYM and 10 kg Falidol powder for planting evergreen climber, rainy season is preferred i.e. July-Sep. Although it can also be planted during February-March. Whereas, the deciduous climbers should be planted during winter i.e. February-March.

Care and management- Regular watering is required after planting the climber. Weeding and hoeing must be done as and when required. During subsequent year pruning is essential to keep the climber in limit and in desired shape.

Description of important climbers

S.No.	Common name	Botanical name	Family	Flower colour	Flowering time	Method of propagation	Remark
1	Rangoon creaper (madhu- malati)	*Quisqualis indica*	Combretaceae	White and pnnkish	Most part of the year	Cutting layering	Flowers are produced in drooping branching
2	Jhumkolata (passion flower)	*Passiflora edulis, P.alba*	Passifloraceae	White, pink, purple	June-Nov.	Suckers layers	Vigorous hardy
3	Madhabilata	*Hiptage beneghalensis*	Malpighiaceae	White with yellow	Dec.-Feb.	Seeds/ years	Sweet scented evergreen
4	Allamanda	*Allamanda cathartica A. Hendersonii*	Apocynaceae	Yellow	April-July	Cutting layers	Easy to grow
5	Coral creaper	*Antigonon leptopus*	Polygonaccac	Orange yellow	Most part of the year	Seed, cutting layering	Lubcrous rooted quick growing
6	Duck flower	*Aristolochia elegans A. Grandiflora*	Polygonaceae	Rose	April-June	Seed, cutting layering	Flower emit repelling odouck
7	Pelicanr/swan flower	*Aristolochia denocalymma Aristolochia alliaceum*	Bignoniaceae	White purple brown	March-June	Layering cutting	Emit a garlic like small
8	Trumpet creaper		Bignoniaceae	Yellow pink mauve	July-Aug.	Suckers cutting	Trampet shaped flower with aerial rootlet
9	Clerodendron	*Clerodendron splendens*	Bignoniaceae	Red deep orangre	Dec.-Feb.	Suckers layer	Beautiful climbr
10	Golden shawer	*Bigonia venusta*	Bignoniaceae		Feb.-June	Layering cutting	Tabular flower grown on compound wall
11	Purple wreath	*Petrea volobilis*	Verbenaceae		Feb.-April	Suckers cutting Layering	Star shaped flower
12	Juhi	*Jasminum auriculatum*	Oleaceae		April-Sept.	Cutting	Sceuted flower
13	Safe bel bridal bouqut	*Porana paniculata*	Convovulaceae	White	Aug.-Oct.	Cutting, layering seed	Head shaped leaves used for screen
14	Heavenly	*Thunbergia grandiflora*	Acanthaceae	Blue with yellow	Feb.-Aug.	Seed cutting	Used for covering wall
15	Vernornia	*Vernornia elaegnaefolia*	Compositae	White	July-Aug.	Seed cutting	Used for screening
16	Money plant	*Pothas aurens*	Areceae			Cutting	

Chapter 32

Importance of Post Harvest Technology

Proper handling, packaging, transportation and storage reduce the post harvest losses of fruits and vegetables. For every one percent reduction in loss will save 3 million tons of fruit and vegetable per year. Processing and preservation technology helps to save excess fruit and vegetables ... season. The technology has become ... and ... food sector. ... commodities in the form of ... mango, pineapple, citrus, grapes, tomatoes ... processed on a large scale.

Principles and Methods of Preservation

Preservation: Preservation means ... but scientifically it may be defined as a ... ... (food) ... spoilage ... foods ... process, by controlling the physical, chemical ... is called preservation.

1. Physical changes: Colour, flavour ...
2. Chemical changes: Carbohydrates, fats ...
3. Microbial changes: Mould, yeasts and ...

Why do we preserve the food?

1. To supply, to increase the shelf life of the ...
2. To make the seasonal fruits available throughout ...
3. To add the variety to the diet.
4. To save time by reducing preparation time ...
5. To stabilize the prices of the food in the market.
6. To improve the health of the population.

Chapter 32

Importance of Post Harvest Technology

Proper handling, packaging, transportation and storage reduce the post harvest losses of fruits and vegetables. For every one percent reduction in loss will save 5 million tons of fruit and vegetable per year. Processing and preservation technology helps to save excess fruit and vegetable during the glut season (off season). The technology has become a necessity to improve the food safety and strengthen nation's food security. The technology helps to boost export of agricultural commodities in the form of preserved and value added products e.g. mango, pineapple, citrus, grapes, tomatoes, peas, potato and cucumber being processed on a large scale.

Principles and Methods of Preservation of Fruits

Preservation: Preservation means just protect the foods against the spoilage, but scientifically it may be defined as a science which deals with the process for prevention of decay or spoilage of the food is called preservation. In other words, just controlling the physical, chemical or microbial changes in the foods is called preservation.

1. **Physical changes**: Colour, flavour, texture and taste etc.
2. **Chemical changes**: Carbohydrate, fats, proteins, vitamins and minerals.
3. **Microbial changes**: Mould, yeasts and bacteria

Why do we preserve the food?

1. To supply, to increase the shelf life of the food for increasing the supply.
2. To make the seasonal fruits available throughout the year.
3. To add the variety to the diet.
4. To save time by reducing preparation, time and energy by fire.
5. To stabilize the prices of the food in the market.
6. To improve the health of the population.

Principles of preservation: There are three main principles:

A. Prevention/delay the microbial decomposition of the food.
B. Prevention/delay the shelf decomposition of the food.
C. Prevention of damage by insects, animals, mechanical causes *etc.*

A. Prevention / delay the microbial decomposition of the food

1. By Keeping out the microorganisms- Asepsis
2. By Removal of microorganisms- Filtration
3. By Hindering the growth and activity of microorganisms- Anaerobic condition
4. By Killing the microorganisms- Exposing at high temperature

1. **Asepsis:** It means preventing the entry of microorganisms by maintaining of general cleanliness, while picking, grading, packing and transporting of fruits and vegetables, increase their keeping quality and the product prepared from them will be superior quality.

2. **Filtration:** Fruits juice, bear, soft drinks, wines etc. enter through bacteria proof filter which is made of asbestos pad or unglazed porcelain type of materials. These filters contain the microorganisms and allow the water or juice to percolate though with or without pressure.

3. **Anaerobic conditions:** It can be maintained by:
   i. Replacing the O_2 by adding CO_2 (carbonation)
   ii. Evacuating the sealed container (fruit juice)
   iii. Use of oils from top of the food (pickles)

4. **Exposing at high temperature:** Fruits can be exposed by high temperature such as:
   i. **Canning:** Food is exposing to a high temperature (> 100°C) which prevents spoilage and inactivate the enzyme present in the food.
   ii. **Irradiation:** In case of irradiation, the food is exposed to the radiations to kill the surviving microorganism by ionizing and non-ionizing radiation like α, β and γ rays. Here, food is exposed to electromagnetic or ionizing radiation or various frequencies ranging from low frequency electromagnate to high frequency *i.e.* gamma rays which destroy the microorganism present in the food.

B. Prevention / delay the shelf decomposition of the food

i. By destruction or inactivate the enzyme – Blanching.
ii. Prevention / delay the non-enzymatic chemical reactions – Antioxidant.

Blanching

1. It is primary treatment which have to soften the tissues to facilitate packaging.
2. To preserve the original colour and flavour
3. To destroy the certain enzyme which are undesirable
4. Elimination of the air
5. Mostly for vegetables
6. Remove microorganisms
7. Remove astringent taste and toxins

Antioxidant: Antioxidant are substances which are used to protect the food gamma deterioration caused by exposure to the air.

1. BHA – Butylated Hydroxy Anisole Vegetable oils, BHT – Butylated Hydroxy Toluene
2. Gellales: Animal fat, Vegetable oil
3. Tocopherols: Animal fat
4. Ascorbic acid: Fruit juices, Citrus oil, Wine, Bears *etc.*
5. Lactic acid: Processed fruits and vegetables, Canned fruits,
6. Phosphoric acid: Vegetable oils, Animal fat and cold drinks

Methods of preservation of fruits:

There are two main basic methods:

A. Bacteriostatic methods
B. Bactericidal methods

A. Bacteriostatic methods

1. Drying of foods
2. Use of chemical preservatives
3. Use of food additive
4. Use of low temperature

B. Bactericidal methods

1. Pasteurization
2. Cooking
3. Canning
4. Irradiation

A. Bacteriostatic Methods

In this method, the environmental conditions are change to prevent the growth of microorganisms, such conditions are called bacteriostatic. These are -

1. Drying of Foods

Drying is just removal of moisture from the food to a certain level at which microorganisms cannot grow is called drying, it can be done by two methods:

i. Application of heat:
   - a. Sun drying
   - b. Mechanical drying
   - c. Vacuum drying
   - d. Freeze drying

ii. Binding the moisture in the food:
   - a. Use of sugar
   - b. Use of salt

i. Application of heat

a. **Sun drying:** Sun drying is the method in which food is directly exposed to sunlight. It is generally done in the places where plenty sunshine is available for long periods e.g. Rajasthan. The dried product in this method is inferior in quality.

b. **Mechanical drying:** This is a method of drying where application of heat is applied by a mechanical dryer under the controlled conditions of temperature, humidity and air flow.

c. **Vacuum drying:** The temperature of the food and the rate of water removal are controlled by regulating the degree of vacuum and intensity of heat input.

d. **Freeze drying:** In this method, the food is dried by sublimation process, *i.e.*, just converting the food into ice without passing through the liquid form of water by means of vacuum plus heat applied in the drying chamber. In this method, product first frozen then water is removed by vacuum and application of heat which occurs simultaneously in same chamber.

ii. Binding the moisture

a. **Use of sugar:** The use of high concentration of sugar bindup the moisture and make the food have a certain level of moisture at which microorganisms are not able to grow.

b. **Use of salt:** The concentration of salt causes the high osmotic pressure and tie up the moisture which inhibit the growth of microorganisms. It dehydrates the food by drying out and tie up moisture as it dehydrates the microorganism's cells. Salt reduces the solubility of O_2 in the food by reducing the moisture. It interferes with the action of proteolytic enzyme. The effectiveness of NaCl is varied with the concentration of salt and temperature.

2. Use of Chemical Preservatives

Chemical preservatives are substances which are added to food just to retard, inhibit or arrest the activity of microorganisms such as fermentation, pacification and decomposition of the food. Chemical preservatives are of two types:

Class-1 preservatives: Common salt, sugar, dextrose, spices, vinegar, ascorbic acid

Class-2 preservatives: Benzoic acid and its salt, SO_2 and the salts of sulphuric acid, nitrates, sorbic acid and its salts, propionic acid and its salts, lactic acid and its salts. Among the class-2 preservatives, only two chemical preservatives are used in fruits and vegetables preservation:

i. KMS

1. It releases the SO_2 and it is unstable.
2. It is used for the fruit which have non water solvent pigment (colourless).
3. It cannot be used in naturally coloured juices such as phalsa, jamun because they have the Anthocyanin pigment.
4. It cannot be used in the product which are packed in container because it acts on the tin containers and oil, Hydrogen Sulphide (H_2S) which has an unpleasant smell and also form a black compound with the base plate of containers.
5. Best to control moulds than bacteria.
6. 350 ppm KMS is mostly used in fruit juice products.

ii. Sodium Benzoate

1. It is salt of benzoic acid and soluble in water.
2. It delays the fermentation in the juices.
3. It is commonly used in the product which are having natural colour such as Anthocyanin pigment.
4. It is more effective against the yeast.
5. 750 ppm Sodium benzoate is mostly used in fruit juices, squashes and cordials.

3. Use of Food Additive

Food additives are substances or mixture of substances other than basic foodstuffs, which are present in the foods as reagent of any aspects of production, processing, storage, packaging *etc.* Food additives are (i) sugar, (ii) salt, (iii) acids, (iv) spices. In case of sugar and salts, they exerts osmotic pressure by water is diffuses from the product through a semipermeable membrane until the concentration reach equilibrium. They kill the microorganisms or do not allow them to multiplication.

i. **Sugar:** The concentration of 68-70% is used for preparation of jam, jelly, marmalades *etc.* sugar act as a preservative by osmosis and not as a true poison for microorganisms. It absorbs most of the available water, so little water available for the growth of microorganisms.

ii. **Salt:** The concentration of salt 15-20% is used for the preparation such as pickles. Salt inhibits enzymatic browning and discolouration and also acts as an antioxidant. It exerts its preservative action by:

   1. Causing high osmotic pressure resulting in the plasmolysis of microbial cells.
   2. Dehydrating food and microorganisms by tying up the moisture.
   3. Ionizing to yield the chloride ion which is harmful to microorganisms, and
   4. Reducing the solubility of oxygen in water, sensitizing the cells against CO_2.

iii. **Acids**

   1. Many processed foods and a beverage needs the addition of acids to impart their characteristic flavour and taste in the final product because acids provide desired flavour and taste.
   2. They adjust the sugar and acid ratio in the food.
   3. Proper balance flavour of the food.
   4. They also play a role for controlling the formation.

   Main acids are the following

   1. Acetic acid (Vinegar)
   2. Citric acid (Lime juice)
   3. Lactic acid (Lactose)

   1. **Acetic acid:** It is commonly used for pickles, chutney, sauce and ketchup, just to inhibit the growth of microorganisms.
   2. **Citric acid:** It is used for preparation of jam, jelly, squash, nectar *etc.* just to increase the acidity.
   3. **Lactic acid:** It is used for the formation of curd from milk, raw flavour, and specific to pickles.

iv. **Spices:**

1. Spices are plant products which are used in flavouring the foods and beverages to enhance the food flavour, colour and palatability.
2. They acts as antibacterial and antifungal activity.
3. They impart as colour agent.

4. Use of Low Temperature

Low temperature retards the microbial growth and enzyme reaction because it retards the chemical reactions. This is not a permanent method because some microorganisms can also grow at low temperature.

1. Cellar storage: (Above 15°C)
2. Refrigerated storage: (0 to 5°C)
3. Freezing storage: (-18 to -40°C)

1. **Cellar storage:** These are the underground room where surplus food can be stored for sometimes, only root crops such as potato, onion can be stored for a limited period.
2. **Refrigeration:** Fruits and vegetables can be stored for 2-7 days. Semiperishable crops, such as potatoes, apples *etc.* can be stored, in the commercial cold storage with proper ventilation, automatic controlled temperature for one year.
3. **Freezing:** It ties up the moisture and increase the concentration of dissolved substances in the food. But, sometimes enzymes are active even below the 0°C. In this case before freezing, 'Blanching' is necessary for vegetable freezing.

B. Bactericidal Methods

In this method, food material is exposed to higher temperature and high temperature helps to killing of the microorganisms due to coagulation of protein. It helps in inactivation of enzyme. Here moist heat is more effective than dry heat. At low pH high temperature is required, as compared to high pH. High temperature can be employed by following methods:

i. Pasteurization: Below 100°C
ii. Boiling/ Cooking: at 100°C
iii. Canning: Above 100°C

i. Pasteurization

There are three methods of pasteurization

a. **Bottle or holding pasteurization**: This method is commonly used for the preservation of fruit juices at home. The extracted juice is strained and filled in bottles, leaving sufficient head space for the expansion of the juice during heating. The bottles are then sealed air-tight and pasteurized.

b. **Overflow method**: Juice is heated to temperature of about 2.5⁰C higher than the pasteurization temperature and then filled in hot sterilized bottles up to the brim, during filling and sealing the temperature of juice should not fall below the pasteurization temperature.

c. **Flash pasteurization**: The juice is heated rapidly to a temperature of about 5.5⁰C higher than the pasteurization temperature and kept at this temperature for about a minute. This method commonly used for canning of natural orange juice, grape and apple juices. It is a mild heat treatment by pasteurization milk is pasteurized by HTST at 72⁰C for 15 Sec. Fruit juices are pasteurized at such temperature and for such periods as would render them sterile, without impairing their flavour. Usually, the juices are pasteurized at about 85⁰C for 25-30 min., according to the nature of the juice and the size of container. Acid fruit juices require lower temperature and less time for pasteurization than the less acid ones.

Juices can be pasteurized in two ways

1. By heating the juice at a low temperature for a high time (LTHT).
2. By heating the juice at high temperature for a short time only (HTST).

ii. Boiling/cooking

The primary objective of cooking is to produce a palatable food. Cooking results in:

1. Destruction or reduction of microorganisms and inactivation of undesirable enzymes.
2. Destruction of potential hazard in the foods which are present naturally through microorganism.
3. Improvement of colour, flavour and texture of the food.
4. It improves the digestibility of food component.
5. Putting the temperature about 100°C by this method, food can be preserved for 10-24 hours at low temperature.

iii. Canning

Canning is done at or above 100⁰C. In case of fruits which are acidic, they are canned at 100⁰C, while in case of vegetables those are non acidic, they are canned at above 100⁰C. Here, high temperature can be obtained by using steam pressure time is varying according to the type of foods. Due to anaerobic condition any survivable organism will not grow.

On the basis of acid, foods are divided into four different groups

1. Low Acid Foods (pH 5.3 and above): Peas, Corn, Lime beans, Meat, fish, Poultry and Milk.
2. Medium Acid Foods (pH 5.3-4.5): Spinach, Asparagus, Beets and Pumpkin.
3. Acid Foods (pH 4.5-3): Tomatoes, Pears and Pineapple, Sauce.
4. High Acid Foods below (pH 3.7): Berries and Sauer kraut, Pickle.

Chapter 33

Canning

Canning: Canning is the process by which sealing of the food product and sterilizing them by heat for long storage is known as canning.

History: The term canning was first invented by N. Appert (1804) in France. In honour of the inventor canning is also known as appertization (Appart is known as the father of canning) and Saddington (1807) in England first described the method of canning. Peter Durand (1810) got first british patent on canning of food in tin container and William under wood introduced canning of fruit on a commercial scale in U.S.A.

Principle of canning: The main principle of canning is destruction of spoilage organism by means of heat.

Process of canning: The process of the canning should be as follows:

1. **Selection of fruits and vegetables**
   - The selected fruit and vegetable should be absolutely fresh.
   - Fruit should be ripe but firm and uniformly mature.
   - Over ripe fruit should be rejected because they are infected with microorganism and give a poor quality product.
   - Unripe fruit should be rejected because they generally shrivel and toughen on canning.
   - All vegetable except tomatoes should be tender. Tomato should be firm, fully ripe and of deep red in colour.
   - Fruits and vegetables should be free from dirt.
   - They should be free from blemishes, insect damage or mechanical injuries.
2. **Grading-** The selected fruits and vegetables are graded according to size and colour to obtain uniform quality.
3. **Washing-** It is important to remove pesticide residue and dust from fruits and vegetables should wash thoroughly.
4. **Peeling-** Removal of outer layer by hand, by steam (potato and tomato) by lye peeling (1-2% boiling castic soda solution for 30 sec. to 2 minutes depending upon their nature and maturity).

Hot lye dissolving the pectin and skin become loose. Any trace of alkali is removed by washing the fruits and vegetables thoroughly in running cold water or dipping 5% citric acid for few second. Flame peeling- It is used only for garlic and onion.

5. **Cutting-** Cut the piece accordingly for maximum accomodation of produce in canning. Seed, stone and core are removed.
6. **Blanching-** It is also known as scalding, parboiling or precooking. Produce should be cooked in boiling water or steam for 2 to 5 minutes followed by cooling.

Advantage

i. Inactivate most of plant enzyme which cause toughness, dicoulration (polyphenol oxidase), off flavor (peroxidase), softening and loss of nutritive value.

ii. Reduce the area of leafy vegetable such as spinach by shrinkage or wilting making their packing easier.

iii. Remove tissue gases which reduces sulphides.

iv. Reduce the number of microorganism.

v. Enhance the green colour of vegetable such as peas, broccoli and spinach.

vi. Remove undesirable acid and astringent taste of the peel.

Disadvantage

i. Water soluble materials like sugar and anthocyanin pigment are leached by boiling water.

ii. Fruit loose their colour, flavour and sugar.

7. **Cooling-** After blanching cooling the materials for easy handling.
8. **Filling-** After cooling, the filling of product is done by two ways i.e. syruping and brining.

Syruping- A solution of sugar in water generally used in fruits. Non acidic fruit require more concentrated syrup. Less acidic fruit, less concentrated syrup. The temperature at the time of syruping is 79-82°C and head space is 3 to 5 cm.

Brining- A solution of salt in water is called as brining. This process generally used in vegetables. The concentration of brine is 1 to 3% and the temperature at the time of brining is 79-82°C with head space is 3 to 5 cm.

9. **Exhausting-** The process of removal of air from cans is known as exhausting.

Advantage

i. Corrosion of tin plate and pin holing during storage is avoided.

ii. Minimize discoulration by preventing oxidation.

iii. Help in better retention of vitamins particularly vitamin C.

iv. Reduce chemical reaction between the containers the contents.

10. **Sealing-** Immediately after exhaustings, the cans are sealed airtight by means of can sealer. During the sealing temperature should not fall below 74ºC.

11. **Processing-** Heating or cooling of canned food to inactivate bacteria. Spore of bacteria can be killed only by either very high or very low temperature treatment or prolong cooking. Over cooking should be avoided as it spoil the flavour as well as appearance of the product. Temperature and time of processing vary with the size of can, larger the can greater the processing time and vice-versa.

    Almost all the fruits can process satisfactorily at a temperature of 100ºC i.e. in boiling water as the presence retard the growth of the bacteria and spores. Further they do not thrive in heavy sugar syrup which is normally used in canning fruits. Non acidic produce like vegetables except tomato and rhubarb require being at higher temperature of about 115ºC to 121ºC.

12. **Cooling-** After processing the cans are cooled rapidly about 39ºC to stop the cooking process. Cooling is done by following methods:

    i. Dipping the hot cans in tank containing cold water, exposing the cans to cold air, spray the cans with cold water.

    ii. If canned product is not cooled immediately after processing. Peaches and pears become dark in colour, tomatoes turn brownish and bitter in taste. Peas become pulpy with cooked taste and many vegetable develop sour taste.

13. **Storage-** Storage of can at high temperature should be avoided. It should be store at dry, cooled and ventilated place.

Flow Chart for Canning Process

Selection of fruits and vegetables
↓
Grading
↓
Washing
↓
Peeling — Hand peeling / Steam peeling / Mechanical / Lye peeling
↓
Cutting
↓
Blanching (mostly for vegetable)
↓
Cooling
↓
Filling — Syrup (30-50%) for fruits / Brine (2%) for vegetables
↓
Exhausting (79-82^{0}C)
↓
Sealing (Temperatures should not below 74^{0}C)
↓
Processing — 100^{0}C for fruits / 116-121^{0}C for vegetables
↓
Cooling (Cooled to 39^{0}C)
↓
Storage

Chapter 34

Drying and Dehydration

Drying- Removal of water from product by influence of non conventional energy source like sun and wind.

Dehydration- Process of removal of moisture by the application of artificial heat under controlled condition of temperature, humidity and airflow etc.

Advantage of dehydration over sun drying

1. The process of dehydration is much more rapid than sun drying.
2. Dehydration requires less floor area.
3. Dehydration is done under very hygienic condition.
4. Sun drying is not possible in cloudy weather or during rain while dehydration or mechanical drying is not dependent on weather.
5. The colour of dehydrated or mechanically dried fruit and vegetable remain uniform due to uniform drying temperature.

Principle of dehydration

1. To inactivate the microorganism by removal of water.
2. Psychometric relationship in fruit and vegetable means relation between moisture and temperature. Where the temperature is more, moisture will be less and vice-versa.

Mechanism of Dehydration

It involves four steps

1. Heat and mass transfer phenomenon
2. Development of dried thick layer
3. Establishment of moisture gradient
4. Establishment of normal Equilibrium Relative Humidity (ERH)

1. **Heat and mass transfer phenomenon:** It provide the food between two heated plate into the close chamber, then the transfer of heat decrease but it would interfere with the step of free moisture.

2. **Development of dried thick layer:** During the drying of the food, temperature force to remove the moisture from the surface of the food at initial stage of dehydration and later stage of drying it becomes slow because of development of dried thick layer, which is due to the loss of more moisture from the outer surface of the product and remaining of moisture in the centre of the food.
3. **Establishment of moisture gradient:** When dried thick layer in formed and it act as an isolation against rapid heat transfer into the food and the forces of heat transfer to the centre of the food is determined and water retain in the centre of the food which have moisture gradient to get out on the surface will not be loose faster and it established a moisture gradient.
4. **Establishment of normal ERH:** The heat transfer of the product and mass transfer to the surface from the centre of the food decreases but drying process will be continue and finally there will be a constant weight of the product and will have a particular level of moisture content. After that there is not any reduction in weight or moisture until and unless atmospheric conditions are not changed.

Process of Dehydration

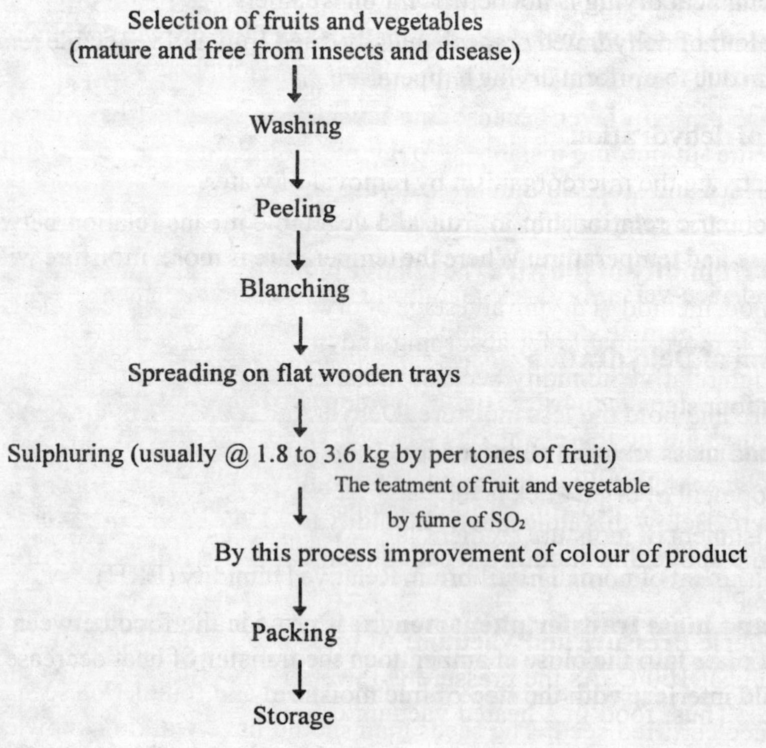

Factors Affecting the Drying Rate

1. **Temperature**: Temperature plays an important role in drying of fruits and vegetables. It provides the force for removal of moisture from the food, so that water is driven out of the food in the form of vapours so it must be carried away otherwise, the moisture will create a saturated atmosphere to the food and made liable to be deteriorated.
2. **Velocity of Air:** Hot air take up the more moisture than cool air, in the same way high velocity of air sweep away more moisture from the surface of dry food, preventing the moisture to create saturated atmosphere which would otherwise slow the subsequent moisture removal.
3. **Surface Area**: Larger surface area provides more surface in compact with the heating medium than the small surface area. More surface area allows removing or evaporating the more moisture from the food particles than the small şurface area. So, large surface area increases the drying rate than the small surface area.
4. **Size of Product:** Sub divided the food into small pieces during the drying because smaller particles reduce the heat to the centre of the food and distance through which moisture in the centre of the food to reach the surface and stop. So, small size of food increase the drying rate than the larger size of pieces of food.
5. **Tray Load**: The tray load is also influenced by tray capacity. Generally we put the food in thin layer because thin layer reduce the heat level to the centre to the surface and distance through which moisture from the centre to the surface and stop. So thin layer drying will be faster as compared to large one. Lesser the tray load, faster the drying
6. **Relative Humidity of the Air:** The relative humidity of air varies with the type of food, method of drying and stage of drying. The air with low relative humidity is more capable for absorbing and holding the moisture than air having high relative humidity because moist air is closer to saturation and can absorb and hold the less moisture. Dehydrated foods are hygroscopic. Each food has its own Equilibrium Relative Humidity (ERH). This is the humidity at which the product neither lost nor gains moisture from the atmosphere. Below this atmospheric humidity level, the food can be further dried while above this humidity, it cannot, rather it picks up moisture from the atmosphere.
7. **Atmospheric Pressure and Vacuum:** At pressure of 1 atm (760 mm Hg) water boils at 100°C. As the pressure is lowered, the boiling temperature decreases. Thus, food in a heated vacuum chamber will lose moisture at

faster rate at low temperature. This low temperature, short time drying is especially important for heat sensitive foods.

Changes during drying

Shrinkage: The food materials do not have perfect elasticity and water is not removed evenly throughout the food piece as it dried causes shrinkage. Often with quick high temperature, the surface becomes dry and rigid long before the center has dried, when the center dried, it pulls away from the rigid surface causes internal splits, voids and honeycomb effect. This affect the bulk density of dried product

Case hardening: If there is a very high surface temperature and unbalanced drying, dry skill will form quickly, before most of the internal moisture would migrate to the surface. The impermeable skin then traps much of the remaining water within the particle, and the drying rate drops off severely. This leads to shrinkage and sealing of the surface (pore dogging) of a food known as case hardening. This is common in foods contain dissolved sugars and other solutes in high concentration. It can be minimized by lower surface temperature.

Thermoplasticity: Fruit and vegetable juices, lacks structure and is high in sugar that soften and melt at the drying temperature. So, even after all of water has been removed, the solids will be in a thermoplasticity condition. However, on cooling, these solids harden into a crystalline or amorphous glass from which is brittle in nature.

Pre and Post Dehydration Treatments for Drying

A. Pre-Dehydration Treatments

Blanching: It is a partial pre-cooking treatment in which vegetables are usually heated in boiling water to inactivate the natural enzymes before processing.

Purpose

1. It is done to inactivate the natural enzymes
2. To remove hardness.
3. To improve colour, texture and flavour.
4. To reduce the bacterial load.
5. To shrink the volume.

Sulphuring: The whole fruits or slices/pieces are exposed to the fumes of burning sulphur inside a closed chamber known as sulphur box. In sulphur box, the products are loaded in the trays. For small scale sulphur box (90 x 60 x 90 cm) which can hold about 11 trays size of 80 x 60 x 5 cm is sufficient. A box holding the 10 trays it requires burning of sulphur about 18-36 kg/tonnes of fruits.

Purpose of Sulphuring

1. To prevent oxidation and darkening.
2. To check the growth of mould.
3. To act as a preservative/antimicrobial agent.
4. To prevent cut fruit from fermenting.
5. To prevent the vitamin loss.

Sulphitation: Sulphite solution is less suitable than burning sulphur because the sulphite solution prevent the fruit poorly and bleaches the nutrients like sugar, acid and flavour compounds. In addition to preventing enzymatic browning SO_2 treatment reduces the destruction of carotene and ascorbic acid which are important nutrients in the products.

B. Post-Dehydration Tretments

1. **Sweating:** Sweating is a process to hold the dehydrated foods in bins for equalization of moisture before packaging.
2. **Screening**: In production of dehydrated food, during cutting operation and in movement of product through processing line, they leave some unwanted size of the product which have to be screened. The unwanted sizes of pieces of products are removed by passing the dried products over a vibrating pathway or perforating metal screens.
3. **Inspection**: The dried product is inspected to remove the discoloured pieces such as skin or steam particles. These are removed manually. The inspection is carried out by packing out the desirable particles while the product is moving on the continuous PVC belt at a speed of about 15-25 per minute.
4. **Heat treatment**: Dried fruits and vegetables are generally attacked by insect even when they are properly dried and stored. Insect not only consume the material but also leave the debris which spoil the appearance of product. To avoid insect infestation, great care is necessary in the construction of practices on godown. In case of heat treatment, dried fruits such as rasins, fig, peaches are dipped in water for dilute solution of NaCl or Na_2 HCO_3 and then redried at 54-65^{0}C to destroy all insects including their formative stages. Dried vegetable may be heated directly without any preliminary treatments. The heat sterilized materials should be packed in clean and sterilized containers which are insect proof.

5. **Fumigation:** It fixes the insect including their eggs. Great care is necessary in using fumigation as some of the substances like CO_2 and hydrocyanic gas are unfavourable and poisonous. Besides, it is also possible that fruit may absorb small amount of HCN (Hydrocyanic acid) rendering the product poisonous. But these days Methyl Bromide is becoming popular for this purpose. The mixture of Ethylene Dichloride (EDC) and CC, Ethylene oxide and EDC are also used for fumigation.

Chapter 35

Preparation and Preservation of Fruit and Vegetable Products

Jam: Jam is a product made by boiling fruit pulp with sufficient sugar to a reasonably thick consistency. Jam is mainly prepared by apple, pear, sapota, apricot, peach, papaya, karonda etc. It can be prepared from one kind of fruits or from two or more kind of fruits. In general jam contains 0.5-0.6% acid and invert sugar should not be more than 40%.

Procedures of the jam preparation are as follows:

FLOW CHART FOR PROCESSING OF JAM

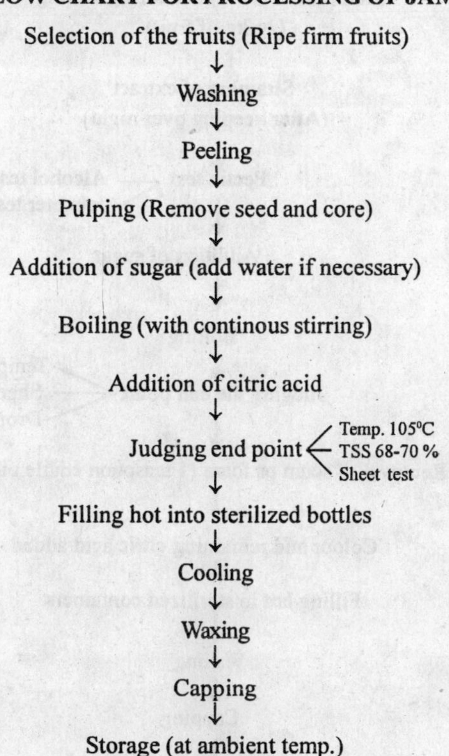

Jelly: Jelly is a semi solid product prepared by boiling a solution of pectin containing fruit extract free from pulp after the addition of sugar and acid. A perfect jelly should be transparent, well set, should have original flavour of the fruits, attractive colour and it should be free from dullness. Jelly is mainly prepared by guava, sour apple, wood apple, loquat and papaya. Apricot, pineapple, strawberry etc. of low pectin containing fruits can also utilize after addition of pectin powder because these fruits have low pectin contain.

The procedures of the jelly preparation are as follows:

FLOW CHART FOR PROCESSING OF JELLY

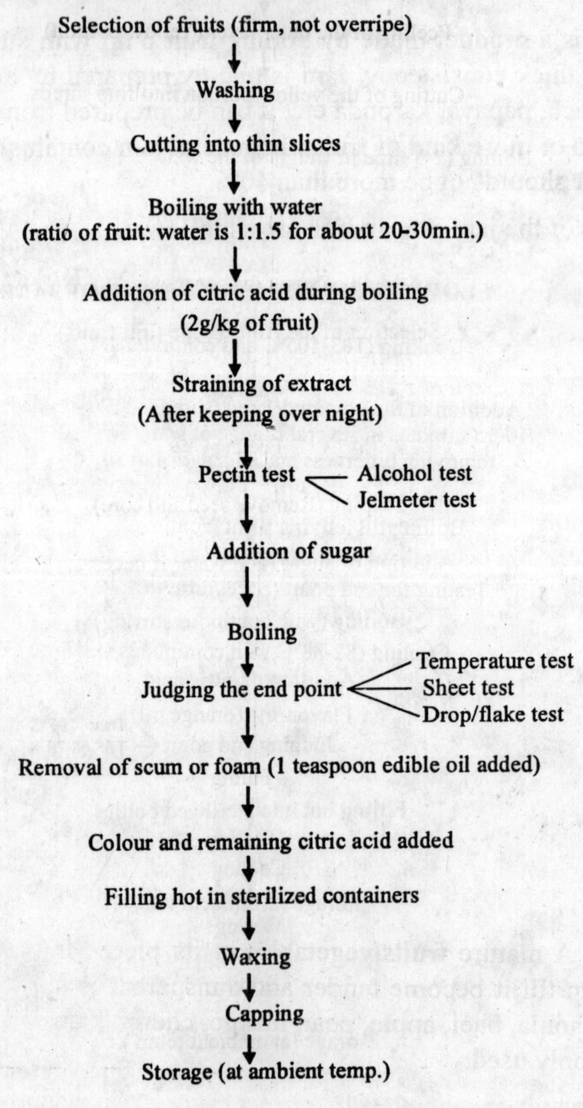

Marmalade: Marmalade is a fruit jelly in which peels of the fruits is in suspended forms. This product is generally prepared from citrus fruits like orange and lemon. The citrus marmalade can be classified into jelly marmalade and jam marmalade. 1 kg pectin extract requires 750g sugar and 62g shredded peel.

The procedures of the marmalade preparation are as follows:

FLOW CHART FOR PROCESSING OF MARMALADE

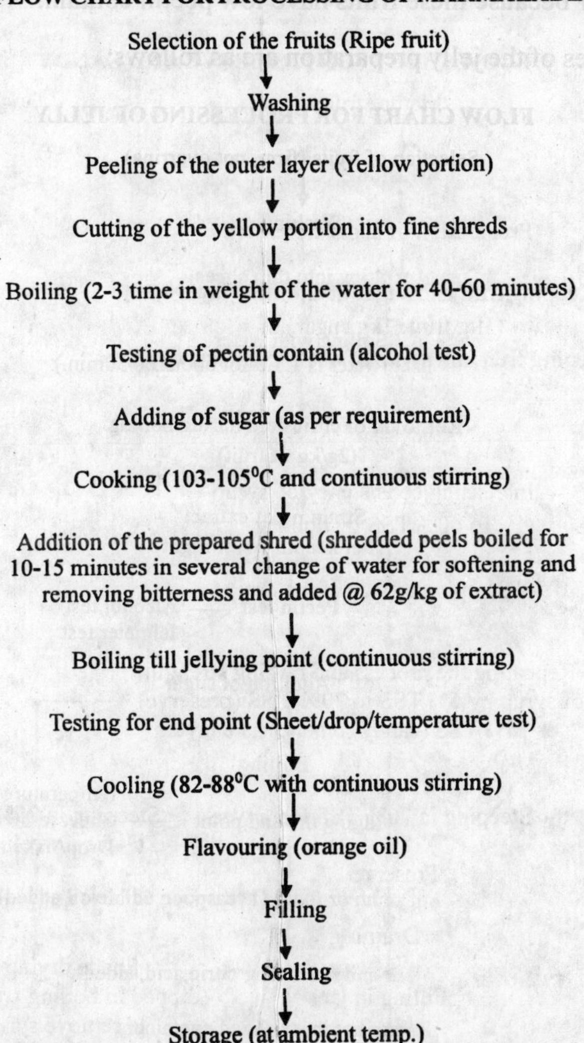

Preserve: A mature fruits/vegetables or its pieces impregnated with heavy sugar syrup till it become tender and transparent is known as preserve. The fruits like aonla, bael, apple, pear, mango, cherry, karonda, pineapple, papaya are commonly used.

Candied fruit: A fruits/vegetables impregnated with cane sugar syrup and subsequently drained free of syrup and dried is known as candy. The most suitable fruits are aonla, apple, pear, cherry, karonda, pineapple, papaya are commonly used. In candy the total sugar content of the impregnated fruits is kept about 75% to prevent fermentation.

The procedures of preserve making are as follows:

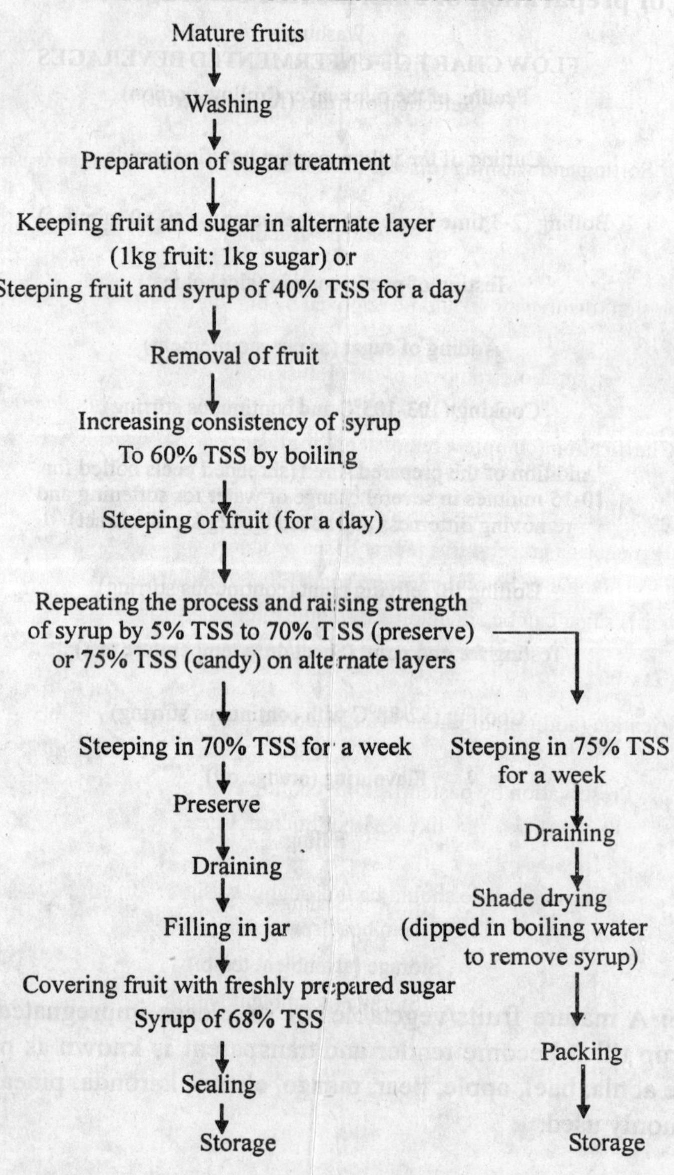

Beverages: The fruit beverages are easily digestible, highly refreshing, thirst quenching, appetizing, nutritionally for superior than many other synthetic drinks. There are two types of fruit beverages i.e. unfermented beverages and fermented beverages. Natural juice, RTS (Ready to Serve), nector, cordial, squash, crush syrup, fruit juice concentrate and fruit juice powder are the main unfermented beverages. The fermented beverages are wine, champaigne, port, sherry, tokay, muscut, neera, cedar, orange wine, berry wine and fenny are the important.

Method of preparation of unfermented beverages

FLOW CHART OF UNFERMENTED BEVERAGES

Selection of fruits (fully ripe fruit)

↓

Sorting and washing (disease portion should be removed then washing)

↓

Juice extraction

↓

Deaeration (disolve air should be removed by high vacuum with the help of dearater)

↓

Filtration (removal of the fruit skin, seed, broken tissue etc.)

↓

Clarification (complete removal of the all suspended material from the juice)

↓

Addition of sugar (except grape and apple) all the juice added the sugar for sweetening and sugar act as a preservative (sugar based product divided into three category i.e. low sugar [30% sugar or below], medium sugar [30-50% sugar], high sugar [50% or above sugar]) sugar can be added directly to the juice or as a syrup made by dissolving in hot water with small quantity of citric acid

↓

Fortification (addition of vitamins and ascorbic acid for enhancing the nutritive value)

↓

Preservation by pasteurization, cooling etc. and adding preservatives like KMS or Sodium Benzoate

↓

Bottling (bottle should be thoroughly washed with hot water and 1.5-2.5cm head space should be keep)

↓

Storage (at ambient temp.)

Squash: It is a type of fruit beverage containing at least 25% fruit juice or pulp and 40-50% TSS commercially. It also contains about 1% citric acid and 350ppm sulphurdioxide or 600ppm sodium benzoate. Generally it is diluted before serving. Mango, orange, pineapple, lemon, lime, guava, litchi etc are commercially used for squash making using KMS as preservative. The coloured fruit like jamun, passion fruit, peach, phalasa, plum, mulberry, strawberry and grapefruits are also used for making squash but due to bleaching effect KMS is not used as preservative. In such types of fruits sodium benzoate used as preservative.

Method of preparation of squash

FLOW CHART FOR PROCESSING OF SQUASH

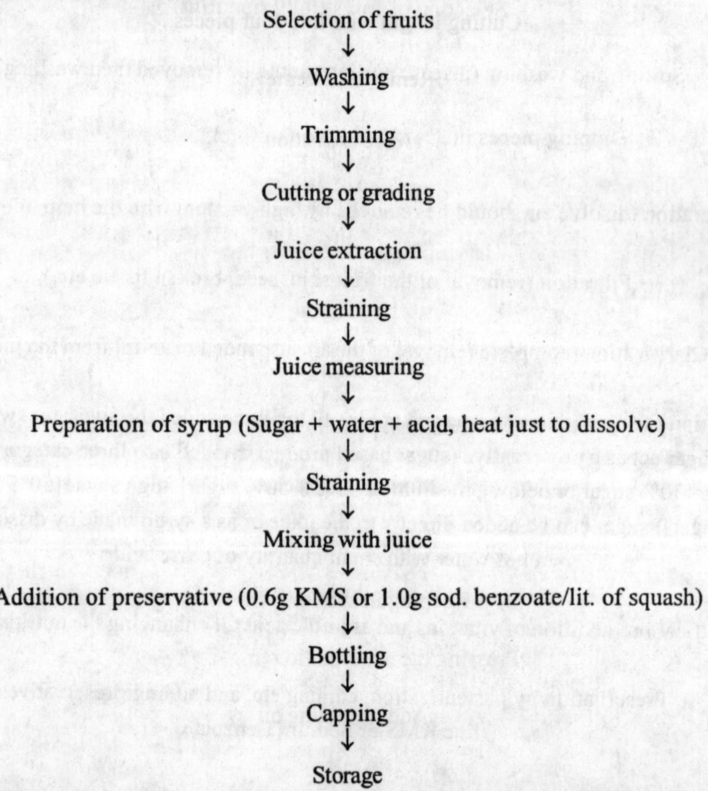

Pickles: Pickles are a product which is prepared by using the common salt or vinegars of fruits and vegetables. It is a good appetizer and adds to the palatability of a meal. It's also helpful to stimulating the flow of gastric juices and thus helps full indigestion. Pickles are mainly preserving by salt, vinegar, oil and it can also be preserved by the mixture of salt, spices, vinegar and oil.

Ingredient of 1kg mango pickles: Mango piece 1kg, salt 150g, fenugreek powder 25g, turmeric powder 15g, nigella seed 15g, red chilli powder 10g, clove headless 8 in number, black pepper 15g, cumin 15g, cardamom large 15g, aniseed powder 15g, asafoetida 2g and mustard oil 350 ml.

Method of preparation of pickles

FLOW CHART FOR PROCESSING OF MANGO PICKLE

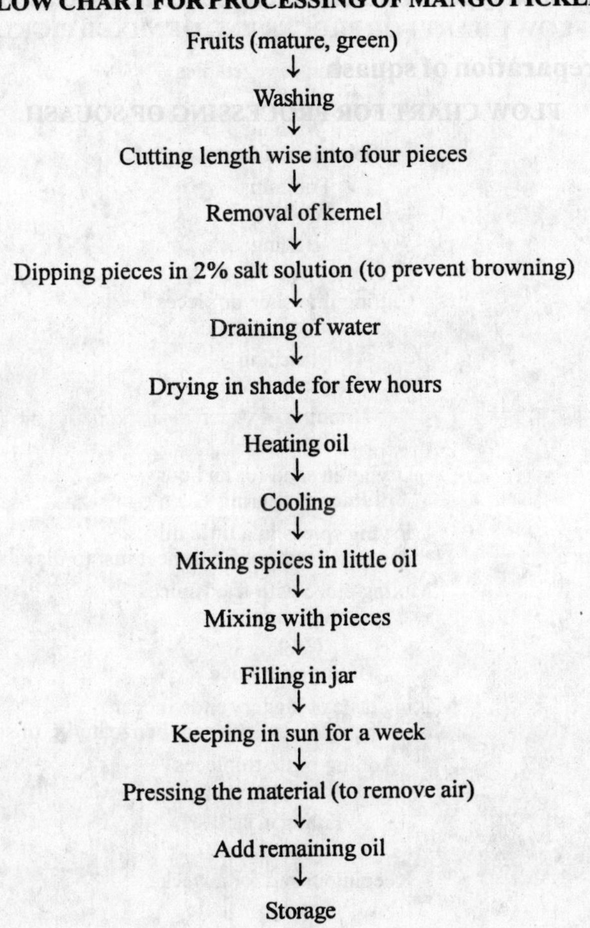

Ingredient of 1kg mixed pickles: Cauliflower + *diced carrot* + turnip slice + vegetable pea each in equal amount of 1kg, salt 100g, ginger chopped 20g, onion chopped 50g, garlic chopped 10g, red chilli powder, black pepper, turmeric, cardamom large, aniseed powder, cumin, fenugreek powder each of 10g, clove headless 5 in number and mustard 50g, vinegar 200ml and mustard oil 450ml.

Method of preparation of mixed pickles

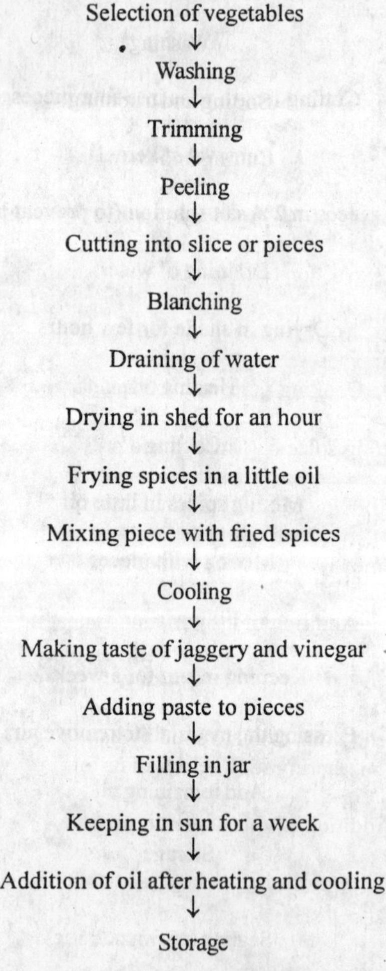

Sauce/Ketchup: Fully ripe red fruits are selected, all green and blemish part are discarded. It is made from strained tomato juice or pulp and spices, salt, sugar and vinegar with or without onion and garlic and contains not less than 12% tomato solid and 25% total solid.

Ingredient of tomato sauce/ketchup: Tomato pulp 1kg, sugar 75g, salt 10g, onion chopped 50g, ginger chopped 10g, garlic chopped 5g, red chilli powder 5g, cinnamon, cardamom large, aniseed, cumin, black pepper powder 10g each, clove headless 5 in number, vinegar 25ml or glacial acetic acid 5ml and sodium benzoate 0.25g/kg final product.

Method of preparation of tomato sauce/ketchup

FLOW CHART FOR PROCESSING OF TOMATO SAUCE/KETCHUP

Selection of tomato fruits (fully ripe and red)

↓

Washing

↓

Sorting and trimming

↓

Cutting and chopping

↓

Heating at 70-90^{0}C for 3-5 minutes (for softening)

↓

Pulping or extraction of juice/pulp (by machanically or by sieving)

↓

Straining tomato pulp/juice

↓

Cooking pulp with 1/3 quantity of sugar

↓

Putting spice bag in pulp and pressing ocassionally

↓

Cooking to 1/3 of original volume of pulp/juice

↓

Removal of the spice bag (after squeezing in pulp)

↓

Addition of the remaining sugar and salt

↓

Cooking

↓

Judging of end point (tomato solid by hand refrectometer/volume by measuring stick i.e. 1/3 of its original volume

↓

Addition of vinegar/acidic acid and preservative

↓

Filling into bottles at about 88^{0}C

↓

Sealing (crown corking)

↓

Pasteurisation (at 85-90^{0}C for 30 minutes)

↓

Cooling

↓

Storage (at ambient temp.)

Ingredient of tomato chutney: Tomato 1kg, sugar 500g, salt 25g, onion chopped 100g, ginger chopped 10g, garlic chopped 5g, red chilli powder 10g, cinnamon, cardamom large, aniseed, (cumin, black pepper powder 10g each), vinegar 100ml and sodium benzoate 0.50g/kg final product.

Method of preparation of tomato chutney

FLOW CHART FOR PROCESSING OF TOMATO CHUTNEY

Selection of tomato fruits (fully ripe and red)

↓

Washing

↓

Sorting

↓

Blanching for 2 minutes

↓

Putting in cold water (to crack skin)

↓

Peeling

↓

Crushing

↓

Addition of ingredients except salt and vinegar and cooking gently to desired consistency

↓

Addition of salt and vinegar and cooking for 5 minutes

↓

Addition of preservative

↓

Filling hot into bottle

↓

Sealing

↓

Storage (at ambient temperature in cool and dry places)

Chapter 36

Physiology of Fruit Growth and Development

Growth: Growth involve cell division subsequently cell elongation. Increase in volume that is associated with fruit growth largely result of cell division or cell elongation or both. In some fruit such as apple, extension of intercellular space may also contribute the growth. Generally growth by cell division in early stage whereas, cell elongation during later stage.

Two distinct type of growth curve are observed when increase in such variable such as fresh weight, volume and dry weight of fruit.

1. Single sigmoid curve
2. Double sigmoid curve

In case of single sigmoid growth curve firstly there is rapid increase in size then after decline so there is only one rapid growth is observed e.g. Apple, pear, tomato, cucumber and strawberry.

In case of double sigmoid two rapid growth period are separated by an intermediate period that is less growth or no increasing growth curve. Double sigmoid growth curve can be used as two successive sigmoid curve thus there are three clearly define stage of growth.

Stage I : Cell division occur ovary and its component grow rapidly except embryo and endosperm.

Stage II : This is characterized by rapid growth of embryo and endosperm. Endocarp is lignified.

Stage III : Rapid growth of mesocarp occur causing final swelling of fruit which is followed by maturation e.g. ber, bael, grape, fig, cherry, olive, apricot, peach and plum.

Maturation : Stage of fruit development during which fruit attain full size of growth is known as maturity.

Developmental phase: Growth and maturation are collectively referred as developmental phase.

Ripening : Ripening is a terminal period of maturation during which fruit attain the maximum edible and aesthetic pulp.

PROCESS OF RIPENING

Ethylene synthesis
↓
Stimulation of oxidative and hydrolytic enzyme
↓
Solublization in soluble cellular compound (protopectin and cellulose)
↓
Changes in cell membrane permeability
↓
Mixing of substrate with their enzyme
↓
Initiation of metabolic process such as respiration (Responsible for biochemical changes)
↓
Ripening

Senescence : Senescence is the period of ripening during which biochemical process of ageing replace the perfective change of ripening.

Changes during development : At the time of development of the fruit two types of changes are observed that is physical changes and biochemical changes. In physical changes increase the size and weight, specific gravity and colour of the fruit. In biochemical changes the continuous accumulation of starch, the rate of sugar is higher, rise in acidity during the early period and respiration rate per unit weight is higher.

Changes during ripening : During ripening physical and biochemical changes occurs. In physical changes green colour changes into respective colour and increase the specific gravity.

Biochemical changes during ripening

1. **Hormone :** Particularly ethylene play a very important role in the fruit ripening. Ethylene synthesize from amino acid (Methionine). During ripening its level increases and other hormone like abscisic acid (ABA) has also been increases (due to synergistic effect) during ripening such as grapes and strawberry etc. The level of GA, cytokinin and auxin decreases (due to antagonistic effect) during ripening of the fruits.
2. **Respiration :** Respiration rate can be used for determining the ripening and storage life of fruit. The level of respiration increase during ripening which is known as respiratory climatric. There are many factors which affect the rate of ripening such as maturity, fat, protein, energy, natural protein and growth regulator.

3. **Pigment:** Pigment are responsible for development of colour that is chlorophyll, carotenoid and anthocyanin. Chlorophyll decrease during ripening, it is degraded by enzyme chlorophyllase. Growth regulator particularly ethylene cause degradation of chlorophyll whereas, GA_3 increase the level of chlorophyll (Regreening).

Regarding carotenoid, xanthophylls responsible for yellow colour e.g. lemon, lycopene responsible for pink colour e.g. tomato and red fleshed guava, beta-carotene is found in mango, papaya and peaches etc.

How they are degraded

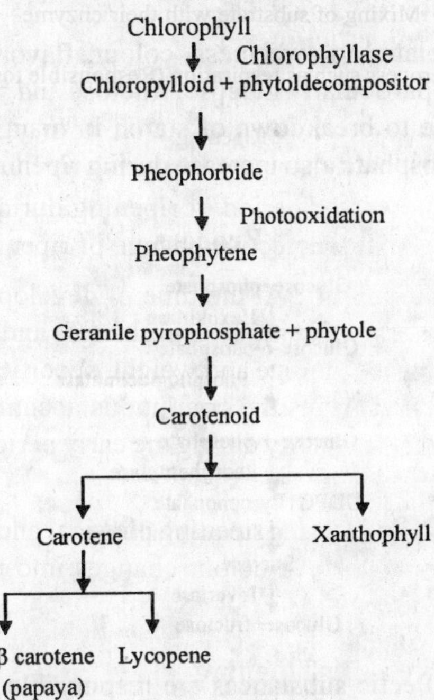

Anthocyanin : Anthocyanin is responsible for red, blue and purple colour development during ripening of various fruits such as apple, plum, phalasa, jamun, fig, pomegranate etc. The level of anthocyanin is higher due to higher synthesis in ripening period. There are different form of anthocyanin like in apple fruits it is found in the form of cyanidin-3-galactoside.

How it synthesizes

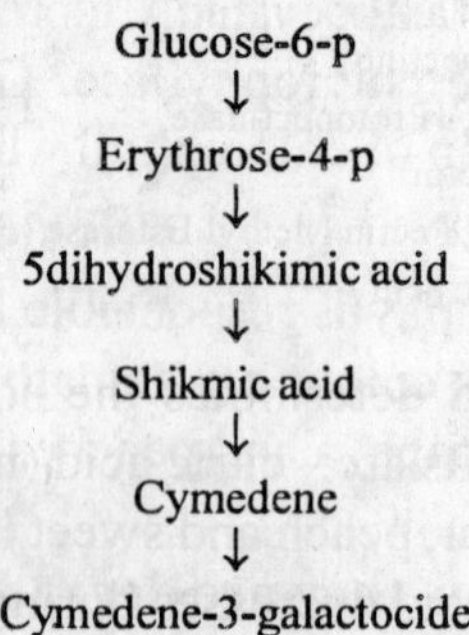

Sugar : Sugar are related to sweetness, colour, flavour and structure of the fruits. Level of sugar particularly glucose, fructose and sucrose increase during ripening of fruit. Due to breakdown of starch in mango and banana level of pentose and sugar phosphate also increase during ripening of fruit respectively.

Process

Glucose+phosphate
↓ Hexokinase
Glucose-6-phosphate
↓ Phosphogluconutase
Glucose-1-phosphate
↓ Phosphomylase
UDPG+Pyrophophate
↓ Sucrose synthetase
Sucrose
↓ Invertase
Glucose+fructose

Pectic substances : Pectic substances are responsible for firmness of fruits. These are mainly three type:

i. Protopectine (water insoluble)
ii. Pectinic acid or pectin (water soluble)
iii. Pectic acid

The level of protopectine decrease during ripening of fruits and pectin content of fruits increase during ripening. Cellulose is also responsible for breakdown of pectin.

Process

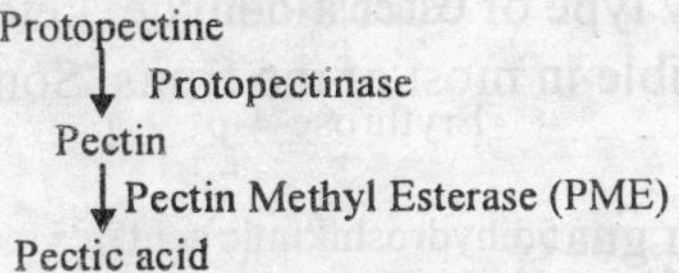

Organic acid : Organic acid determines the sourness of fruit. Some most important acid presents in fruits are:- citric acid (mango, citrus and pineapple), malic acid (banana, apple, pear, peach and sweet lime), tartaric acid (grape and tamarind). Level of organic acid decreases during ripening. Enzyme invertase is responsible for the conversion of acid into salt and sugar and acids are utilized in metabolic process.

Amino acid : Amino acid particularly methionine is precursor of ethylene and it plays an important role in fruit ripening. Total amino acid increases during ripening. Different fruits have different amino acid.

i. Alanine (mango and gooseberry)
ii. Aspartic acid (banana, apple and datepalm)
iii. Methionine (pineapple)
iv. Arginine and proline (grape)
v. Proline (lemon)
vi. Histidine (orange)

Protein and nucleic acid : Fruits have very little amount of protein but it play very important role in ripening. Before climacteric if protein synthesis is to be checked by cyclohexamide (protein inhibitor) the ethylene synthesis and fruit ripening process stops. Hence protein synthesis is an important effect in fruit ripening normally protein content of the fruit during ripening is increases. The level of RNA is increases in climacteric period hence this is the reason that protein content in fruits increase during ripening.

Enzyme : Enzyme is responsible for physiochemical changes in fruits. The level of most of the enzyme increase during ripening. Important enzymes are chlorophylase, catalase, invertase, sucrose synthetase, polyphenoloxidase, pectin methyl esterase, cellulase and peroxidase.

Lipid : Lipid content in fruit is very little amount but it plays an important role in aroma and flavour of the fruits. Ratio of palmitic and palmetalic play very important role for aroma and flavour of mango. If this ratio is less than 0.8-0.9 therefore very strong aroma and flavour like Alphanso and Langara. If the ratio is more than 1 (1-1.5) then there is less aroma and flavour like Neelam and Bangalora.

Volatile compound : Volatile compound are also responsible for aroma and flavour. There are many type of ester aldehyde, ketone, alcohol, hydrocarbon, and acetate are responsible in most of the fruits. Some volatile compounds are as follows:

i. Cynamile acetate in guava
ii. Ethyl acetate in pineapple
iii. Lanoline in citrus
iv. Eugenol in banana
v. Ethyl-2-methyl butyrate in apple
vi. Linalool in grape
vii. Methyl or ethyl ester in pear

Phenolics : Phenolics also contribute for colour and flavour and is also responsible for resistance to diseases. The level of phenolics decreases during ripening. The important phenolics are:

i. Cynamic acid
ii. Flamans
iii. Flavanols
iv. Anthocyanin
v. Tannin
vi. Jugalance

Vitamins : Vitamins are important for nutritional point of view. Fruits are very rich source of vitamins. Carotene is found maximum in mango, papaya and jackfruit. It increases during ripening

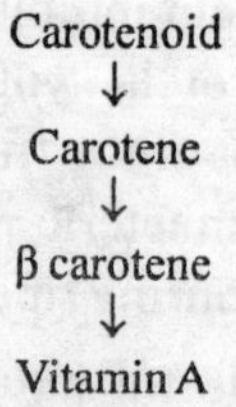

Thiamine (Vitamin B$_1$) : It increases during ripening and mostly found in grape. Riboflavin is found in pineapple and papaya.

Ascorbic acid (Vitamin C) : Most of the fruit crops vitamin C decreases at the time of ripening except papaya. In papaya it increases during ripening.

Ascorbic acid
↓ Ascorbinase
Dehydro ascorbic acid
↓
2, 3 dikitogluconic acid

Minerals : Fruits are very rich source of minerals which have important role in nutrition. There is little change in mineral content of fruit during ripening. Potassium and sodium increases during ripening and level of calcium decreases during ripening.